Life in the
FANTASTIC '40s

Reminisce

A DECADE OF STRENGTH, PROGRESS AND TRIUMPH

Table of Contents

PAGE 36

PAGE 121

PAGE 173

PAGE 67

Swing into the
GREATEST GENERATION!

The 1940s were like no other time in history. Folks who lived through this remarkable decade have no shortage of compelling stories to share. Inspiring, humorous and heart-wrenching, these are the tales of men and women who lived through the turmoil of one of our nation's most devastating wars, yet never wavered in their love and commitment to family, community and country.

In *Reminisce: Life in the Fantastic '40s*, we've gathered more than 450 of our contributors' favorite personal recollections and photographs so you can relive all the trials, innovations and triumphs that made this decade great. Recall heroic military accounts and steadfast can-do war efforts on the home front. Revel in blissful tales of falling in love at first sight and innocent—and sometimes not-so-innocent—good old-fashioned childhood fun. Delight in the enchantment of ready-to-wear fashions and novelty household appliances. And discover why nothing beat the glitz and glamour of American showbiz.

The extraordinary memories, funny stories, personal photos, vintage ads and more inside *Reminisce: Life in the Fantastic '40s* chronicle the unforgettable moments, amazing accomplishments and simple pleasures celebrated in homes across America. This keepsake collection is your personal glimpse into these joyful memories of yesteryear and all the things that made the 1940s simply fantastic!

Best to you all,
The editors of *Reminisce* magazine

1940–1949:
A RETROSPECTIVE

There has perhaps never been a decade as distinctive as the 1940s. The nation was at war in both Europe and Asia, and everyone on the home front was pitching in to do their part. But this generation was also witness to amazing innovations and cultural shifts that helped propel America into a brighter future. So before you turn the page to look ahead, take a moment to look back at the events that made the '40s such a compelling—and fantastic—time in history.

1940

MARCH The radio show *Truth or Consequences* premieres on NBC radio.

MAY Winston Churchill replaces Neville Chamberlain as British prime minister. John Steinbeck wins a Pulitzer Prize for his novel *The Grapes of Wrath*.

JUNE The French surrender to Germany. Adolf Hitler leads the Nazis through Paris.

OCTOBER Moviegoers see Charlie Chaplin in his first speaking role in *The Great Dictator*.

1941

MAY The jeep is invented for U.S. military use.

SEPTEMBER Ted Williams of the Boston Red Sox becomes the last baseball player to achieve a batting average of .400.

NOVEMBER The national monument on Mount Rushmore in South Dakota is unveiled. President Franklin D. Roosevelt signs a bill establishing the fourth Thursday in November as Thanksgiving Day.

DECEMBER Japan bombs Pearl Harbor in Hawaii. The United States declares war on Japan the next day.

Honolulu Star-Bulletin 1ST **EXTRA**

SAN FRANCISCO, Dec. 7.—President Roosevelt announced this morning that Japanese planes had attacked Manila and Pearl Harbor.

WAR!
OAHU BOMBED BY
JAPANESE PLANES

SIX KNOWN DEAD, 21 INJURED, AT EMERGENCY HOSPITAL

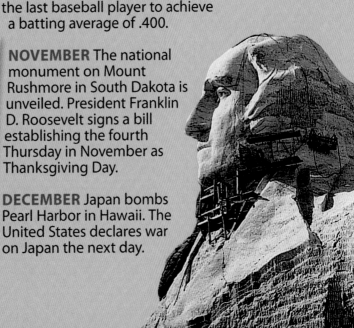

1942

1943

Making their appearance on grocery store shelves this year are Kellogg's Raisin Bran, Hunt Foods and Dannon Yogurt.

JANUARY The heavyweight boxing title is frozen as reigning champion Joe Louis is inducted into the U.S. Army.

JUNE In the Battle of Midway, the outnumbered U.S. Pacific fleet is victorious against Japanese forces.

OCTOBER Bing Crosby records the song "White Christmas," which becomes a No. 1 hit.

NOVEMBER The movie *Casablanca*, starring Humphrey Bogart and Ingrid Bergman, premieres in New York City.

MARCH The original production of the musical *Oklahoma!* opens on Broadway.

MAY *The Saturday Evening Post* features a cover image of Rosie the Riveter by artist Norman Rockwell.

SEPTEMBER Gen. Dwight D. Eisenhower announces the surrender of Italy to the Allies.

1944

1945

NOVEMBER President Franklin D. Roosevelt is elected to an unprecedented fourth term in office.

MAY Meat rationing in the U.S. ends.

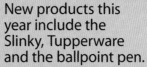

JUNE The Allies storm the beaches of Normandy, France, ultimately overwhelming German forces.

AUGUST The Nazis capture Anne Frank and her family in their Amsterdam hideout.

New products this year include the Slinky, Tupperware and the ballpoint pen.

APRIL President Franklin D. Roosevelt dies. Harry Truman is sworn in as the 33rd president.

MAY Germany surrenders to the Allies.

AUGUST The U.S. drops atomic bombs on Hiroshima and Nagasaki. Japan surrenders, effectively ending World War II.

SEPTEMBER The microwave oven is invented by Percy Spencer.

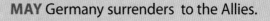

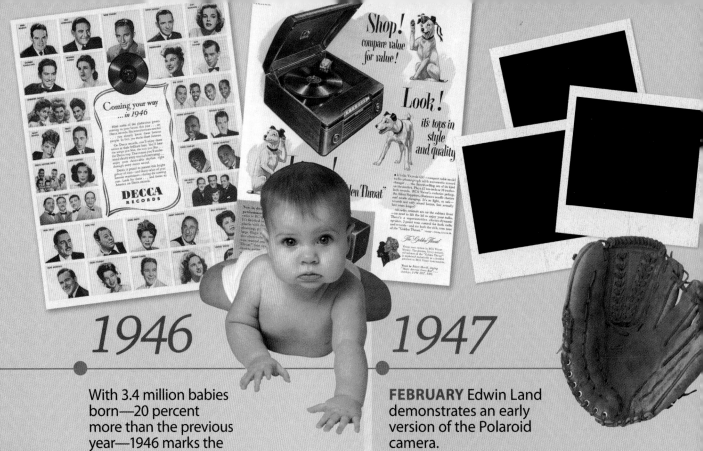

1946

1947

With 3.4 million babies born—20 percent more than the previous year—1946 marks the beginning of the baby boom.

MARCH Frank Sinatra releases his first studio album, *The Voice of Frank Sinatra*.

JULY French designer Louis Réard unveils his latest creation, a two-piece bathing suit for women called the bikini.

DECEMBER The classic Christmas movie *It's a Wonderful Life* is released.

FEBRUARY Edwin Land demonstrates an early version of the Polaroid camera.

APRIL Jackie Robinson plays his first baseball game with the Brooklyn Dodgers, becoming the first African-American in the major leagues.

JUNE Under the title *Rear Annex*, the diary of Anne Frank is published in the Netherlands.

OCTOBER American pilot Chuck Yeager exceeds 662 miles per hour at 40,000 feet, in a Bell X-1 research plane, becoming the first person to fly faster than the speed of sound.

NOVEMBER Princess Elizabeth, heir to the English throne, marries Phillip Mountbatten at Westminster Abbey in London.

1948

JANUARY Mohandas Gandhi is killed by a Hindu fanatic in Delhi, India.

FEBRUARY The National Association for Stock Car Racing—NASCAR—is incorporated.

JUNE The United States and Britain begin the Berlin Airlift, flying food, water and medicine to West Berlin citizens after Soviet forces cut off supply routes.

AUGUST At a hearing before the House Un-American Activities Committee, Alger Hiss faces charges of being a spy for the Soviet Union.

NOVEMBER Despite the infamous headline "Dewey Defeats Truman" in the *Chicago Daily Tribune*, President Harry Truman wins re-election.

1949

A television boom begins this year, when 940,000 households own a TV set.

JANUARY The Academy of Television Arts & Sciences holds its inaugural Emmy awards ceremony.

FEBRUARY A U.S. Air Force crew flies the first nonstop flight around the world, beginning and ending in Ft. Worth, Texas.

JUNE George Orwell publishes his classic novel *1984*.

AUGUST Two rival basketball leagues, the BAA and NBL, merge to form the National Basketball Association (NBA).

Remember Saying?

LETTUCE:
cash

CHAPTER 1

As You WERE

PAGE 37

PAGE 21

PAGE 22

PAGE 28

When the world was at war, countless American men and women left their loved ones behind to defend liberty and uphold justice stateside and overseas.

"I was drafted at 18 and had never traveled," writes Roger Raines from Placerville, California. "I left Kansas City, Missouri, and was sent to Fort Leavenworth, Kansas. I became a code clerk on a machine that converted English into coded letters. I felt like we knew more about how the war was going than most generals.

"I was assigned to a code room in the office of the Supreme Headquarters of American Forces—right below the office of Commanding Gen. Dwight D. Eisenhower. We got a message authorizing D-Day, and a few days later I saw the invasion of Europe on a newsreel.

"Next, we boarded a ship and ended up just outside London. The order came to get ready for another move, and we crossed the English Channel, landing in France. Before long, we moved to Berlin, and I was reassigned to Gen. George Patton's 3rd Army. Not long after that, the war ended."

The men and women who were lucky enough to return home from World War II never forgot their experiences—both heart-rending and spirit-lifting. Turn the page to relive these events through their eyes.

I Spent Christmas 1944 Under A HAYSTACK

A DOWNED B-17 TURRET GUNNER SPENT HIS LAST CHRISTMAS OF THE WAR EVADING GERMANS AND RUSSIANS. *By Silas Crase, Fort Pierce, Florida*

When I left the ball turret of a burning B-17 at about noon on August 27, 1944, I didn't realize I'd be spending Christmas in Slovakia.

I parachuted into a dense forest in southeastern Germany. Over the next five weeks, I avoided capture by the Germans and got over the hills to Slovakia, where I was fortunate enough to meet a member of the underground.

He took me to some of his partisan leaders, who verified that I was an American flier. With winter coming on, they decided it was better to hide me rather than try to get me back to my base in Foggia, Italy.

I stayed with Pavel Rézak and his wife, Hannah, in their log home. I spent much of the time under a six-foot-high pile of hay.

What food I was able to keep in reserve was shared, unwillingly, with the mice. The lice, if they'd been bigger, would have taken their share, too. As it was, they feasted on me.

Home Was Primitive

The Rézaks' house was 24 feet square, with an attic for extra hay and what food they could harvest. There were four-foot-wide benches that ran the length of the house on each side. They served as seats, beds and the dining table.

There was a rock-and-mud fireplace in one corner. It had an oven, above which the three Rézak boys slept.

A separate room housed two cows and a few goats. There was a log wall between the rooms, but the logs weren't chinked so the heat from the house would also warm the animals. The stench was nauseating.

Nearby was a village that Pavel and I often visited at about 1 a.m. to listen to the BBC broadcasts. A family there allowed me a Christmas bath in an old copper tub—my first since before the August 27 flight!

On Christmas Eve, Hannah splurged and we all had an extra helping of unseasoned mashed potatoes, mixed with kraut and covered with cold clabbered milk. After some songs in Slovak and English, I retired to my haystack in another building.

A short time later, I heard the tapping code that meant "Come on up." I came out and found Hannah with a box in her hands and Pavel with a grin on his face.

"Here is a small Christmas gift from the partisan leaders," Pavel said in his halting English.

It was a box of cookies I learned had come from a German truck the partisans had raided. So, indirectly, the Germans provided me with an unexpected Christmas gift.

I insisted we all share the cookies, but they shushed me and sent me back to bed to think of my next Christmas, which they prayed would be with my own family.

On Christmas Day, the Germans came to the village and searched the houses. I stayed hidden in the haystack for more than an hour as I listened to the muffled conversations between the Germans and Slovaks until the Germans left.

GREAT EVADER. Silas Crase lived as a Slovak (cameo at left) while taking refuge with Pavel Rézak and family (top left) in 1944. Silas returned in 1980, when the photo of Hannah and son Dominic (top right) was taken.

Stayed Buried For Two Days

The usual routine was for me to remain under the hay for two days after a German "visit." During that time, the only contact I had with anyone was when Pavel or Hannah came in to get hay for the animals.

When I finally crawled out, I insisted that my cookies be shared or I wouldn't eat any of them. I'd managed to make my cookies last for four or five days without the mice getting any!

I also carved a small model Greyhound bus for each of the boys. The buses had no markings, of course, but Pavel told the boys he had ridden Greyhound buses many times when he was in the United States for several years before the war.

Each time the boys saw me after that, their first words were "Gra-i-hound." The cookies and the little wooden buses were their only Christmas presents.

About May 1, the Russians moved in. Within two weeks, the Slovaks were saying, "Give us back the Boche!"

I also evaded the Russians until June 15, 1945, when I reached the U.S. embassy in Prague.

Now, even after all this time, that Christmas in Slovakia is the one I'll never forget.

The Pencil Stub Memorial

THE DAY THAT LIVED IN INFAMY WAS MEMORIALIZED IN A SMALL WAY BY THIS HIGH SCHOOL SOPHOMORE TURNED AIRMAN. *By Russell Bucher, Albuquerque, New Mexico*

FUNNY MONEY. That was one name GIs gave the scrip they were issued overseas in lieu of "real" money during World War II, says Chester Kirk of Fort Lauderdale, Florida. The lady pictured on smaller "cents" denominations is apparently Liberty. But Chester can't remember who the lady is on the $1 certificate that's pictured above.

It was December 8, 1941. I was a sophomore in high school, and our entire student body was in shock over the attack on Pearl Harbor.

I sat uneasily at my desk in study hall. Not much studying was being done—students were talking about the attack, and I could feel their outrage.

President Roosevelt's address to Congress was piped over the PA system: "My fellow Americans, yesterday, December 7, 1941, a date that will live in infamy, the United States of America was suddenly and deliberately attacked by naval and air forces of the Empire of Japan…"

I was sitting in the back of the room near the wall, tossing a pencil stub in the air, trying to get it to land on top of a wooden control box that hung just above the red fire alarm bell.

It wasn't that I wasn't interested in the President's speech. I'd been saturated with Pearl Harbor news from the minute I heard about the attack. Besides, I was a little annoyed that I was only 17 and too young to enlist.

Outside every recruiting office in the country, thousands of young men were lining up, and I would have gone that day if they'd have taken me.

Instead, I sat there tossing the pencil and listening to the President's speech. After numerous attempts, the pencil landed squarely atop that control box. *Good aim!* I thought.

America marched into war without me. But when my 18th birthday finally came in August, I lost no time riding my bike to the post office and registering for the draft. We'd been at war for eight months, and many of my friends had gone off to fight.

Instead of waiting for my draft number to come up, I could go in as a volunteer inductee. But my parents refused to sign the papers.

"If they draft you, that's different," my father said. "But you're not going until they do."

Son Had a Plan

So I came up with a scheme to get my father to sign. In January I deliberately failed all my midterm exams. He was furious!

"If fighting for your country means that much to you, go get the papers and I'll sign them," he stammered. Mother, in tears, also reluctantly signed.

"As soon as the war's over, I'll go back to high school and get my diploma," I promised.

"In a pig's eye you will," Father snorted. I vowed that day I'd make him eat those words.

I ended up a nose gunner in a B-24 Liberator and flew 32 bombing missions before we were shot down near Prague on August 24, 1944. I parachuted out, was captured and held as a prisoner of war until May 3, 1945.

I sailed back home and into New York Harbor on June 16 aboard the USS Hermitage with 5,000 other former POWs. Three days later, I was home on a two-month rehabilitation leave.

It worked. When I was shot down, I weighed 155 pounds. The day I was liberated, I weighed 92 pounds. After two months of Mom's good home cooking, I was back up to 124.

Following discharge in September, I went back to high school, along with 35 other ex-servicemen. I walked into the study hall where I'd listened to President Roosevelt's address some four years before and looked up at the control box. My pencil was still there!

I decided to leave it as a memorial to all those from our school who served and didn't make it back. And, yes…my father did eat his words. On June 25, 1946, I graduated from high school.

Hub Zemke
Saved Us…TWICE

It happens so often in our lives—we don't fully appreciate what people do for us until some time after the fact.

A classic example of that is Col. Hubert "Hub" Zemke, who became a hero to me twice—not with muscle or firepower, but with brains and leadership.

Hub was a remarkable 30-year-old officer who was once described by a general this way: "Typical fighter pilot, chip on his shoulder…looks you right in the eye…not insolent…just confident."

I met Hub in Stalag Luft I, a camp near the town of Barth on the Baltic Sea coast. We were "kriegies" (short for *kriegsgefangenen*, the German word for prisoner of war).

There were some 9,000 captured American and British RAF fliers incarcerated there. Hub was the ranking Allied officer. I was a B-17 bombardier whose plane had been shot down a year earlier. Some prisoners had been there for almost four years.

Call to Action

At dusk on April 28, 1945, I was walking along one side of a double barbed wire fence dividing the compound. Hub, on the other side, called to me.

"Lieutenant, get this message to Col. Wilson right away!" he instructed. Wilson was the officer in charge of North Compound I.

Glancing at a nearby guard tower to make sure he wasn't being watched, Hub quickly tossed a small coffee can containing the note over the fence. I grabbed it and took it to Wilson.

We were aware that the war in Europe was nearing an end, so I assumed Hub was making some plans for the prisoners. The Russian army was reportedly less than 25 miles away from the camp.

Later, we learned that our camp commandant had been ordered by Heinrich Himmler to evacuate the camp within 24 hours and move it to a location near Hamburg. Because of the ravaged transportation conditions in Germany, such a move would have entailed a forced march of 150 miles.

Hub saved the day by somehow persuading the commandant it would be in the Germans' best interests to get just themselves out of the camp before the Russians arrived.

The next morning when we awoke, we found the Germans gone. Hub's "MP's" were manning the guard towers, and the Stars and Stripes had replaced the Nazi swastika on the flagpole.

But Hub wasn't done. When boisterous Russian patrols stormed in later that day, he had another problem to resolve with his political finesse and power of persuasion.

The Russian commander said they planned to move us to Odessa, a Russian port city on the Black Sea. Hub was outraged—we were just 150 miles from Allied territory, and they wanted to transport 9,000 weary soldiers 1,500 miles to the east?

Hub wanted the 8th Air Force to fly us out to France instead. He sent RAF Group Capt. C.T. Weir to contact British Field Marshal Bernard Montgomery, who helped convince the Russians that it would be impossible for the inmates of our camp to make the long journey to Odessa.

Reportedly, Montgomery met with Marshal Rokossovsky, Commander of the White Russian Army Group. Capt. Weir returned to report that plans were worked out to have the 8th Air Force evacuate Stalag Luft I. A week later, some 300 B-17s came in and flew us to freedom.

—**Oscar Richard,** *Baton Rouge, Louisiana*

HERO RECALLED. Hubert Zemke (center) and fellow fighter pilots pose after returning from a mission. He was later taken prisoner at a German POW camp, where he helped save 9,000 incarcerated American and British RAF fliers.

SONGS FOR SOLDIERS

BOYS (AND GIRL) IN THE BAND

In 1944, I played in this swing band while stationed at the naval air station in Norfolk, Virginia. As you can see from the photo of our first "job," I was the only woman in the band, which played at the Chiefs Club located on the base. The glamorous female singer on the left, whose name I don't know, was a hit with the audience.

We couldn't charge for our services, so a jar was placed at the front of the stage for people to drop money into, if they desired, while they danced by. I think we made $60 the first night. That was used to buy more music. Note the flag direction on the wall; I think that meant that our country was in distress.

My main saxophone solo with the band was "Tea for Two." One evening, we had a second request for the song and received $20—a surprise to us all. The musicians were all very talented, and I felt lucky to play with them.

The Navy provided entertainment for civilians as well as the service members. Sometimes, we were asked to play during the noon hour. People would eat their sack lunches and dance in a space in front of the band.

The band eventually drifted apart when several members were called to duty elsewhere. Some of the men signed their names on my photo. The ones I could decipher are: Charles Ray Wintufe, Darryl D. Cheaturn, Keith Hendrickson, John Stewart, Milton H. Maser, J. Hurdy and our bandleader, Frank Orofino.

—*Madelynn Theilen Herman*, *Eyota, Minnesota*

MORALE IN THE MUSIC

After basic training in early 1942, my dad, Aaron Caplan, had a short leave to go home and then on to field artillery school—or so he thought. Aboard the train, he learned from a porter that he wasn't going to field artillery school. "You're in the Air Corps now," the man said.

One day while in Italy, he heard an airplane mechanic playing a guitar in the barracks. He said it was wonderful to hear music, and it gave him an idea. He put up a notice for musicians, and from the various squadrons he assembled an 11-piece band.

He got permission to requisition the instruments the men needed and sent to the States for orchestrations. The band rehearsed in a barn with

an old, broken-down piano, and when the musicians were ready, the Red Cross arranged a dance in town.

The band's debut, Dad said, unfolded with the glossy perfection of a scene from an old movie. The GIs were in dress uniforms and under strict orders to behave decently. Nurses were officers and didn't go to dances for enlisted men, but there was a good turnout of local girls. My dad got up to make the introduction, and when he turned around and requested "One O'Clock Jump," the band took off.

For any outfit that wanted music, Dad charged $10 for each member of the band, $10 for himself as manager, and all the food and booze they could consume. The band was made up entirely of enlisted men. When officers wanted a dance, they had to come to the enlisted men to ask for it.

One time an African-American outfit came to Dad to request a dance, but the white Southerners in the band objected. Dad told them that the black soldiers were doing the same job they were doing and asked if they would play as a special favor to him. They said, "OK, Cappy, we'll do it for you." The Italian girls danced with the group, and the African-American GIs were appreciative.

Dad always said he wasn't a hero, but at the end of the war he received a written citation recognizing his contribution to morale through his band.

—**David Caplan**, *Chicago, Illinois*

ON TOUR. Deborah Nigro of Hyannis, Massachusetts, proudly poses next to one of the caravans that rode in the Women's Auxiliary Army Corps Caravan Military Recruiting Show during WWII. In the spring of 1943, they toured 15 New England cities in an effort to bring young women into the corps. Each stop featured a patriotic parade and evening variety show. Her GI father played trumpet with the caravan band.

A Debt Of
GRATITUDE

DUTCH WOMAN'S APPRECIATION FOR ALLIED LIBERATORS LED TO A PERSONAL CONNECTION WITH AMERICAN FAMILY.

By Willemyntje "Willy" Slot, Windsor, Nova Scotia

Life in Holland during the Nazi occupation was filled with hardships. We had so little food that many people died of hunger. The Germans would give us four ounces of bread per person per week; it was made with beer and was as hard as rock. By the end of the war, we were eating grass just to survive.

It was a terrible time in other ways, too. The Germans controlled all aspects of our lives, with curfews and rules about what we could and couldn't do, and where we could or couldn't go. All the young men were gone, either sent to work in German munitions factories or in hiding to avoid being sent away.

At one point my family could find nothing at all to eat. So my sister and I left our home in Blaricum for 10 days, walking for miles and sleeping where we could, to search for food. After finally finding some potatoes, we were stopped by two German soldiers in a car. I begged them to let us keep the food to feed my starving family, and to my surprise they did.

Our saving grace was the Allied food drops that came about once a week around 11 a.m. We'd put a big flag with a red cross on it out in a field, and planes would drop bags of flour and dried peas from the Swedish Red Cross. The planes came in so low that we could see the pilots. It was the most beautiful sight!

Breaking the Rules

We weren't supposed to be outside to see the food drops, but we would sit on the roof and watch anyway. German soldiers would check all the bags for concealed weapons before letting us have any of the food.

The flour went to a local baker who used it for bread. Families were assigned numbers, and when your number came up, you got a loaf of bread. It always looked like a big cake to us.

I despised the occupation so much that I joined the Dutch underground when I was 18 and did resistance work for the last two years of the war. Looking back, I wouldn't think of doing it now—it was very risky. But I was young, and we thought we were invulnerable!

The underground did many things, including hiding downed pilots and helping them escape. The only news we received about the war came from German radio, so distributing newspapers dropped by Allied planes was also important to our cause.

But it was dangerous, too. My sister's boyfriend was caught carrying papers, and we never saw him again. If they grabbed you while you were carrying something illegal, you were headed for a concentration camp.

Acting in Secret

I did my part mainly by serving as a courier, carrying things like messages and food stamps. It was all very secret. You never used your real name, nor did you know the real names of the people you worked with.

Once a month or so I met a contact in Amsterdam, about 20 miles away. My father would get a telephone call notifying him it was time for another delivery, and I'd go by train or bicycle.

In Amsterdam, I'd walk by the contact's apartment building, ring his doorbell and walk away. I'd keep an eye out until he came to the door, which was my signal that it was safe to meet him.

I never knew what the messages were about. Once the man made a secret courier pouch by cutting open my cloth powder puff, putting two

small pieces of paper inside, then sewing it back up for me to carry home.

When I returned, my father would call the message recipient and say, "The cake is almost ready." That was the signal to meet me at a certain spot. Once I rode my bike out to deliver a message to a German surgeon who lived in a big mansion; many Germans who had moved to Holland before the war were sympathetic to our cause.

I kept a crystal radio set hidden in my pillow, and one night I heard the most amazing news: The war was over! We ran outside and saw some German soldiers. We tried to tell them the news, but they fired guns in our direction, so we ran back inside.

In the morning, we saw the Dutch flag flying high atop a church tower—and not a German soldier in sight. It was the most beautiful thing we'd ever seen. My parents cried, and we all hugged each other over and over. I'm 87 years old, and I still think about that liberation every day.

After the war, the Dutch government asked citizens to "adopt" the graves of Allied soldiers. I wanted to show my thanks to those who had liberated us, so I adopted the grave of Foster Blake, a turret gunner in the U.S. 8th Air Force. He died in combat over Germany in 1944, and he was buried at the Netherlands American Cemetery and Memorial in Margraten.

Over the years, I tended the grave and represented Foster's parents and other family members who could not take part in commemoration services. On Memorial Day, I always laid tulips on his grave.

A friend of our family made a stainless steel replica of the headstone, which we sent to Foster's mother, Julia, in Bradford, Vermont. She was very pleased and, in return, sent us pictures of her son. But because I could not speak English at the time, we soon lost touch.

A Tearful Meeting

That all changed years later, after I married and moved to Nova Scotia. We enjoyed taking family camping trips in the United States, and during one such trip to Vermont in 1964, I happened to see a Veterans Affairs office in Burlington. I turned and said to my husband, "I wonder if they know anything about Mrs. Blake."

We went inside and I told my story. A man looked up some information and told us that Mrs. Blake still lived in Bradford, where Foster's remains had been reburied in 1948. I said I'd love to visit her, and the man said it would be OK— with her approval.

So he called Mrs. Blake right then and there, and she said she was very eager to meet "the girl with the braids." She was referring to a picture I'd sent her of me putting tulips on Foster's grave.

PAYING IT FORWARD. On a Memorial Day years ago, Willy Slot lays tulips on Foster Blake's grave at the Netherlands American Cemetery and Memorial in Margraten, Holland. Dutch citizens have "adopted" all 8,301 graves at the cemetery, one of 24 U.S. military burial grounds on foreign soil. People are still on a waiting list to adopt graves, more than 65 years after the war ended.

Later we drove to her home for a very emotional meeting. She hugged me and our three children, and we cried a lot. We felt as though we'd known each other for a long time.

I believe many wounds were healed that day. Mrs. Blake was so appreciative of what I did.

But it was nothing compared to what her son and all the other Allied troops did for us in Holland. We adopted those graves because it was important to honor everything that had to do with our liberation. Thanks to them, we were finally free. That was the greatest gift of all.

MANNA FROM THE SKIES

I was 6 years old in my native country of Holland when German troops marched into our streets and searched our homes during World War II.

The greatest event of my childhood came in 1945, when Holland was liberated. Even now, the sound of thunder reminds me of the time when artillery sounds grew louder the closer our liberators got to us.

The other great event happened a few days before that. In much of Holland, the Germans had stopped all transportation. Railroads were torn up, the steel sent to Germany for the war effort. With transport at a standstill, millions of people were starving. People were begging farmers for food, even cooking tulip bulbs. Trees and railroad ties were dug up just to warm our homes.

Near the end of the war, in April and May of 1945, Allied forces responded to the desperate situation by flying low over the countryside with American, British and Canadian bombers to drop off food. The missions, dubbed Operation Manna and Operation Chowhound, miraculously delivered more than 11,000 tons of flour, powdered eggs, military rations and other necessities to the Dutch population, with planes flying as low as 300 feet.

People lined the fields and streets by the thousands, crying and waving at these heavenly guests. My father-in-law wrote a very emotional poem about the event.

What a joy it must have been for those pilots and staff who had the privilege to be on those missions.

—*Richard Oostra,* Blaine, Washington

MINKA...A Soldier's
BEST FRIEND

Although I loved dogs as a boy, we lived in apartments and couldn't keep pets. I didn't have my first real "this is my dog" relationship until I was fighting my way across Germany in World War II.

I was in I&R (Intelligence and Reconnaissance), and it was mid-September of 1944 when we first made our way onto German soil.

Two weeks later, we approached a small village and encountered a heavy barrage from the dreaded and deadly German 88-mm guns.

Jumping from my jeep, I ran for cover in an old barn. There, shivering and quivering—just as scared as the rest of us—was a little dog. I cuddled up with him, and we rode out the artillery storm together.

I named him Minka after an old song I'd loved back in the '30s. We soon became so close that nothing could separate us.

He sensed all situations as though he were human and knew what to do for us to stay together. If I needed Minka to stay put at a certain place until I returned, he wouldn't move until I came back. Out on patrol when complete silence was necessary, Minka never once barked to reveal our location.

Only once was I in danger of losing Minka. We'd received hurried orders to move out in five minutes—but Minka was out browsing somewhere and I couldn't find him!

Joyous Reunion

After advancing some 30 miles forward, I was in a state of panic and knew Minka would be, too. Our bond had become so strong, "heartbreak" was too mild a word to describe my feelings.

Two days later, Minka found me. Apparently, he'd caught a ride up to the front by himself. The joy we felt when reunited was unexplainable. After that, I made sure we were never separated again.

During that winter, if we were in a safe place at night and could use our sleeping bags, Minka would climb in with me and sleep at the bottom, keeping my feet warm.

I can't recall all the things Minka did to amaze the Fighting Fourth, but all the boys loved this intelligent animal. (I found out years later several named their own dogs after Minka.)

When the war in Europe ended, Minka and I enjoyed many days of peace together. But I dreaded the moment we'd be separated—we had been told we could not take animals home with us. I loved that dog, and he loved me.

My mind was in turmoil—as silly as it sounds, the thought crossed my mind that if he was not allowed to go home with me, I would just stay myself.

Finally I devised a plan. I'd train Minka to stay still inside my barracks bag while I carried it onto the ship. But Minka just couldn't seem to comprehend this procedure and why he had to keep still. I tried teaching him for days, to no avail.

When our orders arrived, I drove to Le Havre with a heavy heart, wondering how I'd ever be able to say goodbye. In a complete state of panic, I had one last talk with Minka.

I explained that if he wanted to go home with me, he must get in the bag and remain perfectly still. My talk got through to him, because he didn't move a muscle as I walked aboard.

The Invisible Dog

During the trip, the rest of the boys shielded Minka from unwanted eyes whenever necessary. We fed him from our rations, and I cleaned up the steel deck after him.

Back in New York, I had another talk with Minka before getting off the ship, with the same result. Home free!

What a relief to hit dirt again in New York. Minka hit the first 10 trees he saw! And the train ride home to Greensboro, North Carolina, was a cakewalk—the train people were most understanding.

When I brought Minka home, the family gladly welcomed him to our home. In 1946, I married and my wife and our three children all got to know Minka before he died in 1957.

—**Jon Holden,** *Jacksonville, North Carolina*

Band of Brothers

A BROTHER IN EVERY PORT

During World War II, my father-in-law, Gayle Evers, was at sea for two years on a battleship. The prospect of setting foot on shore when they docked for supplies or repairs was irresistible, but only sailors with immediate family in port were permitted to leave the ship.

On five different occasions, Seaman Evers unflinchingly declared that he had a brother in port. The first four times, he was granted leave and enjoyed several days of exploring.

The fifth time was different. The captain ordered the Shore Patrol to escort Gayle to his brother's location and bring them both back to the ship, where the captain would inspect the brother's credentials.

On that fateful occasion, Gayle's brother George happened to be stationed at an Army base near the port.

After verifying the truth, the surprised captain said, "The whole blasted Japanese navy can't beat me, but Evers, you sure did. Enjoy your leave."

—**William Keller,** Worthington, Ohio

HUNTING FOR BROTHER BY CROSS-ISLAND TRAFFIC

While serving at an Army anti-aircraft gun battery in Manila during World War II, I heard that my brother Oscar was stationed at the U.S. air base at Lingayen on the other side of the Philippine island of Luzon.

I was able to get a weekend pass, but Oscar's base was more than 150 miles away. I hitched some rides from the Marine and Army transport units that were constantly moving about the island. The dirt roads through the woods were awful.

A general in a jeep stopped and asked me where I was headed. I told him that my brother was a mechanic with the Army Air Forces in Lingayen, adding that I hadn't seen him since the beginning of the war three years earlier. He told me to climb on board.

Later, as I walked onto the base, the CO yelled to ask where I was from, and I told him that I had hitchhiked from Manila to see my brother, Oscar Cormier.

I followed him and saw Oscar beside a fighter jet, washing spark plugs in a dish of solvent. I came up behind him and said, "If you don't know what you're doing, why don't you ask someone?"

He turned around and gave me a dirty look, then realized who I was. We were both invited into the officers' lounge, where we partied all night long.

I will never forget that day or that look of surprise on my brother's face.

—**Joseph Cormier**
New Bedford, Massachusetts

LAWBREAKERS. Twins Rocco (left) and Sal Robelotto weren't supposed to be on the same ship in WWII because of the "Sullivan brothers law." They were, just the same. Living in Torrance, California, Rocco wonders if any other brothers "broke" that law.

BROTHERS IN ARMS. Being stationed 150 miles apart didn't stop Joseph Cormier (right) from hitchhiking to visit his brother Oscar (left) while they were both serving in the Philippines.

ON-THE-JOB TRAINING. After the German surrender, Bob Evans (right) of Statesville, North Carolina, found out his brother, Ed, was stationed just 30 miles away. Bob wrangled a pass and the use of a motorcycle—even though he'd never ridden a motorcycle before. Along the way, he slid into a stone wall, blew the front tire and busted the headlight. When Bob finally met his brother, Ed wanted to know where Bob learned to ride a motorcycle. "On the way over," he said.

FAMOUS & FEARLESS

TYRONE TOLERATED TALK FROM FLYING FANS

In August 1943, I was the radio operator on a C-47 that landed at Bolling Field just outside Washington, D.C. The pilots went to the operations building, and the crew chief, after tending to the plane, stretched out in the shade of the left wing.

I was slouched in the door, half-asleep, when I saw a lone figure striding toward the plane. He not only walked smartly, but he was the best-dressed military man I'd seen in my three years in the service.

When I realized he was a Marine Corps officer, I jumped to my feet and bellowed "Ten Hut!" The crew chief and I then saluted Tyrone Power. He was looking for a ride to Newark, our destination, and our pilots agreed to give him one.

Once aboard, we gathered around Tyrone and talked and talked. He was pleasant and tolerated us "kids" very well…but I think he was happy to get to Newark.

—**William Ellis,** *Lewisburg, West Virginia*

VAN DYKE CRACKED THEM UP

Back in 1944, as an aviation cadet in the Army Air Corps, I had the pleasure of serving in the same unit with Dick Van Dyke.

Dick's laid-back attitude and comic wit were a curse for him back then, because he ended up getting more than his share of KP (kitchen patrol) duty. His body contortions, facial expressions and other antics were everyday occurrences, delighting his buddies, but giving gray hair to his superior officers.

Footlocker inspections were a good example. The rest of us in the unit had to endure the stress of passing inspection. But then the fun began when the office reached the locker labeled "Van Dyke."

We'd never seen such a disarray of rumpled clothing! Items that didn't meet military standards were always found among his possessions, resulting in more demerits for poor Dick.

I had the good fortune of visiting with Dick again more recently, at the premier of one of his movies. We had a great time reminiscing about the days when we were aviation cadets!

—**C.R. St. John,** *Tacoma, Washington*

LUCY AND DESI GOT TROOPS LAUGHING

As a private training at California's Camp Roberts in 1943, I was stationed with Desi Arnaz, who was married to Lucille Ball.

The camp wasn't far from Hollywood, so Lucy often drove up on weekends to perform for the GIs.

One Saturday afternoon when Lucy drove up, Desi ran in front of her station wagon and threw himself on the ground. He bowed in submission, facedown in the street, until Lucy got out and tapped him on the shoulder.

Desi got up, and they embraced, laughing. Then they left for the recreation hall to put on a show.

—**Charles Bernard Jr.,** *Lafayette, Louisiana*

FRANKLY, AIRMAN, I DON'T GIVE A QUACK

One very warm afternoon in 1942, a busload of tired men, including me, arrived in Miami Beach to begin training at the Air Corps Officers Candidate School.

We immediately lined up for inspection and were told to keep our heads still and look straight ahead.

As two inspecting upperclassmen came down the line, I could hear them questioning each man. By the time they reached me, I'd broken into a sweat from the heat (and nerves).

The first upperclassman inquired if anyone had given me permission to sweat. "No, sir," I replied.

Then the second upperclassman asked me, "Who is the greatest actor in Hollywood?"

I'm short, so my eyes were level with his name tags. I knew I had to give the right answer, and quickly. Without hesitation, I replied, "Donald Duck."

Trying hard to suppress a laugh, the two upperclassmen moved on to the next man.

Oh, yes…the name tag I was staring at said "Officer Candidate Clark Gable".

—**Woodrow Wentzy,** *Brookings, South Dakota*

LAUGHING MATTERS

PRIVATE PROMOTED BY EMBARRASSED SHAVETAIL

During World War II, the Air Force "froze" all ratings for a long time, and promotions were rare. I was a private but made acting staff sergeant of a six-man inspection/repair crew working on the interiors of B-24s.

When the landing gear was checked, the bombers were put on jacks, and no one was allowed inside. We'd adjourn to a large latrine area to play poker until we could get back inside the airplane.

The rules of dress and protocol in this flight line area were relaxed—we wore no hats and could roll up our sleeves, and we didn't have to come to attention when officers showed up.

A new "shavetail" lieutenant who didn't know about the relaxed rules came upon us one day and demanded an explanation from me on why we hadn't shown him respect by standing at attention.

The master sergeant with the lieutenant pulled him aside and explained the situation. The embarrassed shavetail quickly left.

About two months later, when promotions were finally made, I was surprised to learn I'd made corporal.

Later, I found out why. The master sergeant told me the shavetail had been given a promotion list, and my name was on it.

"I don't know why this name is familiar," the lieutenant had wondered. "But it must be favorable, so we'll promote this Gibbons from private to corporal."

The master sergeant told me he could hardly keep a straight face.

—**Edward Gibbons,** *Sugar Land, Texas*

WHAT'S IN A NAME

One night when I was in Barie, Italy, with the 941st Engineers, my buddy Daniel Hansen and I went to a show put on by the Red Cross.

During the show, we were getting bombed by the Germans. Afterward, as hundreds of soldiers were leaving the theater, Daniel and I got separated.

That's when he started calling my last name—causing all those hundreds of soldiers to scramble for cover!

—**Walter Scram,** *Herkimer, New York*

PINUP PANIC

I was an Armed Guard Naval gunner in 1945, and all of my shipmates on our merchant tanker had pinups on the bulkheads next to their bunks.

I did, too, but my pinups were of the same girl, actress Susan Hayward. She was my dream girl, and even our gunnery officer, Lt. Hughes, would remark every morning during inspection, "I do like your taste in women."

One of my sisters, knowing how enamored I was, sent me a jigsaw puzzle that turned out to be a picture of Susan Hayward.

Then one day, I was told Lt. Hughes wanted to see me. When I got to his quarters, he told me to sit down because he had some shocking news. The blood drained from my face. My mind raced. I just knew something awful had happened to someone in my family back in Chicago.

The lieutenant walked up to me, put his hand on my shoulder and said in a solemn voice, "Susan Hayward just had twins."

—**James Horan,** *Chicago, Illinois*

GLAMOUR GIRL. Golden Globe- and Academy Award-winning film actress Susan Hayward captivated men around the world with her beauty and talent.

Army Photographer's Job Was Anything **BUT A SNAP**

GEN. MARK CLARK WAS A TASKMASTER, BUT THIS SOLDIER GOT A PRIVILEGED VIEW OF THE WAR FROM OVER HIS SHOULDER.

By Ralph Thomas, Canton, Ohio

I was working as a professional photographer when I was drafted—so, naturally, the Army immediately tried to make a truck driver out of me.

Several months later, my request for transfer was granted, and I was sent to the 163rd Signal Photo Company in San Antonio, Texas.

In November 1943, I was assigned as the personal photographer to Gen. Mark Clark, commander of the 5th Army. I was warned the general could be a difficult man to satisfy—his previous three photographers had lasted no longer than six weeks each!

As it turned out, I lasted 13 months and then left—on good terms—to join a combat team with my old outfit.

Gen. Clark was difficult to work for. He was a blur of constant motion, and I had to be ready to go on a moment's notice—most of the time not knowing why or where. Days often started at 4 a.m. and concluded at midnight.

On the plus side, I got to be "in" on some of the war's biggest moments, like the landing at Anzio in January 1944.

As you can see in the pictures here, I photographed the general with many famous figures of the time—President Roosevelt; Generals Marshall, Eisenhower and Patton; British Prime Minister Churchill; King George VI and Charles de Gaulle.

Despite his often headstrong nature, Gen. Clark was a great man. It was a privilege to serve with him.

SMILE! Ralph Thomas (top) sometimes didn't feel much like smiling when he was serving as Gen. Mark Clark's personal photographer in World War II. But, as his pictures show, he got to photograph many world leaders during his 13-month stint.

STRIKE A POSE. Charles de Gaulle (top, left), George Patton (below, left), Henry "Hap" Arnold of the Air Force (below, center) and of course Gen. Mark Clark were just a few of the world's renowned military figures that Thomas had the privilege to capture on film.

THE IMPORTANCE OF BEING ERNIE

I first met Ernie Pyle in the Army press censor's office in Oran, Algeria. It was late November 1942, and he'd arrived that morning by troop convoy from England.

His compassionate, explicit accounts of the British people and their steadfast courage in the face of Hitler's bombings had captured millions of new readers for his daily newspaper column.

Ernie and I were billeted in Oran's drafty old Grand Hotel, which served as headquarters for the Army's Second Corps. I was a photographer, and we worked on several stories together. One featured the 38th Evacuation Hospital, where our wounded were recovering from the battles fought at the invasion of North Africa.

Ernie almost always worked late at night on his columns—I'd hear his beat-up old portable typewriter clattering away in his room down the hall. Typing rapidly with two fingers, he turned out six new columns each week.

Instead of reporting on major tactical developments or the headline newsmakers, Ernie wrote about the GIs, how they lived, fought and sometimes died. It was a pattern he followed throughout the war, and it would win him a Pulitzer Prize and make him America's best-loved war correspondent.

Just after New Year's Day 1943, Ernie left Oran, and I never saw him again. But his daily columns in *Stars and Stripes* told me his whereabouts.

On Wednesday morning, April 18, 1945, two weeks after his 45th birthday, Ernie was advancing with the U.S. 305th Infantry Regiment along a narrow road on the tiny island of Ie Shima, off Okinawa. He was riding in a jeep with Lt. Col. Joseph B. Coolidge when a Japanese sniper began firing.

The jeep skidded to a stop, and its occupants dove into a ditch. All were safe except Ernie, who'd been killed by a single bullet.

—**Bill Wilson**, *Princeton, Indiana*

BILLIARDS FOR THE BOYS (AND GIRLS). Once a week, the servicemen from a Coast Guard radio school in Atlantic City, New Jersey, along with their wives, were treated to a pool party at the local Elks Club. In this 1943 photo, Avery Taylor is cuing up, with his wife, Betty Clark Taylor, watching on to his left. This was the first base at which the Taylors were stationed, and was followed by Corpus Christi, Texas; New Orleans, Louisiana; Mobile, Alabama; and finally back to their hometown of Houston, Texas, after three years of operating shore radio stations for the WWII Coast Guard.

A PAPAL BLESSING

I was a photographer in the Signal Corps during World War II, stationed in Rome. One day when we were granted some free time, a friend and I visited St. Peter's Basilica.

I had a camera, so we stationed ourselves near a door where we'd seen the Pope on his way to his daily audience. Sure enough, the door opened and Pope Pius XII walked straight toward us.

He greeted us and, as I knelt, he gave me a blessing. Then he asked, "Where would you like me to stand?"

The Pope had seen my camera and thought we were there to take his photo. I asked him to stand where a small skylight illuminated the floor like a spotlight.

The Pope raised his hand and posed, as in a blessing. I cocked the shutter and tried to release it.

Off Duty

Nothing happened! I tried it again, but it still wouldn't work. My buddy offered to try, but he, too, couldn't get it to work.

"You are obviously having trouble with that camera," the Pope said.

I apologized and said we didn't want to take up any more of his time. Others were waiting to talk to him and get his blessing.

When my friend and I left, we walked outside and tried the camera again. It worked perfectly!

I was dumbfounded. Maybe it was because we didn't have permission from the proper authorities to take the Pope's photograph. The Lord sure works in mysterious ways!

—*George LaFrost,* Holiday, Florida

A MUCH BETTER FIT. Warren Sarley, shown here in 1945 with his niece Karen, sports a uniform that was less embarrassing to wear in public.

OUT OF UNIFORM

After the Allied invasion of Europe, our captain gave three-day passes to the men of the 660th Engineer Topographic Battalion, Company C, in England.

Only four men were allowed to go on leave at a time, and on this particular time, all four of us headed for Edinburgh, Scotland, and the same studio to have our picture taken in kilts—the photo above pictures me.

The town was quiet and peaceful and had a big dance hall with bands playing every night. But no matter how we were spending our "free time," it was always guaranteed to be a good three days!

—*Rosario Maiorano,* Norwich, Connecticut

CLOTHES HELPED MAKE THE MAN... INTO A SAILOR

In early 1945, I found myself with a couple hundred other recruits at the Great Lakes Naval Station north of Chicago.

The cold weather necessitated the wearing of the heavy wool blue uniforms during boot camp. I paid no attention to the white dress uniform rolled up in the bottom of my seabag.

Upon my completion of boot camp, I was officially labeled Seaman, 2nd Class, and was shipped off to Algiers Naval Base at New Orleans. What a climate change! My wool outfit drenched me in perspiration from the Louisiana heat.

Granted liberty, I burrowed through the seabag to locate the "dress whites" and found them not only to be badly wrinkled but made for a man twice my size. I wasn't about to miss liberty, so I raced up the dock to the New Orleans ferry with my long pant legs rolled up and a blouse that fit like a blanket.

In the reverie of enjoying a new city, I lost all thought of my absurdly fitting uniform. All of the other servicemen seemed to be accompanied by chic females, and I thought that I, too, might find a sweet and pretty girl.

I was feeling proud of myself until one sharp-looking girl, one arm entwined with that of a tall, handsome ensign, reached out and grabbed the long tail of my oversized blouse. She kept tugging, then giggled and said for all to hear, "Hey, boot, where did you get the pup tent? You must have bought it at a sail-maker's store."

Everyone around me, right in the middle of Canal Street, roared with laughter. I tried to lose myself in the milling crowds, and then I spied a tailor shop. I had little cash, but I was desperate. I ordered the tailor to cut my uniform down to size. Later, out into the New Orleans night I strode—no girl and flat broke. Still, I felt like an authentic Navy man.

—*Warren Sarley,* Rochester, New York

LETTERS HOME

ENVELOPE ART GOT DELAYED DELIVERY

During World War II, I found myself attached to a remote LORAN (long-range navigation) station on tiny Cocos Island off the coast of Guam.

With only 31 other personnel there, it was difficult to find new subjects to write about to my wife. So to make my letters more interesting, I drew cartoons on the envelopes. I penned them in color and often used various events experienced in the islands for my subjects.

The cartoons provided something different to dress up my letters. I also hoped they'd help cheer up my wife (pregnant at the time with our first child) by making light of my situation.

What I didn't know until I returned to the United States was just how popular my mail had become!

When I arrived in San Francisco, I went to the Fleet post office to pick up my mail before it got forwarded to the island.

After the postal clerk learned who I was, he told me that the letters I'd been writing to my wife were routinely held there so each shift working at the post office had a chance to see the drawings and catch up on the latest events at the island base!

Eventually my mail did get through, as you can see from the censors' stamps and postmarks.

—*Wayne Harwood*
Delmar, New York

QUICK NOTE BETWEEN BATTLES

This postcard was handmade by French staff operating a large castle near Chaumet, France, that served as a rest area for Allied troops in World War II. I sent it home the week before Christmas 1944.

I was serving in the 141st Field Artillery Battalion, which had been in combat for over a year without a break. The French cooks at the castle could make even powdered eggs taste good. While there, we got a hot bath and clean clothes.

After a week, it was back to my unit to continue the fight. I was lucky to go home in August of 1945.

—*Carroll Johnson, Frankfort, Indiana*

NOSTALGIC LETTER FROM THE PACIFIC

My husband, Marine Corps Pfc. Nathaniel Wright, was with the U.S. occupation forces in Japan for Christmas 1945. On Sept. 24 while stationed in Honolulu, he sent home a Christmas package for his family, including a touching letter he'd written in Oahu to his parents and sisters, 16-year-old Pat and 5-year-old Bonnie.

I did not see my husband's letters from this time until after his death in 2009. Here's the Christmas letter, which he signed "Bunk," a Southern nickname for a first or only son.

"Dear Folks,

"Here it is Christmas again, and Santa Claus holds sway over the Wright household. It's a little different this year, though. I'm not there to break the Victrola records or knock the balls off the tree and stuff like that. However, don't let this take away from the joy of the occasion. I'll be thinking about you and remembering all our other Christmases. There's always a certain magic about this time of year. I remember the kick I used to get out of wandering downtown among the crowd, looking in store windows and listening to carols, playing the Victrola when nothing but the tree lights were on, and the 'Runt' (kid sister Bonnie) on Christmas morning, and Pop snoring on the couch that night. Oh, well, this is only a temporary absence, and maybe next year I'll be home for all these things.

"The gifts in this box are just a few things I picked up in Honolulu, a little sample of the tourist trade. Hope ya like 'em. Also enclosed are a few photos taken in Honolulu. They're pretty grotesque, but at least they're me.

"Have a good time and don't worry about me. Just write and tell me how 'Sandy Claws' treated you all. Merry Christmas and a very Happy New Year.

"My love to you all,

"Bunk."

—Sue Wright
Glenside, Pennsylvania

Remember Saying?

GOBBLEDYGOOK: *wordy*

WOMEN AT WAR

OVER THERE...IN CANADA

It was 1943, and I felt strongly about the war. But at age 18, I was too young to be a U.S. WAC. So I did the next best thing: I joined the Canadian Women's Army Corps (CWACs).

We freshly minted CWACs marched to a multinational beat on a parade ground in Kitchener, Ontario: not just "O Canada," but "Over There," "Tenting Tonight," "It's a Long Way to Tipperary" and, yes, "God Save the King."

In six weeks of basic training, we learned to march, salute and climb into upper bunks and troop trucks. I became an expert at tying a military tie, shining buttons and using a gas mask. I also learned such Canadianisms as "aboot" for about, "leftenant" for lieutenant, "petrol" for gas and "zed" for Z.

While I never made it beyond the rank of private, I got a plum assignment to the directorate of public relations OHMS—On His Majesty's Service. Serving in Montreal and Ottawa, I wrote press releases and magazine articles about the CWACs and the men of the Canadian regiments, including some Americans who'd enlisted in Canada before the U.S. officially entered the war.

Traveling by train, lugging my kit bag and manual typewriter, I'd sleep in an upper berth while an officer took the lower one. An unforgettable assignment awaited me in Halifax, Nova Scotia, where I met a troop ship bearing badly wounded soldiers. Many were carried ashore by stretchers. Despite their injuries, they still tried to salute the officers and wave or wink at the female nurses, soldiers and civilians.

In April 1945, after the death of President Franklin D. Roosevelt, I joined a thousand or more weeping Americans and Canadians for a memorial gathering at the U.S. Embassy in Ottawa.

Less than a month later, we cried happy tears after news of victory in Europe came clacking loudly over the teletype. After the war, as a 20-year-old veteran and a resident of Yonkers, New York, I went to college on the GI Bill.

—*Barbara Cole Feiden,* White Plains, New York

CALL TO DUTY. Gutsy 18-year-old Barbara Cole Feiden proudly poses in her CWACs uniform. She excersied her writing muscle by working as a journalist from 1943 until the war's end in 1945.

SWEEPING SUCCESS. On the back of this postcard, one WAC wrote, "This is just the way we do it. My bed is a double-decker, and I am on top. We don't have blue floors. Louise"

MAKING WAVES

"You'll be sor-eee," they yelled as I walked through the gate to WAVES boot camp at Hunter College in the Bronx on January 6, 1944. I was dressed in my best coat and wore a matching Juliette hat that sat neatly in the center of my carefully arranged pompadour.

Hundreds of us from all over the U.S. were herded into a huge auditorium, where we waited to find out what we'd volunteered to do. That's also where we were issued the only part of our uniforms we'd get until weeks later—heavy Oxford shoes and the little "roller style" WAVES cap.

When I put that cap on, my beautiful pompadour came down around my ears like sausages. It was then I wondered if those hecklers at the gate had been right.

But it worked out okay, and over the next six weeks, I became good friends with my roommate.

—*Marion Voltz*
Dunedin, Florida

SIGNAL WACS SAW EXOTIC LOCALES

During my two years overseas with the 6715th Communications Company, 2629th WAC Battalion, I wrote 250 letters to my immediate family.

I spent eight months in Algiers and 14 months in Italy, and one might think from my letters that we did nothing but dance and relax in Capri and Rome. But outgoing mail was heavily censored, and recreational activities preserved our sanity amidst the terrible war.

Algiers was exotic and exciting, and we encountered a great variety of military personnel everywhere. One repulsive memory of those months involved the five-inch grasshoppers that jumped into our trucks as we rode to work.

While in Caserta, Italy, in the autumn of 1944, our choir joined forces with a drama group that used the small theater in the palace where I worked as a typist. Our group presented *Our Town* by Thornton Wilder, and Col. Wilder was even present to autograph all of our programs!

—*Mabel Smith Sushinsky*
Parma, Ohio

Memorable Moments

FIRST LADY VISIT. "I was stationed at a small Navy outpost in the Galapagos Islands during World War II," writes Arnie Konkol (far left) of Black River Falls, Wisconsin. "One day, Eleanor Roosevelt, who was on her way back to the United States, stopped at our post and visited the sick bay. I was 19 then."

O.D. DOWN UNDER. "This is me, as a 2nd lieutenant serving in Australia, standing in front of my quarters in August of 1942," relates R.B. McAtee of Arlington, Virginia. "The .45-caliber pistol on my hip indicates that I was Officer of the Day."

FLYING WITH DAISY. "My dad, Robert Smith, on the far right in this 1944 photo, was a mechanic for this B-24 Liberator when he was stationed at Seething Air Base near Norwich, England, during WWII," says Stan Smith of Columbus, Nebraska. "I don't know these fellow mechanics from the 448th Bomb Group of the 8th Air Force, but the man on the far left did the painting on the plane. The 'Daisy Mae' was Dad's favorite plane and the one he worked on most. The spot Daisy is seemingly pointing at is a patched hole from damage received during one of about 35 missions flown by the crew."

V FOR VICTORY.
When Frank Farmanian enlisted in the Navy in 1942, so did several of his fellow employees at the *Los Angeles Daily News*. When the group was sworn in on October 14, they formed a "V" for a *Daily News* photographer. "That's Frank third from the bottom of the V in the left flank," says his wife, Alice, of Glendale, California. Frank and his buddies all came home safely and worked for the *News* until it closed in 1953.

DREAMS WENT ADRIFT. "In 1944, I was gun captain aboard the liberty ship *CHM Jones*, anchored near Belfast, Ireland, and the shore looked ever more inviting to my armed guard crew and me," says Hilton Floyd of Pascagoula, Mississippi, in the white cap. "We built the little boat with visions of visits to nearby ships or a trip ashore for a beer. After the trial run, we tied the boat to the stern of the ship and looked forward to a break in the monotony. It wasn't in the cards, however, as the *SS CHM Jones* swung at anchor all night, and the little boat's line was chafed in two. At dawn, all that remained of our work was a short line of rope to show where it had been."

The War is Over!

ADVENTURES ABROAD AND STATESIDE

After 18 months in the jungles and a short stint in the Philippines, I was eligible to return to the States, arriving at Camp Atterbury, Indiana, to await discharge. I was on a pass in Columbus in August when everyone went wild as the word spread that the Japanese had surrendered.

Excitedly, I ran down the street in hopes of getting some spirits for celebrating before the liquor store closed. The next thing I remembered was waking up in the hospital.

I was told that in the celebration, someone had dropped something out of a second-floor window and hit me in the head, knocking me unconscious. I was out of commission for the party, but the war was over!

—**William Swegan,** Sonoma, California

HOMECOMING ANNOUNCEMENT

I was on a ship headed back to the U.S. when we heard the news that World War II was over. I was a technical sergeant and ordnance section chief of the 96th B-17 Bomb Group, and I was now to be mustered out.

As I watched the tugs put our ship into her berth in New York Harbor, I saw a broadcast tower about 30 feet below us marked "MBS." I remembered that the Mutual Broadcasting System covered my hometown, and when I saw a man with an MBS microphone, I whistled.

My wife, who was listening 1,500 miles away in Dodgeville, Michigan, heard it and told her dad, "Nobody but Frank whistles like that!"

Then I hollered, "Hey, Dodie, I'm in New York!" That confirmed what she'd read in the paper and heard on the radio. My two brothers and I were very happy to come home to stay, and I still thank God for the gift.

Before leaving the East Coast, we were served a steak dinner at Camp Kilmer, New Jersey. The white-coated waiters were German prisoners of war. We were thankful that this was the last time we'd be meeting our adversaries.

After many days, I arrived by train in Houghton, Michigan, around midnight and saw my wife waiting on the platform. Our first embrace lasted 15 minutes—I just couldn't let her go. The next stop was her dad's home, where I met my 2-year-old son for the first time.

—**Frank Taucher,** Hancock, Michigan

EARTH-SHAKING NEWS.
"Aboard the *USS Tulagi*, we had a small radio over which we heard Tokyo Rose, the queen of World War II propaganda, announce our sinking more than once," says Paul Shy of Kansas City, Missouri. "In this photo, we're listening to a report that an atomic bomb had been dropped on Hiroshima and the Allies were demanding unconditional surrender. We huddled around the radio and wondered whether a bomb could be that powerful and if surrender was possible without invasion. The answer to both questions, of course, was yes."

THE PARTY JEEP. "This photograph from Victory Day in Europe—May 8, 1945—appeared on the front page of a newspaper in Cape Town, South Africa, with the headline 'Third Reich Ceases to Exist,'" says C. Douglas Mitchell of Springfield, Virginia. "I'm the sailor (radioman, 2nd class) on the passenger seat, fifth from left. We American sailors were part of the Navy's Armed Guard crew from the *SS Taos Victory*. The Armed Guard was formed to man the guns and communications on merchant ships, very hazardous duty early in World War II."

WELCOME HOME. "My father, James H. Roberts, is at the table on the float in the 1946 welcome-home parade," says James W. "Jim" Roberts of Marysville, Pennsylvania. "He was instrumental in organizing these sorts of things. Sitting at the table are (clockwise from front left) Dalus Ashenfelder, Ed Straw (face obscured), Charles Arter, my dad, Ed Crandall (in Navy whites) and Bob Bitting. My uncle Ned Ember is at the piano. I'm the 18-year-old at the wheel behind the float, driving Dad's 1909 Sears motor buggy. My mother, Stacia, was riding along with me."

LIBERATING THE PHILIPPINES

ABUYOG'S ROYAL TREATMENT

In 1944, I was an artillery mechanic in the 77th Division, and my 404th Ordnance Medium Maintenance Company was moved to a small village called Abuyog on Leyte Island in the Philippines.

A young Filipino named Ernie was overjoyed to see American troops outside his village and came to visit me often. He spoke fluent English with a slight accent.

Since the battle was going well, our commanding officer let us have some days off.

Ernie asked us to go to the farm with him, and my captain granted permission.

On Saturday morning, Ernie took me to a riverbank where his friend was waiting in an outrigger canoe. On the river, Ernie whistled and heads popped up all along both banks. "They know you are coming," he said.

After about an hour, we came to a path and got out of the canoe. Ernie stayed behind me as a large old man came toward me, carrying a knife.

I was a bit scared, but the man was all smiles. He handed me the knife and said, "You are American hero! We are free again!"

The people from the farming village surrounded me, shaking my hand and hugging and kissing me. They were all crying and saying, "Thank you, American hero, we love you! We love Gen. MacArthur, too. Thank you for returning to our island."

I was overwhelmed. They offered me gifts of live chickens, eggs and fruit and led me to a bamboo building, where a large table was set up with all their favorite dishes.

The man who gave me the knife said, "Eat! We made just for you."

I was treated royally. Ernie and the other villagers showed me the importance of why we were fighting to stay free.

When we later left the area, the whole town came out and waved goodbye. What an experience!

—*William Clark, Bellmawr, New Jersey*

Height of Patriotism

Lt. Bernard "Bud" Stapleton of Orlando, Florida, was sent into Tokyo on Sept. 3, 1945 (the day after the surrender), along with an interpreter and a photographer, to confiscate any photographs of the Hiroshima bombing. Seeing all the Japanese flags flying made Bud decide to wave the Stars and Stripes. This photo, taken by Martin Sontheimer, was seen around the world and also by Gen. Douglas MacArthur, who was furious. It seems MacArthur was planning to raise his own victory flag—the one flown in Potsdam after the German surrender, which was sent to MacArthur by President Truman. "You can't imagine what it's like to be chewed out by a five-star general," recalls Bud.

CHAPTER 2

On the
HOME FRONT

PAGE 60

PAGE 53

PAGE 62

PAGE 63

There were plenty of ways to support the war effort in our own communities. Americans young and old pitched in however they could to ensure an Allied victory.

"During World War II, 75 young girls in my hometown of Wichita Falls were too young to work as 'Rosie the Riveter.' So we became 'Hobby Helpers' instead," says Olyve Hallmark Abbot of Fort Worth, Texas. "Named after Col. Oveta Culp Hobby, head of the Women's Army Auxiliary Corps, our junior WAAC unit was the first of its kind in the United States.

"Our unit's first project was a drive to collect silk or rayon hosiery, slips, gowns, blouses, dresses and even bedspreads. Factory workers rewound these fabrics so they could make parachutes. When the nationwide effort to collect scrap metal slowed down and the situation became desperate, our group switched gears and became scrap-metal salvagers.

"The organization not only taught the youngsters loyalty to country, but how to contribute to the community. You can imagine how proud we were to do our part on the home front!"

From scrap metal collections and victory gardens to rationing and bond drives, those of us at home helped fight World War II in our own way. Read about many of these war efforts here.

PATRIOTIC POSTER GIRL. Margie Stewart's career took off in the mid-1940s. In 1943, she appeared in her first movie, *Bombardier*, with actor Richard Martin (at right) playing her love interest. In June 1945, she went to Europe to promote the sale of war bonds to adoring GIs, like this ecstatic group in Reims, France (above).

Margie, the GIs'
GIRL BACK HOME

A SMALL-TOWN GIRL TURNED STARLET MADE SOLDIERS SWOON AS THE U.S. ARMY'S POSTER GIRL.
By Margie Stewart Johnson, Studio City, California

During World War II, millions of GIs knew me by my first name. Now, at age 92, I still marvel at how that came to be—how a small-town girl from Indiana became a department store model, a Hollywood actress and the U.S. Army's only official pinup girl—all in just a few years.

My adventure began in 1937, when I left home in Wabash to attend Indiana University. During my first year, I was elected freshman princess, a title that included a free trip to Chicago. It seemed like the perfect place to spend my summer vacation, so I talked a girlfriend into joining me.

We knew we'd need jobs to stay in Chicago for the summer, so we hit the pavement daily, looking for work. After two weeks with no luck, we were almost ready to give up and go back home. But as luck would have it, we wandered into the right place at the right time: the Frank Lewis photography studio.

There we met Russell Stone, an advertising executive who was looking for two girls to pose in a rowboat on Lake Michigan for an ad featuring Johnson outboard motors. That was the beginning of my career as a model.

Shortly after that, a family emergency called my roommate home, so I knew that if I wanted to stay

on my own, I needed a steady job. Luckily, I was hired to model at Chas. A. Stevens, a women's department store in Chicago. The pay, which seemed wonderful at the time, was $24 a week!

Hollywood Bound

In 1941, I decided to join my parents, who had moved to California, and landed a job modeling for the upscale Bullocks Wilshire department store in Los Angeles. Within a year, MGM Studios offered me a contract. I refused because I thought they would immediately change my name, dye my hair and pluck my eyebrows—and none of that was my cup of tea!

But later that year, RKO Pictures offered me a one-week trial contract. If I liked being a starlet for a week, I could stay on. During my trial run, I performed a skit with Edgar Bergen and Charlie McCarthy at a birthday party. Charles Koerner, RKO's production chief, noticed me and offered me a full contract at $75 a week.

The first movie I appeared in was released in 1943: *Bombardier*, starring Pat O'Brien and Randolph Scott. I played Mamie, a girl who falls in love with a character played by Richard Martin. I was also in *Gildersleeve's Ghost* and played small parts in many other movies.

Patriotic Response

During that time, I spent many Thursday nights talking and dancing with scared, homesick GIs at the Hollywood Canteen. The club provided free food, dancing and entertainment to servicemen waiting to go overseas. I also went on hospital tours with the USO in California, Texas, New Mexico, Oregon and Washington.

By this time, Mr. Stone, who had given me my first modeling job, was a retired Army major. He went to the Pentagon with an idea for bolstering troop morale around the world, persuading the brass to let me pose for a series of three posters. I felt thrilled and privileged when he asked me to participate. I got a token fee of $5 per photo shoot; advertising staffers chose all my clothes, accessories and poster themes.

The first poster bore the messages "Please Get There and Back" and "Be Careful What You Say or Write." George Hurrell, the famed Hollywood photographer, shot the sessions in 1942 in Los Angeles.

The response to the posters was so strong that Eleanor Roosevelt tried to stop distribution because she feared they were making the GIs too homesick!

But as letters from the troops began to pour in, asking the identity of that girl in the posters, she finally relented. In fact, so many letters came in that I was asked to pose for 11 more posters, which soon became known as the "Margie posters." In all, around 94 million posters went to American soldiers around the globe.

Entering a New Theater

Asked to tour the European Theater of Operations to promote the sale of war bonds, I set off for France on June 8, 1945. I was billeted at the Ritz Hotel in Paris and used that as a base camp.

One of my duties was to visit Army camps and offices for *Stars and Stripes*, the weekly newspaper for GIs. At one office in Germany, the officer in charge asked me to write a caption for a photo of officers who would receive bronze stars the next morning. I said OK, as long as he wouldn't give me the credit. I'm glad he didn't; the next morning, the paper came out with this headline: "Brass Receive BS Medals"!

We visited camps all over France, Belgium, England and Germany. I was the first American to enter Germany in civilian clothes; I could not believe the devastation there. I ate a lot of GI rations and lost six pounds. But I just tightened my belt and went on.

Whirlwind Adventures

While in Munich, I ran into a soldier from Manchester, Indiana, whom I had dated back in Wabash. Talk about a small world!

The next day I flew in an aircraft carrier to Austria to deliver some mail. Later, back in Munich, as we rode in an open jeep, a sniper shot at us—so it was time to leave Munich! We boarded the airplane, and the crew put me in the co-pilot's seat.

During the flight, they turned the controls over to me and told me to follow the Rhine River. Before landing, a voice came over the speaker, asking the crew to bring the "co-pilot" to the tower. I thought I was in trouble—but the men just wanted to meet Margie!

During a 24-hour flight home, I helped serve meals and tried to sleep, to no avail. We landed in Washington on Aug. 14, 1945—V-J Day—and found the streets alive with celebration. The general who asked if he could help me with my luggage couldn't have known that its contents included a German helmet and a loaded Luger pistol! With that general's help, I just breezed right through customs.

During my trip to Europe, I met and fell in love with Capt. Jerry Johnson, who was assigned to take charge of my touring itinerary and accompanied me wherever I went. We were married by the mayor of Paris in his office on July 7, and again by an Army chaplain in the American Church of Paris, which we were told was necessary to make it legal.

In 1946, when our son Stephen was born, I retired from my acting career to take care of him.

As I look back on those years, the opportunity to be the Army's poster girl fills me with pride and gratitude.

'TEN-HUT! PINUP GIRLS CAUGHT GIS' ATTENTION

Margie Steward was one of hundreds of pinup girls who buoyed troops' morale, and imaginations, during World War II.

While it's hard to pinpoint where and when the first pinup appeared, one thing is certain: Press agents eager to advance young starlets' careers were happy to sate GIs' appetites for photos of comely young women. *Yank*—a weekly magazine that reached 2.6 million soldiers in WWII—served as a worldwide conduit for those images, along with calendars, postcards and other magazines. *LIFE* magazine, for example, raised civilian awareness of pinups in a July 7, 1941, issue that featured a coquettish Dorothy Lamour, displaying considerably more than just her acting prowess.

Other photos remain pop-culture icons to this day. Consider the 1943 publicity still of a coy, swimsuit-clad Betty Grable, with her "million-dollar legs" insured by Lloyd's of London. Twentieth Century Fox studios reportedly circulated 5 million copies to soldiers.

Then there's the photo of a sultry, negligee-wearing Rita Hayworth that appeared in the Aug. 11, 1941, issue of *LIFE*. Or the 1943 publicity still for the movie *The Outlaw*, featuring a pistol-packin' Jane Russell, seductively resplendent in a hay pile.

The glory days of traditional pinups began to fade in 1953, when Marilyn Monroe appeared in the first issue of *Playboy* wearing only an alluring look. The ensuring proliferation of explicit men's magazines made the old-fashioned pinup girl—who left something to the imagination—a quaint notion.

But during their World War II heyday, there's no denying that gorgeous pinup girls, posted in footlockers, barracks and even plane cockpits, boosted soldiers' spirits—one glorious, glamorous and glossy black-and-white photo at a time.

—*Ken Wysocky*

I LIVED THE HIGH LIFE

TURBULENCE, TIGHT QUARTERS AND TALKATIVE SOLDIERS MADE EVERY FLIGHT AN ADVENTURE FOR A 1940S STEWARDESS!

By Anna Mae Craig, Saratoga, California

I worked as a stewardess with TWA in 1943, back when that job was considered one of the most glamorous jobs a young woman could have.

After growing up in Gary, Indiana, and attending Purdue University for a year, I'd decided I wanted to do something for the war effort, so I applied for a job with TWA as a hostess or ground agent.

When I got the telegram inviting me to interview for hostess training, I was excited. But when I saw the other applicants in the waiting room looking so poised and sophisticated, I didn't think I stood a chance.

To my surprise, I was the only one chosen from the bunch. I later found out it was because I looked "wholesome."

My parents didn't think it was safe for me to live in Chicago, so I stayed with them near Gary. This meant a 3-hour commute each way. I had to walk seven blocks lugging a suitcase—often in the middle of the night—to catch the South Shore train to Chicago, then ride the streetcar to Midway Airport.

Ugly Shoes and Nylon Blues

Our uniforms consisted of a sky-blue skirt and jacket with a navy camisole and an overseas-style hat. Nylons were so scarce I'd cry if I got a run. I can recall my roommate coming home from a flight and taking her nylons off—just in time for me to put them on!

Our shoes were plain brown oxfords—ugly but practical during turbulence, when we were buffeted back and forth while passing out "burp cups" to airsick passengers.

Our aircraft was the trusty DC-3, and our crew of three consisted of pilot, co-pilot and me, the hostess. The passengers were mostly military personnel, who had priority with the airlines.

I empathized with the soldiers and airmen who were either going to war or coming home, but I was sometimes emotionally drained by their stories.

Flights then were longer, more turbulent and less predictable, but they were much more exciting! Besides burp cups, I'd pass out chewing gum to help ease pressure of stopped-up ears.

Served Food on Cardboard

The galley was drafty and cramped and had a strong "metallic" smell. Sometimes the food tasted metallic, too—and nothing looked too appetizing on those cardboard trays.

I was responsible for the flatware. Every night I'd have to take it off the plane to my hotel room to wash it in the basin!

In those days of smaller planes and fewer passengers, we could give more personalized service than they do now. I visited with passengers, and they sometimes showed their appreciation with letters of commendation.

Those years were truly the best of my life. I flew the first delegates to the United Nations and occasionally saw celebrities. Though bad weather often stranded us in dull places, having a long layover in an exciting city was adequate compensation.

One stormy night, a tall, handsome naval officer boarded my flight. From then on, my flying days were numbered—a few months later, I married that good-looking Navy pilot.

In the years since, I've seen airliners increase greatly in size and sophistication. Still, the jumbo jets with their luxurious accommodations and super power just don't thrill me like that modest little DC-3 once did as it quivered at the end of the runway, ready for takeoff.

Winds Pushed Balloon Bombs into the U.S.

My father, Oscar Bryant Hill, and my brother Owen had a moment of fame after they made a discovery in the woods. One day in December 1944, while they cut wood near Kalispell, Montana, they came across a Japanese incendiary balloon bomb.

During World War II, the Japanese released these balloons in an attempt to burn down American forests and deplete a valuable resource. If disturbed, the undetonated bomb could have exploded and caused injury or death.

They returned to Kalispell and reported what they found to the police, bringing with them a rubber string from the bomb as evidence. Later my other brother, Burnell, and I would take that small piece of rubber to school for show and tell, making us VIPs in possession of an item from the enemy forces.

The local sheriff notified the FBI, and when the agents arrived, Dad and I drove them back to the location of the balloon.

> ## "The Japanese released these balloons in an attempt to burn down American forests."

The story goes that my dad insisted everyone help load up his truck with wood slabs—the outside pieces cut by loggers while squaring a log—before hoisting the balloon on top of the load for the drive back to town. Gasoline was scarce at the time, and Dad wasn't going to waste another trip without a load of wood! He made a living collecting wood slabs and selling them for household fuel.

News of the discovery was kept secret for nine days as the balloon was examined, but soon *Time* and *Newsweek* ran articles on the find. *Time* even reported that my father and brother found the bomb and credited them with acting quickly and intelligently afterward.

Papers in our area ran the story, too, along with a photograph of my dad showing the location of the bomb. He was a local hero for a short time before things quieted down and the great balloon discovery became just another family story.

—**Donald Hill,** *Corona, California*

DOIN' MY PART

GET YOUR STAMPS HERE!

During World War II, I sold war bonds in Buffalo, New York. War stamps cost 25 cents each; a filled book cost $18.75 and allowed you to redeem $25 after 10 years. Sales were slow because I had to sell stamp by stamp.

My Aunt Ruth and Uncle Art owned a restaurant where the employees patriotically purchased stamps with part of their paychecks. Each week I'd ride a streetcar and two buses to go down to the restaurant and sell war bond stamps.

On Fridays, my mother and dad would take me to a local radio station, where I joined other children to announce our sales on the air.

Celebrities visiting Buffalo often made guest appearances on the show. The one I remember best was Zasu Pitts. I'd never even heard of her (I think her fame was somewhat limited), but I recall her wearing a lot of makeup and a feather boa.

She was introduced by the master of ceremonies and made a few patriotic statements. I stepped up to the microphone next and announced, "I'm Marjorie Beahan, and I've sold $32 worth of United States Defense Stamps this week." Miss Pitts graciously planted a big kiss on my forehead!

I doubt anyone else remembers that program, but it will always rank as my favorite since I got to be "on the radio" every week for several months.

—***Marjorie Vandenack,*** *Yutan, Nebraska*

DEFEND WITH DOLLARS. "This photo was taken in 1944 during a war bond rally held in the Sacramento Memorial Auditorium, which seats 4,000 people and was built to honor World War I veterans," writes Paul Richins of Paradise, California. "My father, Heber Richins, is the security officer dressed in black in the middle of the picture. The photo was issued by the Sacramento Air Service command and sent to participants. It probably appeared in local newspapers at the time."

BUZZING BROTHER. When Tom Gill (inset) came home in 1943, he was able to fly over his house and give a little brother and his buddies a thrill they never forgot.

MY BROTHER WAS
TWICE A HERO

COMING AND GOING, THIS 1943 AVIATOR GAVE THE FOLKS BACK HOME SOMETHING TO REMEMBER HIM BY.
By Dewey Gill, Minneapolis, Minnesota

I tracked the sky as my sixth-grade buddies wrestled on our front lawn. Tom had told me to watch to the south about 4 o'clock on Friday afternoon, so I was first to spot the plane.

"There it is!" I hollered. "I bet it's him! See it? See it?"

My friends promptly stood up and followed my pointing finger to the flying speck in the sky. I'd invited them over to see my brother, Tom, come home for the weekend in his BT-13, a trainer he flew as an Air Corps instructor in Texas.

It was September 1943, and Tom had his orders for Europe, where he'd fly a B-24. He was due to ship out soon, and he'd talked his commanding officer into letting him fly the trainer home to Milwaukee to say goodbye to his family.

The plane crawled northwest across the clear, bright sky. In the quiet of that afternoon, we could hear the drone of its engine.

Suddenly the plane turned and began to spiral

downward—one loop, then a second and a third. I never figured out how Tom was able to pinpoint our neighborhood, our block and even our house from 10,000 feet. But by the time he completed the third spiral, he'd fixed his target.

Time for a Dive

Down he came, engine screaming, in a power dive. We were cheering, oblivious to the risk.

Down and down he came, straight at the house—straight at us, unwavering in his aim. Closer and closer he came with his thundering engine growing louder. Our eyes widened. We covered our ears.

In a moment we could see his helmet, and then we could see his gloved hand, waving at us as casually as if he were in a parade!

Finally, no more than 100 feet over us, Tom jerked the stick and the plane's nose shot up, skimming over the trees and houses with only a few feet to spare.

My friends and I shrieked and rolled on the ground in excitement. It was absolutely fantastic!

Tom was my hero—and I was a hero to my buddies for having such a daring brother. I'd made a promise to them and he'd delivered in stunning excess.

But the neighbors were not so taken. There were calls to the local Air Corps base about Japanese attacks and complaints about rattling windows and fallen china.

Farewell Flight

The complaints were relayed to Texas, where Tom's commanding officer promised the proper discipline. (We learned later that he got little more than a slap on the wrist.)

The following morning as I got ready to go to school and was saying goodbye to Tom, I begged him to buzz the school before he left town.

"What kind of brother are you?" Tom scolded. "I'm in plenty of hot water already, and now you wanna make it deeper for me! Sorry, Dew-boy— no more fancy stunts."

But outside, away from Mother, Tom caught

> **Suddenly the plane turned and began to spiral downward—one loop, then a second and a third.**

hold of me and said, "Keep an eye out around 10. No guarantees, understand. But I'll see what I can do." He winked and we shook hands.

By 9:50, we heard him. He zoomed over the playground, circled the smokestack at our fourth-floor level, dipped his wings in farewell and circled the smokestack twice more, smiling and waving as he zipped past the windows.

Then he gunned the engine, rocketed up and swung away to the south toward Texas. That was the last time I ever saw him.

In late 1944, Tom's B-24 was ripped by German anti-aircraft fire over The Hague in the Netherlands. After he got the crew out, Tom tried desperately, unwisely, to save his ship.

When he knew at last it was too late, he bailed out of the B-24, but by then he was too low for his chute to open.

In saving his crew, Tom was a hero. But he'd already proven that to me on a sunny Friday afternoon that will ever remain in my memory.

THIS JUST IN

During World War II, Dad faithfully listened to news broadcasts by H.V. Kaltenborn.

Dad had a large map on the wall, and as German troops advanced across Europe, he'd trace the route. He wanted to catch every word, so nobody made a sound during the broadcast.

We lived near the Lexington airport, and one time as Dad was listening, a noisy airplane flew over, drowning out the radio.

With eyes still glued to his map, Dad yelled, "QUIET!"

"Well, Ike," said Mom reasonably, "you can't make the plane stop."

We all laughed—that was the one time we'd made any noise. Even Dad's mouth scrunched up as he tried to keep from breaking up.

—*Virginia Thompson,* Frankfort, Kentucky

The Sweet Smell of Excess

The heady aroma of chocolate swirled all about us, making it difficult to concentrate on what the woman standing before us was saying.

"Keep in mind that you may eat all the candy you want, as many different kinds as you see, as long as you are employed here at the Hershey chocolate factory," she instructed. "But you are not allowed to take any home with you."

Wow! Was this going to be great. Four 16-year-old buddies and I had just landed in chocolate heaven! Turning five teenagers loose to work here for an entire summer could mark the end of the chocolate industry as everyone knew it.

The year was 1944, and good help was hard to come by because so many able-bodied men and women had gone off to fight the war. But my friends and I were available.

We jumped at the chance to work at the Hershey factory, just a 15-minute ride from our homes in Middletown, Pennsylvania.

Air Thick with Promise

As our orientation continued, we saw huge metal vats of molten chocolate, wafting a delightful fragrance into every inch of the huge production facility. With a deep sense of appreciation, I noticed that if I held my mouth open and breathed deeply, I could almost taste the chocolate. Looking at my buddies and seeing their heads tilted back and their mouths opened slightly, I knew that they were experiencing a similar sensation.

Finally we were assigned to our new supervisor. Noticing the expressions on our faces, she grimaced as if she knew exactly what we were thinking: Bring on the chocolate!

We were off in separate directions the instant she left us. I headed for a pallet piled high with open cartons of Hershey Kisses. Scott had found the almond bars and had already devoured one by the time I unwrapped my first double handful of Kisses.

A Dangerous Discovery

Bucky wandered off and found stacks of unusually thick chocolate bars, each with six squares that could be broken off and eaten separately.

We learned later that they were D-ration bars for our fighting forces and that just one square contained enough nutrition to take the place of an entire meal. Bucky ate two whole bars—enough for four days' nourishment!

He didn't know that at the time, of course. But later that afternoon, he didn't look so good. The next day, he couldn't eat anything at all—candy or otherwise.

The rest of us fared a little better on our second day, although our chocolate intake went from gobbling to nibbling.

When I got home that second day, I wasn't the slightest bit hungry for dinner, dessert or anything else. Needless to say, after our third day on the job, not a single piece of chocolate passed our lips!

—**Earl Weirich**, Chesapeake, Virginia

SMOKE MEANS TROUBLE

Do <u>Your</u> Gas Coupons "Go up in Smoke"?

If your car is a "smoker," it's likely to be a "gas-eater" . . . pouring part of your priceless ration out the exhaust, *wasted!* That's because smoke is usually a sign of excessive engine wear. And these days, that might mean a car laid up for the duration.

Excess wear and wasted gas can be *prevented*. One of the best preventives is a motor oil that doesn't break down in the blast furnace heat of modern motors . . . *Insulated* Havoline.

Insulated means that Havoline is extra-tough . . . especially processed to protect your motor at extremes of both heat and cold. Havoline is *distilled*, too . . . free from carbon-forming impurities that take the pep out of performance.

Don't wait till *your* car becomes a gas-wasting "smoker." Change to Insulated Havoline Motor Oil today!

The Texas Company feels that one important part of its war-job is to KEEP YOUR CAR ON THE JOB. *You're welcome to drive in to any Texaco Dealer's for a check-up of tires, battery, chassis and motor lubrication system.*

You're Welcome at TEXACO DEALERS

HAVOLINE
REG. T.M.
MOTOR OIL
DISTILLED AND
INSULATED

TEXACO
T
REG. T.M.

CANTEEN DEPOT. Mary Plimmer (above, holding tray) waits with helpers to serve World War II servicemen and women like those in the top two photos.

Our Canteen Was an OASIS OF KINDNESS

IT TOOK A LOT OF COFFEE, SANDWICHES AND CARING FOLKS TO FEED 1.5 MILLION HUNGRY SERVICEMEN AND WOMEN!

This story recounts Mary Plimmer's experiences organizing and working at the Streator Free Canteen in Illinois during World War II. Her niece, Sister Ann Rena Shinkey, a Reminisce reader from Streator, shared the story.

In 1943, the residents of Streator, Illinois, often went to the busy Santa Fe Railroad depot to catch a glimpse the many troop trains that traveled through our city during World War II.

We saw many hungry young men and women dash across the street to a small restaurant to get something to eat, but the trains never waited long enough for all to be served.

To deal with the problem, the Parents Service Club, to which I belonged, founded the Streator Free Canteen. We eventually served some 1.5 million servicemen and women—absolutely free!

We set up a work table in one corner of the train depot and began contacting local merchants to ask for donations of food and kitchen utensils. On a very cold Nov. 28, 1943, we opened our canteen. It was 5 a.m., and 10 ladies were on hand to work.

We'd made coffee at home and brought it to the station in thermos jugs. Since we had no cups to serve it in, we'd gone from door to door asking for empty cottage cheese containers.

When the first train rolled in, we handed out paper sacks that contained sandwiches and some homemade cookies. On that first exciting day, we served lunch to more than 300 soldiers, most of them traveling from Chicago to San Francisco. Although it was hectic, we all agreed that it was worth the warm feeling that filled our hearts.

Workers Went Without

We realized just how many service people were passing through our town the first time we ran out of food! Undeterred, we ladies took up a collection among ourselves to buy more for the next day. Some of the club members even went home and ground up their family's roast to make sandwiches for the troops!

Coffee was perked in every home we could contact, and when the next train arrived, we were ready to serve. The project grew like wildfire. It seemed that everyone in town was eager to do their part of the war effort.

Someone donated an icebox, and ice was furnished free every day. Merchants gave us large coffeepots, carpenters built long tables and farmers dropped off sides of beef and pork. Other generous farm families gave us bushels of apples and pears. There never seemed to be enough tomatoes to satisfy hungry soldiers who said the produce reminded them of their gardens back home.

Sometimes, though, these young soldiers needed more than just food. Quite often, boys would ask us to call their parents and tell them they were OK. We made a special effort to handle all such requests.

As word of our project spread, some famous celebrities visited us. Amos and Andy of the famed radio series stopped by. And when Claudette Colbert and Shirley Temple visited, they told us how amazed they were at the generosity of our town.

Canteen Was Unique

But I think the troops were the most amazed. They didn't hesitate to tell us that, in all their travels, they'd never found anything like our canteen—and all for free!

In the beginning, some doubted we could feed so many hungry servicemen, but those of us who believed in the canteen never once thought it would fail. We served the soldiers every day without fail between November 1943 and May 29, 1946, when the canteen finally closed.

We shed some tears and had a few laughs on that closing day, but we were proud. The Streator Free Canteen was our personal contribution to our country—one we were happy to make.

SMALL TOWN EMPHASIZED "WE'RE ALL IN THIS TOGETHER"

Having just graduated from boot camp at Hunter College in Bronx, New York, we Navy WAVES (pictured above) headed west to our assignments by train in 1943.

With so many troop cars attached, including those for the Army and Marines, the train struggled in the mountains, and the baggage and dining cars were detached. This put us in a fix for food, and the engineer telegraphed ahead about the problem.

In all the commotion, we didn't realize that it was both a Sunday and Decoration Day as we stopped in a little town. The stationmaster there had gotten the word out about us, and the townspeople cut church services short and opened stores that had been closed.

Families brought their Sunday dinners to the station, with men, women and children carrying all sorts of food from home and the stores to feed us. It was truly a wonderful day, and I cried along with many of those residents as they gave us hugs, kisses and hearty handshakes. Some even gave us what little change they had on them.

My big regret is that, with all this going on, I didn't make note of the town's name. But we left with our bellies full and our hearts filled with love and appreciation.

—*Helen Anderson Glass*, *Tucson, Arizona*

Writing Letters

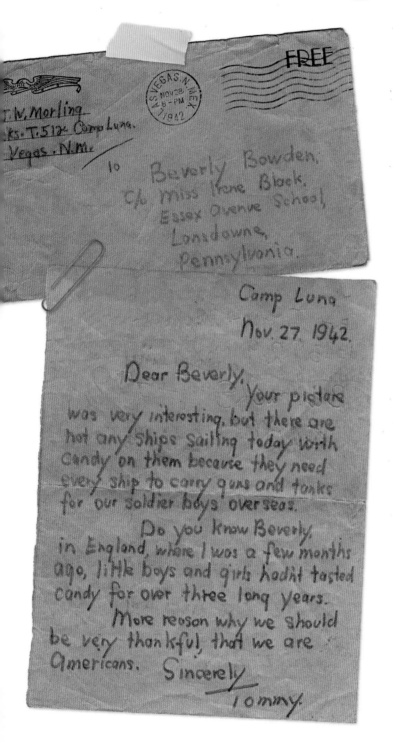

I. W. Morling
ks. T. 512 Camp Luna.
Vegas. N.M.

to

Beverly Bowden,
C/o Miss Irene Black,
Essex Avenue School,
Lansdowne,
Pennsylvania.

FREE

Camp Luna
Nov. 27, 1942.

Dear Beverly,
Your picture was very interesting, but there are not any ships sailing today with candy on them because they need every ship to carry guns and tanks for our soldier boys' overseas.

Do you know Beverly, in England, where I was a few months ago, little boys and girls hadn't tasted candy for over three long years.

More reason why we should be very thankful, that we are Americans. Sincerely
Tommy.

ADOPTING A SOLDIER

In 1942, as a second-grader at Lansdowne Elementary School, our class adopted a soldier, Pvt. Tommy Morling of Camp Luna in Las Vegas, New Mexico.

I still treasure his responses to the letters we students in Miss Black's class wrote, and I remember when he came to visit us.

In one letter, he mentioned that he worked on the camp newspaper, *The Luna Glow*, but that he wanted to get back to the war.

A letter to me (left) dated Nov. 27 read, "Your picture was very interesting, but there are not any ships sailing today with candy on them because they need every ship to carry guns and tanks for our soldier boys overseas.

"Do you know, Beverly, in England, where I was a few months ago, little boys and girls hadn't tasted candy for over three long years.

"More reason why we should be very thankful that we are Americans."

—**Beverly Bowden Keating,** Shrewsbury, Pennsylvania

LETTERS GREW FROM SCRAPS

During World War II, my girlfriend Claudia and I were picking strawberries along the B&O Railroad tracks running through our small Ohio town when we heard a passenger train coming. Seeing the train approaching from the west, we soon realized it was troop train headed for the East Coast. We waved and hollered, and the men hung out the windows, waving at us.

Before the entire train had passed, we saw pieces of paper drifting out of the windows. We gathered up several pieces and discovered there were names and addresses written on them. I took several and gave Claudia the rest.

That evening I wrote the first of many letters. I went to the post office twice a day for what seemed like forever until I receive three letters from the soldiers to whom I'd written. They were stationed in Europe. We corresponded for quite a while before our letters grew less and less frequent. Pretty soon the war was over, and I hoped that the soldiers had gotten home safe and sound.

It was my contribution to the war effort.

—**Bev Harrold,** Fostoria, Ohio

WAITING AND WORRYING

After my husband left to go overseas during World War II, I waited and wondered for over a month.

Our rural mail carrier wasn't the most friendly man around—in fact, he was often downright grumpy. But looking back, I realize he was probably just as worried about his son (also in the service) as I was about my husband.

Every day, about the time the mailman was due, I'd run down to the mailbox and wait. And day after day, I'd be met with the same words: "No letter today."

Then, one bright, beautiful morning, I heard the familiar honk of the mailman's truck—only this time he'd started honking way up the road!

I went flying across the yard and down to the mailbox. The mailman had a big smile on his face when he handed me the mail—there was a tiny V-Mail letter on top.

My heart was racing a mile a minute and I could hardly make out the words through my tears, but there in the upper right corner of the letter I read, "Somewhere in Czechoslovakia." At last, I knew!

That was the longest month of my life, but after 50 years, the memory of the letter I received that morning is as fresh in my heart as if it were yesterday.

—**D. Reed,** *Goshen, Indiana*

WATERMAN AD

The soldier in the ad at right takes me back to '43 and '44, when I wrote V-Mail letters to a soldier overseas. He said my newsy, everyday letters were truly a blessing while he was fighting and kept him in touch with a safe, sane world. Also, I wrote with a Waterman's pen—it flowed so easily.

—**Patricia Newhall,** *Barrington, N.H.*

Remember Saying?

IN CAHOOTS:
conspiring

Write him today!

REMEMBER—he likes to get letters from home as much as you like to get letters from him. So write—and write often.

Today the fountain pen is an essential on all fronts of this war—in maintaining morale at home as well as with the fighting men—in the education of students now going back to school—in the conduct of America's war industries. Waterman's is meeting today's situation by providing the finest pens and inks in the company's history—while making every effort to conserve the nation's precious materials.

Waterman's Commando... *the New Super-Pen.* Specially built for speeded-up America. Tough, fast, dependable, with real military clip; it's the pen for servicemen, students, *everyone,* and priced at only **$5.** Other Waterman's $2.95, $3.50, $8.75 and up.

Waterman's Ink. The world's favorite—safely used in millions of fountain pens for 50 years. 8 brilliant colors, including Washable Blue for school. Great volume assures highest quality—makes possible the low price of only **10¢.**

Waterman's

Our Neighbor's
FIRST AIR RAID

AS LONG AS MOTHER HAD A BOX OF CHOCOLATES—AND HER TEETH—ALL WAS WELL IN THE BOMB SHELTER.
By Ann Morrisette-Rudy, Manhattan Beach, California

As long as Mother had a box of chocolates —and her teeth—all was well in the bomb shelter.

Soon after America declared war on Japan, those of us living on the West Coat were alarmed to hear that Japanese submarines or planes might launch an attack.

"What?" shrieked my mother. "We must prepare for the worst!" She wasn't alone—in our small town, just down the peninsula from San Francisco, everyone was on the lookout for enemy soldiers floating earthward under parachutes emblazoned with the rising sun.

A man wearing a yellow hardhat and looking skyward for enemy planes marched through the streets with fliers that detailed our "orders:"

"When the warning siren blasts, turn out all lights. Lock all doors and keep drapes and blinds closed. Go to your garage and back out your car, keeping lights off. Stay in your garage with blankets and enough food to feed your family for two days."

Mother read the flier, then sat down and frantically fanned herself with it. But she soon rallied long enough to gather warm blankets, pillows, stout shoes, a bar of soap, 10 cans of chili and a box of chocolates.

"All right, girls, this is war!" she declared to my two sisters and me. "We must be brave. Each of us will have a job when the attack comes."

Delegated Responsibilities

She put my oldest sister in charge of backing out the car. My other sister was to wake the dog and make sure he got into the garage with us.

"What about me?" I asked.

Mother eyed me thoughtfully. "Well, you're only 14, but you can do something worthwhile, too," she assured. "Be sure to remind me to put in my teeth."

Proud to serve

Unfortunately, Mother had failed to read the small print on that flier, which informed that a

CAPTAIN DAD

My father was air raid warden for our block in Southern California during World War II. For monthly drills, he'd don his white metal hat and alert the whole neighborhood by tapping a triangular metal device hanging from a wood frame.

Our garage bulged with oddly shaped hand-pumped fire extinguishers. They were to be used in case of attack and were kept approximately filled by my sister and me during the four-year period.

Servicemen were abundant in our area in those years and in need of wholesome, inexpensive activities. My mother and grandmother helped organize the local USO chapter to provide companionship, food, music and activities for "the boys."

When my sister and I (below) were given the chance to help serve, we were so excited! Our parents even gave us our own Women's Army Corps uniforms, which we proudly wore not only at these special times, but also at the weekly "honor our military" days at the grammar school we attended.

Patriotism really was infectious during those years. We learned about teamwork, and we each had an important role to play in the eventual victory. "I can make a difference" and "How can I help?" have been primary in our lives ever since.
—**Diane Leverett-Kieffer**, *Malibu, California*

practice alarm was to be sounded that evening. When the siren went off in a long series of short blasts, Mother flew from her bed, screaming, "AIR RAID! AIR RAID!"

Snapping to attention, we three girls carried out our jobs. The car was backed out of the garage, the dog was awakened and I dutifully reminded Mother of her teeth.

(Mother apparently wasn't the only one who was worried about her teeth during air raids. A joke made the rounds later in which one person said, "Wait until I get my teeth." A second person replied, "What for? They're dropping bombs—not sandwiches!")

Go East, Young Mom

We were determined to stay in the garage. But once the chocolates were gone and Mother decided it was too cold, we retreated to the house to await the all-clear signal. By the time it finally sounded, Mother had decided to rent the house and move inland (clearly she was not a heroine like Greer Garson in *Mrs. Miniver*).

Not that Mother didn't do her part. The small Nevada town where we ended up asked for volunteers to pack survival kits for those living on the West Coast. Mother was eager to do her part and helped with the effort. Fortunately for all of us, those living at the front never had to use any of the kits she packed.

Milkweed Helped
WIN A WAR

YOU MIGHT THINK OF MILKWEED AS A WEED, BUT THIS HUMBLE PLANT PLAYED A BIG ROLE IN WWII.

By Wendell Smith, Muscoda, Wisconsin

Milkweed pods are one of the beauties of autumn, their tiny seeds released to float through the air carried on silky white fluff.

But there was a time when the silk of the common milkweed was much more than a sign of the season. It helped save lives.

During the 1940s, schoolchildren, Girl Scouts, Boy Scouts, 4-H groups and others fanned out across much of the U.S., scouring railroad rights-of-way, road ditches and weedy field corners in search of these pods and the fluff they bore. It was a serious search, because milkweed floss was going to war.

It was filling in for kapok floss, produced by the seed pods of tropical trees and once used to fill the Navy's "Mae West" life jackets. In the early days of World War II, advancing Japanese forces moved into the Dutch East Indies and took control of the kapok plantations. So the United States turned to milkweed floss as a substitute.

Although the tropical kapok trees and the milkweed plants are entirely different, it was determined that the floss from the seed pods was very similar.

The *Science News Letter* reported on Sept. 9, 1944, "The buoyant waterproof floss in 2 bushels of pods is just enough to stuff one of the 1.2 million life jackets the Navy needs to protect the lives of fathers, brothers and friends at sea. It will keep the survivor of a torpedoed ship

afloat in a storm-tossed ocean for 140 hours."

I was among the many schoolkids who picked milkweed pods. In our tiny Nebraska village of McLean, the schoolchildren enjoyed a day off from school going east and west out of town along the Burlington Railroad right-of-way, where milkweed grew in large numbers.

The pods we gathered were placed in mesh onion bags and hung to dry on the fence that separated the schoolyard from the adjoining cornfield. These bags hung from fences surrounding hundreds of rural schools. The government would pay 20 cents for a properly dried bag of pods.

In 1943, with the collection confined mostly to Michigan, enough pods were gathered to make 93,000 pounds of floss. By the following year, the collection effort had spread to include 26 states, with a goal of 1.5 million pounds.

Though it's been over 50 years now, each fall when I admire the white silken strands floating on the breeze, I can't help but recall that autumn day in Nebraska when my friends and I helped milkweed go to war.

BE PREPARED. The Boy Scout motto of "Be Prepared" was obviously a fitting one for the fire department in Belford, New Jersey, on this day during a World War II scrap drive. It appears the boys of Troop 27, and their adult supervisors, were using the local fire engine to haul their scrap metal and old newspapers to the collection point. "I have been a photo buff since I was a boy," says Jack Lentz of Middletown, New Jersey. "I was also in the Boy Scouts. I took this photo in the early '40s of the Scouts and some fire company volunteers collecting material for the war effort. There were some firefighters along in case the engine had to be put into service."

BOYS PITCHED IN WITH SCRAPPY EFFORT

As the winds of war blew over our small town of Clinton, Indiana, in 1942, everyone wanted to help with the war effort, including Chuckie Cogan (seated next to me, right) and me.

Deciding to collect scrap metal, we scoured the neighborhood for old pots, pans, pieces of iron and just about anything we could load onto our little wagon. Some neighbors were not pleased when they found things missing!

In the end, we proudly deposited our collection in the salvage depot across from Chuckie's house. We both felt very patriotic and proud to help our troops.

—**Collett Hill,** *Bedford, New Hampshire*

TOY SOLDIERS CALLED TO DUTY

In 1938, when I was 9 years old and living in Norfolk, Virginia, I was given a mold to cast lead soldiers and a ladle to melt the lead. The mold made one marching soldier and another one lying prone, aiming a rifle.

To get lead, I kept an eye out for gum and cigarette wrappers with lead-foil lining and for toothpaste tubes, which in those days contained lead.

Our gas stove served as the foundry for my smelting, and I requisitioned an iced tea spoon from my mom to skim the slag off the melted lead just before filling the mold.

By 1941, I had recruited quite an army—close to 100 soldiers in all. Being an only child, I used them as rainy-day companions. Sometimes I was the beloved general of my troops. Other times I'd attack them by throwing bombs—actually, they were darts. If I missed, the darts went through the rug and stuck in the floor.

When scrap metal drives became popular, I finally decided to literally send my soldiers to war, believing the military needed reinforcements. My dad helped me pack my troops and carry them off to the lead collection depot.

It was a tearful separation as the troops left me for other duties. But I soon found a greater patriotic calling. At age 11, I joined the Boy Scouts. By age 18, I was an Eagle Scout (photo at right).

At 19, I joined the National Guard and, after more than 20 years of service, retired as a lieutenant colonel.

—**Edward Wall,** *Chesapeake, Virginia*

HEARTWARMING. Norma Connell was a hostess at this 1942 USO Valentine's Day dance in Waukegan, Illinois.

Good Times

35 DRESSES

Late in 1941, I became the assistant director of a United Service Organizations club in Columbia, South Carolina. The mission of the USO was to provide a "home away from home" for servicemen and women by offering recreational activities. Our volunteer duties were many—we hosted dances, bingo parties, pie nights, spaghetti suppers and community sing-alongs. We also visited the sick at Fort Jackson Hospital.

My most unusual duty turned into something I became well known for. It all started the day a soldier asked if I'd stand up at his wedding. His bride was coming from another state to marry him, and she didn't know anyone in Columbia.

I must have done all right because word of my "talent" got around. By the end of my first year with the USO, I'd been a bridesmaid 35 times!

Each bashful bridegroom's approach followed a pattern. First he'd send a buddy to the club to talk to me. Then, encouraged by my acceptance, the bridegroom himself would come in, go over details of the wedding and show me photographs of "the prettiest girl in the world."

The weddings were happy occasions for me as well as for the couples. Often there were enjoyable luncheons or breakfasts after the ceremonies. I usually received a corsage and sometimes even a gift. (I still have several of those gifts among my mementos of that time.)

I served as a bridesmaid so often for the boys of the 8th Division that one of the chaplains actually presented me with an 8th Division pin, making me their official bridesmaid.

Word of my activities reached a local newspaper, *The Columbia Record*, and was picked up by the Associated Press. Eventually, the story even came out in the military paper *Stars and Stripes*. With all that publicity, my "business" boomed, leaving me with a host of happy memories of those long-ago days with the USO.

—**Jean Brabham McKinney,** *Anderson, South Carolina*

ALWAYS A BRIDESMAID. Jean McKinney (below) was no stranger to wedding season. She was a bridesmaid 35 times!

Remember Saying?

PENNIES FROM HEAVEN:
easy money

USO CLUBS WERE A HOME AWAY FROM HOME FOR SERVICE PERSONNEL

During World War II, my father, John Bredenberg, was stationed at a naval hospital in Corona, California, as a hospital apprentice, second class.

While stationed there, my father said that service personnel were only allowed to leave the base when they had liberty, which was every other weekend. Everyone on the base was divided into two groups—starboards and portsides.

The USO is where many service people went for their weekend away. These clubs had a family atmosphere, and everyone could play games like cards or checkers, and feel a little more at home away from home.

There was plenty of food served and you didn't need to pay for the evening's events after entering.

There was a lot of entertainment provided for service people, and dancing was an important part of the evening. Usually they danced to the records of Big Band greats like Harry James, Glenn Miller and Sammy Kaye. Sometimes there was a live band.

Women hostesses for the club were selected in advance and could attend by invitation only. They had strict rules to abide by.

This picture (above) was taken at the USO club in Riverside, California, 14 miles from the naval hospital in Corona. On this night, there was a harvest festival, hence the foliage and archways in the background.

—**Louise Steinman,** *Arvada, Colorado*

ON THE JOB

WORK CAME TO A GRINDING HALT

I was a "welderette" at the Commercial Iron Works in Portland, Oregon, building ships for World War II, when it was announced over the loudspeakers that President Roosevelt had died.

Within seconds, you could have heard a pin drop in that otherwise noisy shipyard. Big, burly machine workers stood with their heads bowed and tears running down their cheeks.

—**Babe McIntosh**, *Denton, Montana*

WONDER WOMAN

During World War II, Jimmie Mae Byrd Whitsell (below) did her part by taking the job of a man who was serving in the armed forces. She connected and repaired electric meters for Florida Power and Light Co. in Miami.

According to her proud daughter, Hazel Grifol of Mary Esther, Florida, Jimmie Mae also volunteered eight to 12 hours each week as an air raid warden. "To this day, Mom is our hero!" Hazel says.

—**Jimmie Mae Byrd Whitsell**, *Mary Esther, Florida*

WAR WORK IN THE BIG CITY

In 1943, my cousin Yvonne Gilchrist and I (pictured above with another young lady) traveled by rail with a group of young women from Fayetteville, North Carolina, to Harrisburg, Pennsylvania, to be trained for wartime civil service jobs. We'd never been on a train or even out of state, so we didn't sleep a wink all night in the sleeper car.

Yvonne recalls how great it felt to finally get off the farm after graduating from high school. In Harrisburg, we learned to work on planes; I was in the paint shop and Yvonne in repairs.

Returning home to Fayetteville after six months, we took jobs at Pope Field. We rented a room from Mr. and Mrs. Flute on Maclay Street. Yvonne recalls that Mrs. Flute offered her a glass of root beer once, and she told her that we didn't drink beer.

That wasn't the only culture shock for us rural natives. When we went out to eat at a fancy restaurant in downtown Fayetteville, there were gas lanterns everywhere. "I backed into one and caught my hair on fire," remembers Yvonne. "We were such country hicks!"

—**Mary Smith Rosser, as told to daughter Connie Rosser Riddle**, *Apex, North Carolina*

READY TO SERVE. Cadet nurses at Indiana's Billings General Hospital treated hundreds of wounded soldiers during World War II, says Ann Cain Hinser of Monroeville (also a cadet nurse, but not pictured). "It was my first job after graduation from Lawrence Central High School, near Indianapolis," she says.

ROSIE THE RIVETER SISTERS

In August of 1943, five of my sisters and I took jobs assembling B-24 bombers at Consolidated Vultee Aircraft Corp., which later became General Dynamics, in Fort Worth, Texas. This photo (right) was taken inside a B-24 when we appeared on the Army Air Force radio program. I am second from the left and my sisters, from left, are Jewell, Freda, Marie, Daphne and Dell.

—*Rubye Marston,* Fort Worth, Texas

Life's Little Luxuries
IN SHORT SUPPLY

SISTERS OF SKIMPING

Pictured above in our office attire in 1943 are (from left) Vione Stroud McArthur, me, Vesta Sadler, Neva Jones and Felton Brady Creek. We worked at the Office of Price Administration, more commonly known as the rationing office, for Roosevelt County in Portales, New Mexico. Rationing was essential during World War II.

My mother, who took the photo, surprised me with a 19th-birthday luncheon for my co-workers and me. Neva was the chief clerk, Vesta was assistant clerk and the rest of us were clerks. We three were all 1942 high school graduates earning approximately $80 a month.

—*Ladelle Frazier Williamson,* Lubbock, Texas

MOM'S EFFORT WAS LOST ON HIM

One year during World War II, Mother saved her meat rationing stamps all summer long so she could make a special meal for my serviceman uncle, who was about to be sent overseas.

When the big day finally came, Mother proudly served fresh produce from our victory garden along with the crowning touch—a big platter of Spam.

My uncle ate the homegrown vegetable but wouldn't touch the Spam. He said he'd eaten it for breakfast, lunch and supper the past six months!

Mother was a bit upset, but I was delighted—I got to eat two helpings of that rare treat!

—*Lorrimer Owens,* Chesapeake, Virginia

DURING WARTIME RATIONING...

During wartime rationing back in 1944, bubble gum was as precious to kids as silk stockings were to their mothers. Noticing a drugstore advertisement saying "Double Bubble available, two per customer," my sisters and I were first in line.

With overwhelming self-control, we walked home planning how to make our bubble gum last as long as possible. By the time we reached the house, we had it all figured out and were just about to unwrap our first cherished piece of Double Bubble when our little brothers and sister appeared.

We knew they'd fuss if we didn't find a way to share, so it was time to brainstorm. Our solution? Each of us girls chewed half a piece of our gum until noon—and then the little ones chewed it the rest of the day.

We all lived happily for the next two days!

—**M.K. Mahoney,** *Barstow, California*

SHEEP WOULDN'T WAIT

During World War II, when so many things were rationed, there were stamps, tokens and citizen boards controlling just about every commodity. Due to manpower shortages, board members were sometimes chosen more on the basis of availability than expertise.

In the area of California where I lived, that made it difficult for farmers who had to approach rationing boards in larger cities like Fresno.

Since rationing allotments were based on quarterly averages, board members often had difficulty understanding why a farmer might, for example, need more fuel in spring for plowing or in fall for harvesting.

A classic example occurred when a shepherd from Lemoore requested an allotment of canvas to make lambing pens for newborn lambs in February. Most lambs are born in spring, but the shepherd's canvas request amounted to more than his average quarterly allotment.

This gave the board a serious problem. They told the shepherd that he should do a better job of planning, and reschedule his lambing period for the month of May when the weather would be warmer.

The shepherd replied that he had discussed this with the sheep, but the timing was nonnegotiable with the ewes. Without lambing pens, many newborn lambs would freeze to death while the board was debating the weather.

When the newspapers and radio stations picked up the story, it wasn't long before the shepherd had his canvas!

—**Walt Gearing,** *Loma Linda, California*

BY THE BOOKS. War ration books were issued to each American family during World War II, dictating the amount of gasoline, tires, sugar, meat, shoes, nylons and other items any one person could buy at a given time. Nancy Novak of New Berlin, Wisconsin, shared these from her family's personal collection of WWII ephemera.

FATHER'S VIOLIN
MADE V-E SPECIAL

Whenever I watch a parade and our country's flag comes into view, my thoughts go back to my father, John Strek, whose love of country was displayed with pride on V-E Day, May 8, 1945.

I remember that day clearly. Father, upon hearing of the war's end in Europe, marched up Main Street in Sayreville, New Jersey, in joyous celebration.

Father loved music. He'd brought his violin to America from Poland, where he was raised among other music lovers.

Paul Masur, the town barber, shared Father's love for music. It was while Father was in Paul's barber chair that the two learned of their mutual love of the violin and made arrangements to play together.

When Paul closed his shop at the end of the day, the two men would retire to the back room and spend hours playing violin pieces by their favorite composers. At one of these many musical meetings, they took time out to discuss the war and their sons, both of whom were in the service.

Father said to Paul, "When the war ends, I promise you that I'll march up Main Street playing my violin, even if I have to do it alone."

Paul smiled. "John, you won't have to do it alone. I'll join you." So, on that evening, a promise was made, though neither man knew when or if it would ever be kept.

The third man who marched with the violinists knew nothing of the plan. Ben Modzelewski, our neighbor, did not play the violin but was moved by the spirit of the occasion.

Paraded as Promised

On the historic day when the news flashed over the radio, Father rushed home from his office, grabbed his violin and headed for the barbershop.

As Father was leaving the yard, Ben asked what was going on. He was given a hurried explanation and immediately understood their plan.

Ben's eyes fell on the American flag that flew from his house each day of the war. He grabbed Old Glory and ran to join Father and Paul.

Together, the three men marched up Main Street, all in step, two violins and the American flag. As they passed through town, people rushed out of their homes. Some fell in to step behind them—men, women and children all became part of the impromptu parade, while others lined the sidewalks, waving, cheering and holding signs, as seen in the photos above.

When they reached Borough Hall, a large crowd had gathered. The men led them in singing "God Bless America" and played other patriotic songs, while Ben held the flag high.

The patriotic march so impressed the borough fathers that they gave the three men an honorary place in the official parade held later to honor all the local men who had served.

Thus was fulfilled a promise made by two violinists in the back room of a barbershop. And still today, 53 years later, Father's violin serves as a silent reminder of that memorable day in his life.

—*Edna Cornell, Sayreville, New Jersey*

Up on the Rooftops

On Nov. 11, 1942, our Boy Scout troop from Staten Island, New York, was invited to participate in an Armistice Day ceremony in Times Square.

World War II was raging in Europe and the Pacific then, so there was a special feeling of patriotism and pride in the air that day. At 11 a.m., our bugler, Horace Watts, played roll call from atop the Hotel Astor. Two minutes of silence followed, during which the police stopped all the traffic in Times Square.

Taps was then sounded by Horace, after which I played an echo from the roof of the Bond Clothing Store on the other side of the square.

That day remains even stronger in my memory because, within two years, most of the boys in my troop would be in the military.

—**Louis Schultes,** *Bridgewater, New Jersey*

CHAPTER 3

Hello, HOLLYWOOD!

PAGE 70

PAGE 78

PAGE 89

PAGE 80

Years ago, a theater could be found on nearly every Main Street in America. As soon as we stepped inside, we knew we were in for a treat!

"'Going to the show' during the '40s was like entering another world for a few hours," remembers Barbara Kacer from Aurora, Indiana. "The elegant theater in our town had ornate columns and a large balcony reached by a wide, curving staircase.

"We all loved the Betty Grable movies and the scary Wolfman and Frankenstein features, but my personal favorite was *Cover Girl* with Rita Hayworth and Gene Kelly. The song they sang in that movie, 'Long Ago and Far Away,' is still fresh in my mind.

"Our fantasies and fun didn't end when we left the show, either. As children, we'd spend many Saturday nights acting out the movies we'd just seen. The only problem was that, as the youngest of our group, I usually ended up being the villain."

We couldn't get enough of show business, whether blockbuster movies, knee-slapping radio comedies or that newfangled contraption called television. The Hollywood glamour of yesteryear is alive and well on the following pages.

A Toast to the King of
CHAMPAGNE MUSIC

ONE READER UNCORKS MEMORIES OF PERFORMING ON THE ROAD WITH LAWRENCE WELK.
By Jayne Walton Rosen, San Antonio, Texas

I was the second "Champagne Lady" to sing with Lawrence Welk's orchestra. Our adventures between 1939 and '47 could fill a book!

I grew up singing for local radio stations and dance bands in San Antonio. After graduation, I worked as a staff singer at WOW radio in Omaha.

Touring Nebraska, Lawrence heard one of my shows. His singer had left, so he called the station manager to see if he could talk to me about joining his band. In summer of 1939, at age 22, I went on the road with Lawrence Welk's Champagne Orchestra. It was an interesting life.

Many of our appearances were one-nighters in small ballrooms with no dressing rooms. Have you ever tried putting on a formal in the backseat of a car in zero-degree weather?

Imagine putting a coat over that formal and donning snow boots to venture out behind the ballroom and wait in line to use the outdoor privy.

Playing the wonderful Trianon and Aragon Ballrooms in Chicago got us off of one-nighters for a few weeks and offered the chance to get our formals cleaned. (After three months of one-nighters, our clothes could stand up alone!)

"Go That-a Way"

While on the road with the band, I did most of the driving. Lawrence would get out the map and tell me which highways to take, then go to sleep.

One time in Wisconsin at 4:30 a.m., I slammed on the brakes when I came to a large body of water with a chain across it and a sign reading "Next ferry 6 a.m."

Lawrence woke up and wanted to know what the trouble was. Well, the trouble was I couldn't drive on water! We lost 80 miles that night.

Small towns often had hotels along Main Street, typically on a second floor above a restaurant. Rooms usually had a thick rope tied to a radiator to use as a fire escape.

We were in a little Iowa town one night when I awoke to sirens and people screaming in the street below. The hotel was on fire!

Lawrence and all the boys had run downstairs before the flames blocked the stairway. They were yelling up at me to grab the rope and jump!

I did, and endured rope burns for weeks. After that, I asked Lawrence to buy me a folding rope ladder that attached to the windowsill. I carried it on the road for years.

Adventures on Asphalt

I'll never forget when Lawrence rented a sleeper bus to take us on a tour of one-nighters. One rainy night when the main highway had flooded,

AN' A-ONE, AN' A-TWO. Jayne Rosen (far right in top photo) treasures her great musical experiences while performing in the famed Lawrence Welk band.

the driver told Lawrence he knew a shortcut. Shorter it may have been, but at about 4 a.m., the bus overturned in a muddy ditch!

Our instruments were broken, the sheet music was everywhere and the Hammond organ flew to the front of the bus. Luckily, no one was hurt.

All 21 of us climbed out the windows and stood there on the highway in the pouring rain.

Lawrence hiked to some farmhouses, and in a few hours, three huge tractors came up the road to help right the bus.

Meanwhile, the boys and I had started walking to get something to eat. We found a truck stop six miles away and ate everything in the place. Lawrence rented cars and instruments, and we continued on schedule.

Once during World War II, Lawrence took his accordion and I took my voice to Walter Reed Veterans Hospital. We spent hours going from bed to bed trying to bring a smile to those boys' faces.

Some of them had danced to our music during better times. I'll never forget one boy who'd stepped on a land mine. He was terribly injured, yet he smiled at us. Lawrence and I both left his bedside in tears.

I've stayed in touch with the Welk family and was with Lawrence and his wife, Fern, in 1992, a short time before he passed away. I have nothing but sweet memories of Lawrence Welk—a great bandleader and a wonderful man.

Our Song

YOU JUST NEVER KNOW

"Why don't you sit here? You two look good together."

With those words, the director brought 17-year-old Clark Handley over to a table to join me, then 15-year-old Nancy Newton. That was how it all began on Jan. 4, 1943, and what a prophetic comment it was.

We were working as movie extras at 20th Century Fox studios in Los Angeles for the filming of *Hello, Frisco, Hello*. The scene was an 1890s nightclub, where actress Alice Faye was singing a new song, "You'll Never Know." Clark and I looked at each other as we heard the song for the first time—love at first sight, with a beautiful background.

We were both students at Los Angeles High School but had never met. Because so many film people had joined the armed forces, we got the opportunity to work as extras. We watched other scenes being filmed, but the highlight remained the scene when we heard our song being sung over and over.

Clark and I started dating right away, and two weeks after we met he wrote a note asking me to go steady, "now and hopefully for the rest of our lives." I said yes, and we dated until he joined the Army Air Corps on his 18th birthday, in April. He became a B-17 pilot, and when he came home, we were married Nov. 18, 1945.

We lived in England for a time and traveled through Europe, Africa and South America because of Clark's work for Chevron Oil Co. Nearly every year, no matter what country we were in, we heard "You'll Never Know" being played at some point. The end of the song says it all about our first meeting: "You'll never know if you don't know now."

—*Nancy Handley, Anaheim, California*

'SKYLARK' INSPIRED

The year was 1944, and I was 17. I spent a lot of time at the local skating rink, where I became friends with a couple who skated three times a week. They were head over heels in love and skated only with each other.

One of the popular songs of the day was "Skylark." I'd sit that one out so I could watch my friends skate together.

They'd meld into one fluid movement and softly glide around the rink with arms entwined, she with her head on his shoulder and he with his lips pressed to her hair. It was a lovely sight, tinged with a touch of sadness since he'd soon be going off to war.

Today I can't even remember their names. But every time I hear Johnny Mercer's beautiful ballad, I can close my eyes and picture that loving couple, aware of only each other.

I like to think that he came home safe from the war and that they stayed in love…and that they're out there even now, still "skylarking" together.

—**Helen Schuster,** *Philadelphia, Pennsylvania*

THE NOT-SO-SECRET MESSAGE

In 1943, I was working my first full-time job as a cashier at the Eastern Telephone Company in Cortland, Ohio. At the time, I was dating a young man named Harold, who worked as an announcer at a radio station in Sharon, Pennsylvania, 25 miles away.

Harold tried to visit me on weekends, but because of gas rationing, he never knew until Friday whether he'd have enough fuel to make the 50-mile round-trip. Plus, the hectic schedule of a radio announcer didn't always provide time enough for a phone call.

So Harold came up with an idea to alert me. He told me to listen to the radio during my lunch hour on Fridays. If he could make the trip to Cortland, he'd play "Jukebox Saturday Night."

I told my friends about Harold's clever idea. Soon it became apparent that I'd never have to worry about receiving my message—it seemed like everyone in town was listening to the radio right along with me.

It wasn't unusual for someone to open our office door on a Friday afternoon and call out, "Harold's coming!" Or I might be walking down the block to have lunch and hear someone on the street yelling, "Hey, Twila—Harold's coming!"

I treasure the memories of the three years I spent with the good people of Cortland, Ohio. Eventually that radio announcer and I married and we've enjoyed many Saturday nights out since.

—**Twila Smith,** *De Soto, Texas*

THEY MET IN ST. LOUIS

Our song was the title song to the movie *Meet Me in St. Louis*. The night I met my future husband, we went to a movie in St. Louis at the Avalon Theater. I was really thrilled to be with that handsome guy, who was a friend of my sister and her boyfriend.

After 40 wonderful years together, my husband is gone, but the sound of that song still puts a warm glow in my heart.

—**Mary Lee Weber,** *Licking, Missouri*

You can be sure…if it's

Westinghouse

All radio-phonographs may look pretty much alike to you . . . but there can be a big difference in the listening. You will get far more enjoyment out of a set that's built *up* to a standard than you will from one that's built *down* to a price. And you don't have to be an expert to tell the difference. You can be *sure* if it's Westinghouse.

Westinghouse radios and radio-phonographs are available in a wide variety of models. The one shown here is the 186, which has exclusive Automix record changer, Electronic Feather reproducer, and Rainbow Tone FM. The two-front cabinet is a Westinghouse classic. Home Radio Division, Westinghouse Electric Corp., Sunbury, Pa.

Listen…and you'll buy **Westinghouse**

Listen to Ted Malone every morning Monday through Friday ABC Network

Remember Saying?

DUCKY SHINCRACKER:
good dancer

JUST WILD
ABOUT HARRY

A 1943 TRAIN TRIP TO CHICAGO TO SEE HARRY JAMES WAS A DREAM COME TRUE FOR TWO TEENAGERS.
By Dorothy Smith, Hanover, Indiana

The radio was the center of attention in our house during the winter of 1943. Dad, of course, waited anxiously for the war news. But, as a 14-year-old freshman at South Shore High School in Chicago, I kept my ears tuned for the music.

Each evening around dinnertime, Harry James did a 15-minute segment on the air. One night, I heard a brief announcement that the James band would soon broadcast live from downtown Chicago and that a limited number of free tickets were still available!

That very minute, I sat down and wrote a letter requesting six tickets. I was hoping to take several friends along to see and hear our music idol, whose records we played endlessly.

After days of suspense, a slim white envelope arrived in our mailbox. My promptness in writing had paid off—but it contained only two tickets.

One for me and one for…? It didn't take long to

decide on my friend Norma. She was just as wild about Harry as I was.

The broadcast would air on a weeknight at 6:30 p.m., but the tickets indicated we had to be at the Opera House by 6.

After school, Norma and I went directly to the train station and took the Illinois Central to the Randolph Street station. Then, feeling very adult, we hailed a taxi.

It was 5:15 when we arrived outside the Opera House, and a crowd was already gathering. More people arrived after we did, and when the doors opened shortly before 6, the crowd surged forward into the hall.

Every seat was filled by the time the curtain parted at 6 p.m. and the orchestra came into view, playing as the houselights dimmed. The broadcast may have lasted only 15 minutes, but the band didn't sell us short—they played for a solid hour!

Some couples jitterbugged in the richly carpeted aisles, and all the rest of us bounced in our seats. The trip home was like a dream, the music still running around in our heads.

The next day at school, Norma and I were the center of attention. Although the band was

performing in Chicago for a week, I must have been the only one in my high school to write for tickets. Norma and I agreed it was the high point of our freshman year.

FRANKLY, KIDS SWOONED OVER SINATRA

Remember the "swooning teens" of the '40s? For a while back then it seemed like the moment a Frank Sinatra tune was played, some young girl dropped to the floor!

The first time I experienced this fainting phenomenon was one afternoon in the small-town grocery store my parents owned. Pop was ringing up a sale, and I'd just picked up a loaf of bread when the radio behind the counter swung into a Sinatra melody.

Suddenly, a scream pierced the air. When I turned to see what the commotion was, I saw that two teenage girls had fallen to the floor.

Pop's reaction was relaxed—he'd already seen this happen a time or two. While I stood frozen on the spot, he calmly switched off the radio, then stepped out from behind the counter and helped

the two girls to their feet. After a few brief words of reprimand, he returned to his work.

Later, when I saw Frank Sinatra perform at the Stanley Theater in downtown Pittsburgh, the effect was the same, only more intense. Young fans waited in a line extending down the block and around the corner. As music boomed from inside through a loudspeaker, the smitten teens began to tumble. Occasionally, a girl would catch her swooning friend and gently ease her to the sidewalk.

Swooning was uniquely and solely for "Mr. Blue Eyes." No matter that the theater seats were hard wood or that there wasn't much space on the floor between rows—dedicated swooners toppled undaunted.

His fans today have found safer ways of expressing themselves. But I'll bet every one of those "ex-swooners" vividly remembers the days when she fell for Frank.

—*Mary Martucci,* South Bend, Indiana

A Trip to the
THEATER

FIRST DATE DISASTER

One night in 1940, when I was a junior in high school, my brother and his girlfriend invited me to go out with them to hear a small band playing.

While there, I began receiving a lot of attention from one of the handsome band members. As you can see from the photo above, he had brown eyes and dark hair, and I thought he looked like Tyrone Power.

Before the night was over, he'd asked if I'd like to see a movie on Friday night. Would I ever!

Friday was rainy, and Bernie arrived dressed for the weather, wearing a fedora, a raincoat with big buttons, and galoshes with clips that clicked out a beat as he walked. When we reached the theater and walked down the aisle, I could feel the eyes of my classmates upon us, everyone sizing up my date.

I was leading the way when I heard a woman yell out in pain. Looking back, I saw a gray-haired lady half out of her seat with her head resting on my date's chest. He was frantically trying to unwind her hair from around one of those enormous buttons.

Just then, the lights dimmed and people began yelling, "Sit down!" Finally, Bernie managed to set her free. I sat down on my seat, but Bernie forgot to put his seat down and sat on the floor.

As I listened to muffled snickers behind us, I began wondering what I ever saw in this nervous klutz. Next he whipped out a pair of horn-rimmed glasses (no wonder he'd sat on the floor—he couldn't see!).

Everything went smoothly during the movie, but when the lights came back on, there was a large clump of gray hair twisted around the button of Bernie's coat. I was so embarrassed I wanted to die and couldn't wait to get home, planning never to see him again.

Well, I guess I must've gotten over the humiliation, because we've been married now for over 50 years. And I still think he looks like Tyrone Power!

—**Mae Bernagozzi,** *Babylon, New York*

THE EXCITING DAYS OF SATURDAY MATINEES

When I was a young boy during the late '30s and early '40s, the Strand was the only movie theater in our small Connecticut town.

Well-provisioned with our huge three-for-a-dime candy bars, my friends and I headed for the show every Saturday afternoon. For 10 cents a ticket, we were treated to adventure, intrigue and suspense.

Potbellied old Mr. Viola had owned the Strand since the days of silent movies. With flashlights in hand, he and his three grouchy sons would patrol his theater's darkened aisles looking up and down the rows for troublemakers. Sometimes, my friends and I were so rambunctious that we fit that description rather well.

A stern "You'd better quiet down!" was usually our first warning. If we acted up again, we were threatened with forcible ejection from the theater. What happened after the third warning? We never found out.

Perched on the edges of our seats, chewing feverishly on Milky Ways or Mounds, we kept our eyes glued to that magical screen, anxiously awaiting each hair-raising development.

The feature was almost always a Western. Hopalong Cassidy, Roy Rogers, Gene Autry, Ken Maynard, Buck Jones and George O'Brien were but a few of the heroes who galloped across the screen with six-guns blazing. The co-feature was usually a Charlie Chan, Sherlock Holmes, Eastside Kids or Mr. Moto whodunit.

But the added attraction we looked forward to most was the continuing weekly adventure serial. As those lawbreakers were brought to justice by movie heroes like Dick Tracy, Captain Marvel, The Shadow, Batman and Zorro, the heroes' wholesome images left an indelible mark on youngsters of that era.

I'll always have a warm spot in my heart for those exciting Saturday afternoons of my youth—Mr. Viola's stern warnings and all.

—**Andrew Alfano,** *Oldsmar, Florida*

Marquee:
ANN SHERIDAN IN
"WINGS FOR THE EAGLE"
ALSO NEWS & TRAVEL
+SALUTE TO OUR HEROES-
BUY WAR BONDS HERE

RIVIERA THEATRE

J. J. NEWBERR

FRANKENSTEIN TAUGHT HER A LESSON

Growing up in New Jersey during World War II, I frequented a small neighborhood movie house.

The theater operator owned a rather large cat that was allowed to roam the movie house. I loved to pet that cat whenever I was there.

One memorable weekday, I skipped school to see *Frankenstein Meets the Wolf Man*, a movie I knew my mother wouldn't approve of. Hoping no one would recognize me, I bought my ticket and slipped into the darkened theater.

The movie was spellbinding—especially for a nervous 12-year-old girl skipping school. At the most dramatic moment, just as the Wolf Man was confronted by Frankenstein, something heavy landed in my lap!

I let out a blood-curdling scream, causing the projectionist to cut the movie and turn on the lights. There on my lap sat the cat, contented as ever. The theater manager never found out who did the screaming…and I never skipped school again.

—**Doris Dermitt**, *Windsor, New York*

STILL ROLLING. Ed Knapp worked at the Riviera Theatre in Three Rivers, Michigan, in 1942. It's still in business! "On Saturday afternoons at the Riviera, we had a comedy, a cartoon, previews, a chapter of the serial running at the time, the feature film and what was called a 'guest feature'—a movie that had run a few months earlier," he says. "That was four to five hours of continuous entertainment! Big crowds came to see the Three Stooges, Gene Autry and Tim McCoy. And another very popular serial was *The Lone Ranger*, partly because it was on radio."

Brushes With Fame

GINGER ROGERS TAUGHT ME TO TRY

I was 15 in 1942, and working that summer for the Medford, Oregon, Postal Telegraph delivering telegrams and using the Teletype.

That summer we planned a big bond drive and rally in Medford, and Ginger Rogers, who lived about 40 miles away and visited us on occasion, was to be the honored guest. The high school pep band, in which I played clarinet, was scheduled to perform at the rally.

I was at work on the day of the rally when I learned that all the boys in the band would be wearing sports jackets. I didn't have one, so I called my mother.

Since I couldn't leave work, Mom came to the office, and we pooled our money and she went shopping, but unfortunately, she didn't have enough for a jacket my size. She bought a coat-type sweater instead, but there's no way I would wear it onstage. Rather than embarrass myself, I went into the back of the office and sat there, dejected.

Jerry, my boss, tried to convince me to go onstage. About that time, Miss Rogers came in and learned about my predicament. She walked over, straightened my tie and helped me put on the sweater. "Now get your horn and let's get out there," she said.

Taking my arm in hers, she marched me up the stairs. Everyone was cheering for her, but when I tried to sit down, she pulled me to the microphone.

"I want you nice people to meet my special guy," she said. "He had to work all day and didn't have time to go home and change. I told him if he didn't come up here and play for me, I wouldn't come up either."

Then she turned and planted a great big kiss on me before turning me loose! My girlfriend sat next to me in the band, and during one of our breaks, she pointed to my reed and said, "You have more lipstick on your reed than I do!"

I immediately removed the reed and put in a new one. For many years I saved that reed. I often took it out and remembered Miss Rogers' kindness.

She made a bashful young boy feel special that night, and her encouragement changed my outlook on life.

—**Bill McCord,** *Central Point, Oregon*

I WORKED BACKSTAGE WITH THE ANDREWS SISTERS

It's a wonder I got the job at all. It was early in 1945, and I had just accepted the position of assistant producer for a new musical comedy show starring the Andrews Sisters. A big fan, it was days before I could talk to LaVerne, Patty and Maxine Andrews without gulping!

Soon, the workload dispelled any remaining shyness in me. I quickly learned that the show's story line had "the girls" owning a dude ranch. Gabby Hayes played the foreman and Pigmeat Martin, a popular black comedian, was the cook. Guests ranged from actors to composers to singers.

It wasn't always easy. Gabby Hayes, the famous Western actor, worked without his teeth, so he needed to be given lines he could pronounce. And Pigmeat Martin, though hilarious, couldn't read. He required short, memorable lines.

The guest on our first show was Bing Crosby, with whom the Andrews Sisters had worked many times before. From the minute the four of them started singing the Cole Porter song "Don't Fence Me In," the studio audience was on its feet applauding.

Another time, when we were working with Bob Hope, I was told to put a script together. The producer swore me to secrecy as to who had actually written it.

But when Mr. Hope saw the script at rehearsal, he winked at me and said, "Nice job, kid!" I walked on air for weeks.

—*Evelyn Walker, Los Angeles, California*

MET A JAZZ GREAT

I've loved piano nearly all my life, and I still feel excitement when I recall some of the great jazz pianists I've had the honor to meet.

After I got out of the Navy in 1948, my favorite place to hear great jazz was on 52nd Street in New York, at spots like the Onyx Club, Jimmy Ryan's and the Hickory House. The Three Deuces nightclub was where Art Tatum and his trio played nightly. Despite being blind, Art was the greatest pianist of them all.

Late one night, my wife and I, along with my wife's sister and her date, were talking to Art after his performance.

"You people really dig jazz, don't you?" Art said. "Want to hear some more?"

We said yes enthusiastically.

"We're going to a special place of mine in Harlem," Art continued. "My car is out front."

Art's limousine was waiting outside, but with the four of us and his 300-pound chauffeur, "Tiny," there wasn't room for Art! So the greatest jazz pianist of all time summoned a cab and followed us on up to 125th Street.

As we entered a small, packed, dimly lit club, Art made his way to a little upright piano where a young man was playing "Georgia."

The man moved to his left, never missing a beat, as Art slid alongside. Magically, that little upright became a Steinway Concert Grand. I heard things in "Georgia" that night I never thought possible—and we didn't leave that club until the sun was rising!

—*Frank Hurlbutt, Lindsborg, Kansas*

GARY COOPER'S "BEST" BUDDY

I was our high school photographer in Grand Junction, Colorado, during the late '40s.

One afternoon after covering a local parade, I was walking to my car when a mechanic at the local Chevrolet agency called me over. He informed me that Gary Cooper was inside the garage having repairs made to his Cadillac.

With camera in hand, I approached, made a quick introduction and asked if I might take his picture. Mr. Cooper graciously agreed. After it appeared in the school newspaper, I sent a copy to Mr. Cooper's address in Hollywood. Later, I received a nice note thanking me.

While attending college in Los Angeles, I stayed at a boardinghouse, and my story and photo of Gary Cooper made the rounds there. In fact, I told it so often that Gary Cooper and I eventually became "friends."

One evening, a group of us was leaving a Hollywood movie theater when one companion said, "Jack—there's your buddy, Gary Cooper."

My friends pushed for an introduction to my "buddy," so I knew I had to act. As Mr. Cooper approached, I stepped up to him and very quickly explained who I was and how we'd met. He smiled, shook my hand and talked briefly with each of my friends before leaving. In just a few seconds, Gary Cooper made me a hero that night...and yet I'm certain he had no idea who I was!

Outside of *High Noon*, that evening's performance may have been his greatest role.

—*Jack Welch, San Jose, California*

Jimmy Durante Was A Genuine Nice Guy

SAVED BY THE "SCHNOZZOLA"

I was a teller at the Culver City, California, Bank of America in 1940. One day, Jimmy Durante walked into the bank with three men, and they stepped up to my window.

Jimmy had written $200 checks to the men, which they cashed. Then I cashed a $600 check for Jimmy himself.

I tried to be careful, but apparently I wasn't careful enough. The men recounted their money, and then Jimmy strolled back to my window and asked if I'd like to count his again.

I was embarrassed to think I'd shorted him, but when I recounted, I found I'd given him $200 too much! Jimmy could have walked away without saying a word, but he didn't. I could have kissed him at that moment!

—*Bonnie Hammond*, *Silverdale, Washington*

NEARLY KNOCKED SCHNOZZES

My sister Betty and I moved from New Jersey to New York City in the early '40s and lived in a girls' club called The Parnassus, near Columbia University.

One day, I was rushing from Radio City to catch the subway home and literally ran into Jimmy Durante and Garry Moore. We almost knocked each other down!

Jimmy looked at my Irish pug nose and said, "We certainly were at opposite ends of the line when they gave out noses."

We all laughed, then they asked where I was going. When I said I was trying to catch the subway, Garry said, "Come on, we'll help you."

With that, we ran into the street as Garry used two fingers to whistle for a cab. One arrived in no time.

"Get in, we'll ride with you," they said. And they did, all the way to West 115th Street. They also insisted on paying the fare! I don't know where they were going, but I'm sure it wasn't in my direction. They were just two considerate, wonderful gentlemen.

—*Rosemary Egan Blackburn*
Pittsfield, Massachusetts

SNOUT'S HONOR. A big schnoz never got in the way of the careers of Jimmy Durante (left) and Danny Thomas, who went nose to nose in this publicity picture sent by Joe Bleeden of Las Vegas, Nevada, who was Durante's publicist for nearly three decades.

KINGS OF COMEDY. Richard Bernard "Red" Skelton (left) and Fred Allen, best known for their comedic sketches, were two of the most popular American entertainers during the Golden Age of Radio. Their ability to make people laugh with their quick wit, playful antics and absurd characters quickly elevated them to radio stardom.

RED WAS OUTRAGEOUS

Our family listened to most of the great radio comedians like Jack Benny, Fred Allen, Amos 'n' Andy and Fibber McGee and Molly. But we kids liked Red Skelton most of all—probably because we had such a difficult time persuading Mother to let us listen to his show.

She refused at first because she thought we were saying "Red Skeleton" and was convinced it was a horror show.

We finally persuaded Mother to listen "just this once." When she realized it was a comedy, she let us listen. Even then, she did so reluctantly—she thought Red's "Mean Widdle Kid" character disobeyed his mother too much and set a bad example.

—**Louise Tippett**, Galena, Illinois

FRED ALLEN'S MANY 'FACES'

During the 1940s, Sunday evenings were filled with laughter at our house as one comedian after another appeared on the radio. Starting at 7 p.m., it was Jack Benny, followed by Eddie Cantor, Edgar Bergen and Charlie McCarthy and my all-time favorite, Fred Allen.

Fred's real-life wife, Portland Hoffa, had a high-pitched voice and played a "dumb Dora" character. She usually entered calling, "Mr. Allen, Mr. Allen!"

Fred always answered in surprise, "Why, it's Portland!"

Sometimes Fred would play the part of One Long Pan, a Chinese detective (based on Charlie Chan) who, despite continually misinterpreting clues, would blunder his way to a solution. I can recall One Long Pan opening the wrong door and walking into a clothes closet—only to explain that it was actually a "clues closet."

Another popular segment was "Allen's Alley," in which Fred strolled down a city alleyway knocking on doors. There he'd meet characters like Pansy Nussbaum (played by Minerva Pious), who spoke with a Russian accent and invariably complained about her husband, Pierre.

"You were expecting maybe Weinstein Churchill?" was her typical comedic response.

Another favorite character of mine was Titus Moody, a taciturn New Englander. He once went to a "silo warming" where a rare delicacy was served—owl country-style.

And who could forget Senator Claghorn, played by Fred's announcer Kenny Delmar? He was a Southern politician who liked magicians—but only if they had a confederate in the audience!

Yes, although Fred Allen is long gone, I'll never forget his wonderful sense of humor.

—**Lucille Posner**, New York, New York

When TV Was New

GRANDPA'S MIRACULOUS TV

In the late 1940s, my grandparents were one of the first families in the neighborhood to purchase a black-and-white television. I'd often visit to watch our favorite programs, Arthur Godfrey's and later Lawrence Welk's shows.

One evening, I received an excited call from my grandfather, who asked me to hurry over to see something amazing. It seems that when Grandpa turned on his TV that evening, a miraculous thing had happened—no more black and white, but a color picture!

My uncle and aunt were there as well, and none of us could explain how this came about. But we joined in Grandpa's pleasure.

As we left, my uncle, who could hardly contain his laughter until we got outside, let us in on the secret. He had picked up a sheet of plastic from an ingenious manufacturer. It was tinted green along the bottom and blue along the top, simulating grass and sky, and could be attached to the TV screen.

After a couple of days of Grandpa calling all the family about his amazing TV set, my uncle confessed to his prank. Grandpa wasn't amused, but he soon forgave us all for the innocent attempt to bring a little color into his life.

—**Doris Danner,** East Boston, Massachusetts

MONDAY NIGHT LIVE!

In 1946, fewer than 100 people in Los Angeles owned televisions—and those who did received as many hours of test patterns as programming.

Only two hours on Monday nights were devoted to live shows on W6XAO. I'd enrolled in a UCLA course on TV production, which ended with a student drama broadcast on the air.

The station director later accepted my offer to arrange a series of Monday night telecasts. This photo is from a boxing program I did after meeting Mozelle Dinehart (widow of actor Alan Dinehart) at an amateur fight held on the Burbank ranch of former heavyweight champion Jim Jeffries.

Mozelle, a former starlet, was delighted to be in front of cameras again. She provided commentary while Gene "Spider" Mock sparred with Johnny Garcia, a Golden Gloves champ.

—Brad Atwood
Laguna Beach, California

A DRAW FOR THE NEIGHBORS

The Tele-Tone was one of the first television sets sold to the public in 1948 by Detroit Edison, where I worked at the time. I purchased a Model 149 featuring a 7-inch screen for my parents, which raised their status in our neighborhood. My parents, us seven children and many friends and neighbors filled our home to marvel at the sights on TV.

In time, a magnifying bubble screen was sold to cover the regular screen and bring the image up to 10 inches. The $99 cost of the TV was worth every penny. It was working when it was packed away, and I'm curious to see if it still works today.

—Pat Caswell Drinkwater
South San Francisco, California

LEADING LADY. Beatrice Gray with actor Bob Steele, who was happy to let her get her close-up.

Those Wonderful
WESTERNS

ACTRESS RECALLS HIGH FUN ON SET OF LOW-BUDGET COWBOY MOVIES.
By Beatrice Gray, Los Angeles, California, as told to Michael Williams, Sevierville, Tennessee

It was the spring of 1943 when I first met Walter Chrysler Jr., a business tycoon whose family owned large interests in both the auto and film industries. In fact, they owned the movie studio Monogram Pictures.

A friend took me to a party that Mr. Chrysler was hosting. At the time, I was 32 and working as a showgirl in a Los Angeles nightclub.

Mr. Chrysler and I began to talk. He told me about some movies he was making and asked me to meet actor Bob Steele.

He soon returned with Bob, a leading man in several Westerns. Bob stood 5-foot-6, and producers were looking for a leading lady to play opposite him. Many actresses were taller than that, so my 5-foot-5 height was an advantage.

The following year, I played opposite Steele in *The Utah Kid* and *Trigger Law.*

I'll never forget my first day at work. Bob met me and started showing me around. Then he showed me the horse they had picked out for me. The poor creature looked lifeless. I was disappointed, because I was raised on a farm and expected better. Bob said the horse might not look like much, but he was spirited.

Well, I got on and spurred the horse, which took off. It jumped over creeks, logs and fences, and I lost control. Bob and the other cowboys jumped on their horses and started after me. By the time they caught up, I had the horse under control. We all breathed a sigh of relief—and they enjoyed a laugh at my expense.

The workings of a low-budget Western set were a far cry from what I had anticipated. I was surprised to learn I would do my own makeup and hair and pick out my own costumes from the wardrobe department.

All the filming was done outdoors, with no

studio lighting. More than once, I heard the director shout, "We're burning daylight!" If time was lost, the script was cut. I once saw the director and writer tearing out entire pages! It was amazing that they could make a story work with such drastic changes.

And what I had thought about cowboy actors soon proved to be untrue. I'd heard they were a crude, rough-and-tumble bunch. But all the actors were perfect gentlemen. I never heard any swearing. I respected them and they respected me. On weekends, the cast and crew were often invited to actor Johnny Mack Brown's ranch for barbecue. We'd ride horses, play horseshoes and socialize. Those are fond memories.

Of all the cowboys I worked with, Bob was a favorite. Most other actors wanted the cameras on them at all times. Bob wasn't like that. He was always willing to let me get in front of the camera for a close-up. He would tell me, "Nobody wants to see my ugly mug."

Over the next two years, I made several movies with Monogram Pictures, including *Stranger from Santa Fe*.

In the '40s, I also appeared in *Joan of Arc* and *Abbott and Costello Meet the Killer, Boris Karloff*. Working with Abbott and Costello was such a thrill. Behind the scenes, they played pranks and were always joking. I also worked with Cecil B. DeMille in *Unconquered* and *The Story of Dr. Wassell*.

Over the years, I appeared in hundreds of TV commercials. In 1996, I starred in the made-for-TV movie *A Memory for Tino*. But if I could relive any part of my life, it would be those glorious years in the 1940s and '50s.

THE CROWD LOVED COWBOYS

Since I grew up in the 1940s, cowboy heroes on the big screen were an important part of my world. I waited all week for the 2 p.m. Western matinee at the Isle Theater in my hometown of Cumberland, Wisconsin.

I recall Gene Autry's movie *Boots and Saddles*. Gene and his horse, Champion, had to win an exciting race to get a horse contract with the army. After a series of mishaps and close calls, all riders were eliminated except for Gene and the bad guy.

"Come on, Champ!" Gene called out. "You can do it, boy."

As they neared the finish line, the screams from the audience intensified, drowning out the sound of the horses' hooves flying across the screen.

"Come on, Champ!" To this day, I can still feel the electricity of it all—especially that grand moment of victory when Champion carried our hero over the finish line to beat the bad guy by just seconds. The thunderous applause that followed seemed to rock the building to its foundation.

—*Gary Gray, Hunt, New York*

COMIC BOOK HEROES. "My love for Western comic books began in 1941, before I could even read," remembers James Valentine of Edgewood, Texas. "I was 4 years old, and Mother would read to me from her Western pulp magazines. I liked the drawings of cowboys so much that soon I began collecting comics. Gene Autry and Red Ryder quickly became my heroes. I later added Roy Rogers, Tom Mix, Hopalong Cassidy, Monte Hale, Lash LaRue and Straight Arrow to my collection."

Reel-to-Reel MEMORIES

THOSE OLD GUYS GET BETTER-LOOKING EVERY YEAR

I was 13 years old when I first saw the 1949 movie *Little Women* starring my two favorite actors—June Allyson and Peter Lawford, my true love.

At the end of the film, Laurie (Peter Lawford) married Amy (Elizabeth Taylor). But Jo (June Allyson) married Professor Bhaer, an old man who carried an umbrella! I sobbed my heart out.

By the time I got home from the movie, I had swollen red eyes and eyelashes caked with tissue fuzz.

Thirty years later, when I saw the movie on television, I realized that the "old man" was the handsome Italian actor Rossano Brazzi. My tastes had changed—Jo did all right after all!

—Nancy Blodgett, *Albion, Michigan*

PICTURE PERFECT

In the '40s, pictures of movie stars were for us girls what baseball cards were to the boys. My friends and I always saved our money then so that when the new movie magazines hit the newsstands, we were ready.

Modern Screen was my favorite and often included six full-color photos. It didn't matter whether those stars were my favorites, because I could always find someone to trade with.

June Allyson and Van Johnson were my "dream team." Friends could easily talk me into giving them four or five photos of Tom Drake or Judy Garland for one June or Van.

The best deal I ever made was three photos of June and two of Van for one Betty Grable. That photo happened to be the pin-up picture of Betty for the men in the service. Little did I know how famous that pose would become.

All these years later, I still enjoy the movies of June Allyson and Van Johnson…and I still think I made a good deal on those photos!

—Sue Leaster Hanson
Mentor, Ohio

A TRUE GENTLEMAN. Italian actor Rossano Brazzi portrayed Professor Friedrich Bhaer, Jo March's love interest and later husband, opposite American actress June Allyson in the 1949 film adaptation of Louisa May Alcott's acclaimed children's novel *Little Women*.

THRILLED BY TARZAN

Growing up in the '40s, I loved Tarzan movies. I'll never forget Johnny Weissmuller as Tarzan, Maureen O'Sullivan as Jane, John Sheffield as Boy…and, of course, Cheetah the chimpanzee.

Each time a new Tarzan movie was released, my sister, two friends and I would hop a bus and ride into the city. Our Saturday afternoons were spent in the darkness of the Plaza Theater.

The Plaza usually ran double features. By timing our arrival right, we could see two showings of Tarzan for the price of one. We'd try to memorize the lines, and sometimes we even took along paper and pencil to jot down the dialogue.

Following an afternoon of movie watching, we could hardly wait to return home. There, in a wooded parcel with a grapevine for swinging, we'd reenact our version of the movie we'd just seen.

Tarzan's mighty yell echoed through those woods along with his favorite command to motivate the jungle animals: "Ungowa!"

—**Carol Kurowski,** *Albuquerque, New Mexico*

ADOPTING THE SQUADRON

The 1948 movie *Fighter Squadron* was filmed mostly at Wurtsmith Air Force Base near my hometown of Oscoda, Michigan, on the shore of Lake Huron. The movie brought Robert Stack, Edmond O'Brien and the rest of the cast and crew to our small town.

Almost every evening, they'd drop in at the Hill

Top Tavern, where their presence created quite a sensation among both local customers and tourists. My grandmother Grace Hopcroft, who owned the tavern, posed for the photo above with Robert Stack.

The cast and crew arrived and departed by the Detroit & Mackinac Railway. The townspeople were sorry to see them leave and gave them a final farewell at the train depot, which has since been torn down.

—**Jane Hopcroft Whitford,** *Oscoda, Michigan*

Radio Recollections

I WAS A BREAKFAST CLUBBER

Money was tight and people were tense back in 1945, but for a 5-year-old kid sitting at the kitchen table listening to *The Breakfast Club*, life was great.

We lived in Norwood, Pennsylvania, where my father worked as a welder in a shipyard. With housing nearly impossible to obtain, my parents, sister and I and another couple with a daughter moved into the same side of a large two-story duplex and split the utilities and kitchen privileges.

Although I was only 5, the couple, Faye and Bernard, soon became my friends. Most days they let me share breakfast with them. I loved going downstairs in the morning and drinking "milk coffee" with my adult friends as we listened to *The Breakfast Club* together.

Out of our big black radio came Don McNeill's distinctive booming voice. The music was wonderful, the singing was great and the jokes made us laugh (although sometimes I wasn't sure what everyone was laughing at).

We listened and enjoyed the wonderful music of so many, often tapping our toes. Bernard sometimes tapped his spoon on the rim of his coffee cup. With eggs frying in the skillet, coffee in our cups and the sun shining through the window, we could forget for a moment that war was raging in distant lands.

On occasion, fans of the show would send in the most unusual things! One time it was a 100-pound watermelon from Hope, Arkansas. *The Breakfast Club* gang ate that huge melon on the air as millions of listeners heard them chomping away.

Those years were among the most difficult in this nation's history, and *The Breakfast Club* helped us get through them. The spirit of those times will always linger in our hearts, as will my precious memories of Don McNeill and his "Breakfast Clubbers."

—Vernice Garrett, *Texas City, Texas*

MAD CHICKEN MADE FOR AN UNFORGETTABLE EPISODE

One night when I was 12, my parents went out and I was allowed to stay home alone for the first time.

That night, *Lights Out* presented an episode titled "Chicken Heart." I turned off all the lights, laid down in front of our console radio and began listening to the most frightening radio program I'd ever heard.

I still remember the story—it was about a scientist studying a chicken heart. The heart began beating in a salt solution, even though it had been removed from the chicken. Then it somehow fell to the floor and started to get bigger and bigger, crushing everything in its way.

By the end of the program, the scientist had fled in an airplane, but he knew the heart would eventually fill the universe with its mass.

I guess I wasn't the only one riveted by that program. Several years later, I heard comedian Bill Cosby tell about the time he heard the same *Lights Out* broadcast.

—Wilson Winch, *Independence, Missouri*

HE KEPT UP WITH THE PARADE

During World War II, I was a radio operator in the 3rd Battalion of the 26th Marines. While on Iwo Jima, I discovered my AM radio could receive a station from the States.

The station was directed to the Philippines and played several minutes of music between what I think were coded messages to the Philippine underground. On Saturday nights, they broadcast *Your Hit Parade*, and I made sure I was tuned in.

Eventually I was sent up to the line and had to leave the AM radio behind and take an FM model. However, I made arrangements with a friend to rebroadcast *Your Hit Parade* on the FM frequency so that I wouldn't miss it.

I'll never forget one Saturday night when the company commander, Capt. Donald Castle, crawled over to my foxhole, peered over the edge and saw me flat on my back with the radio earphones tight to my ears. He asked what I was doing.

"Listening to *Your Hit Parade*, Skipper," I replied.

He shook his head and crawled away. I don't think he believed me.

—Wes Kuhn, *Casper, Wyoming*

USING OUR IMAGINATIONS

During the mid-1940s, my sister and I looked forward to Saturday mornings and our favorite radio program, *Let's Pretend*.

Sitting on the living room carpet in front of the floor-model Philco, we'd listen as the half-hour program, acted out by child performers before a live studio audience, was broadcast over WJR in Detroit.

At the beginning of each program, the host, Uncle Bill Adams, would announce: "Cream of Wheat, the great American family cereal, presents *Let's Pretend*!"

Then, to a lilting theme song, a children's chorus would sing: "Cream of Wheat is so good to eat, that we have it every day. We sing this song, it will make us strong, and it makes us shout hooray!"

How absorbed we were with the stories of Puss 'n' Boots, Rumplestiltskin, Jack and the Beanstalk and Cinderella.

And when Uncle Bill shouted, "Hello, Pretenders!" my sister and I would shout back, "Hello, Uncle Bill!" Soon our younger siblings were joining us in calling our favorite radio "Uncle."

Incidentally, we never did care very much for Cream of Wheat.

—Leonard Peterson, *Lansing, Michigan*

THE LONE RANGER RIDES AGAIN! "When I was growing up in Pittsburgh in the '40s, the flickering streetlights at dusk signaled to me and my friends that the Lone Ranger would soon be galloping across the airwaves," writes Lee Felbinger of Green Lane, Pennsylvania. "When we were kids, the announcer saying 'And now a word from our sponsor. . .' was almost as exciting as 'Hi-yo, Silver!' It brought us to the edge of our seats in anticipation of new premiums to be offered for a dime and some box tops. By the time I'd joined the Navy, I had quite a collection of Lone Ranger premiums. When I returned, it wasn't long before I was hooked again!"

I Was Snowed by
KAY KYSER

SHE FLUNKED HER FINAL AT THE KOLLEGE OF MUSICAL KNOWLEDGE!
By Jeanne Cavender, Canton, Ohio

KOLLEGE GRAD. Bud Roberts (right) of Port Angeles, Washington, met "The Old Professor," Kay Kyser, when the *Kollege of Musical Knowledge* came to the Santa Ana Naval Air Station in 1943. Bud didn't win on the show, but his friend Clifford Strickler did. The ex-prize fighter won a $25 war bond for correctly identifying a "blue plate special," adding, "I've aten many of them." His mom later wrote him, "Clifford, your grammar hasn't improved."

High schoolers in the '40s, my friends and I loved the Big Bands and spent hours in the record shop spinning platters before deciding to buy them.

When we read in the paper that Kay Kyser and his *Kollege of Musical Knowledge* would be at the Palace Theatre in Cleveland, a group of us decided to go.

The show was on a Saturday night, and a heavy snow was falling as we piled into the car for the 65-mile drive. We sat on the edge of our seats trying to see the highway.

It was the fashion then for girls to wear a cardigan sweater backward, with a string of pearls. I was right in fashion…except for the knee-high rubber boots I also wore because of the snow.

We made it to the theater, where we were given numbered tickets as we entered. Soon after we found our seats, Kay came on stage in his trademark cap and gown as the "Old Puh-Fessah."

Put to the Test
Kay began calling out ticket numbers to get contestants for his *Kollege of Musical Knowledge*. One by one, the contestants made their way to the brightly lit stage. When my number was called, I couldn't believe it!

I plodded to the stage and up the stairs in those clunky old boots, scared to the bone. There were so many people in the audience! I wondered why I had put my sweater on backward—I felt like a fool!

Ginny Simms, Ish Kabibble and all the gang from Kay's "Kollege" were there along with the band. During the first part of the show, we contestants were asked questions.

As I stood there in those bright lights with all those faces looking at me, I could hardly remember what my name was, let alone answer any questions.

When it was my turn, Kay asked me a simple question—"Name three bandleaders whose first names have only three letters."

Right off, I named Bob Crosby. Then, after frantically searching my memory, I came up with Cab Calloway. Then I went blank!

In the meantime, Kay was dancing all around me on the stage, flapping his arms and raising his eyebrows. The audience went wild with laughter!

What's My Name?
No matter what he did to draw my attention, I was still as blank as an empty blackboard. After he'd milked this for a good laugh, Kay kindly asked me if I knew his name. Then it dawned on me—too late, of course. I'd missed my chance.

Kay and his crew smiled kindly as I left the stage and plodded back down the steps. I was lucky I didn't stumble as I made my way back to my seat halfway up to peanut heaven!

All my friends were kind to me, too—no one made fun of my embarrassment. But I could already imagine what my mother would say when I got home!

"Why were you wearing that pretty sweater backward?" she asked. "And why didn't you remove your boots and put on some shoes?"

I knew she was right. And to top it off, why had I been speechless on stage after all my years of speech lessons and elocution?

Yes, it was mortifying at the time. But now I have only great memories of the night I "flunked out of Kollege."

Queen for a Day

I'll never forget the day in March of 1946 when I came home from high school to find my mother, Amy Oberg, seated in the living room wearing a homemade cardboard crown on her head.

She'd just been chosen as the out-of-town "Queen for a Day" on Mutual Broadcasting Company's *Queen for a Day* radio program. The only prize Mother received from the *Queen for a Day* people was a package of Gotham Gold Stripe nylon stockings.

Instead, our local affiliate radio station, KORN, stepped forward and presented her with a host of special honors, services and prizes solicited from local businesses. After a day of meals, prizes and a crowning ceremony, my parents stayed in the Bridal Suite at the Hotel Pathfinder, where 21 friends and relatives gave them a shivaree at the hotel. (They never had one when they got married.)

She later fondly reminisced about her day in a book of family history. "This is all a very pleasant memory," she wrote. "Many times it seems that it is the woman who has everything who receives honors like that, so it was very special for an old farm woman like me."

—**Betty Oberg Hoffman,** *Florissant, Missouri*

CHAPTER 4

Kiddin' **AROUND**

PAGE 109

PAGE 99

PAGE 107

PAGE 111

Growing up, every kid had a favorite place to play. Maybe it was the backyard or a park down the street. For some, it was the front stoop.

"In the 1940s, I was lucky to grow up in a lovely brick six-family house which featured an ornate iron fence and a large stoop," explains Catherine Ferrara Zoida of Howard Beach, New York. "That stoop was more than an architectural feature.

"There, my sisters and I imagined flying on magic carpets or sailing the high seas on pirate ships. We played games, picnicked, cut out paper dolls and shared our secrets and dreams. The broad top of the stoop served as a stage for dancing and singing to our favorite Betty Grable musicals.

"When we were older, boys were allowed to sit with us. They occasionally held our hands, and sometimes they'd even steal a kiss. Now our stoop is gone, but I'll never forget all the memories we made there."

Whether we were playing outside or attending to our studies, falling in love or making mischief, the 1940s were a special time to grow up, as you'll see in this chapter.

Some Enchanted
EVENING

IT WASN'T PERFECT, BUT A DATE TO A VALENTINE'S DAY DANCE WAS THE START OF LIFELONG LOVE.
By James E. Redmond, Marana, Arizona

Mary Ann Williams was not the easiest person to date when we were teens in Louisville, Kentucky. Her parents allowed her just two dates a week, on Friday and Saturday nights. The only other window of wooing opportunity came on Sunday afternoons, when guys were allowed to stop by her house, sit in the living room and visit with her and her parents.

And the competition was heavy. Seven of us had her squarely in our sights: two of them in college, one in the service and the rest of us in high school. I had to be fast on my feet to book one of Mary Ann's rare open dates.

All that changed on one magical evening, Feb. 14, 1941, when anything seemed possible.

She Was His Valentine
For several years, Valentine's Day had been special to Mary Ann and me. To continue that trend, I knew I'd have to make my move early—but no more than a month in advance, by her parents' rules—to be the first to ask her to a Valentine's dance at the Shrine Temple.

The dance loomed large for me. Mary Ann would turn 16 in June, and I really wanted to know where I stood with her. So after she accepted my invitation, I came up with a plan for the evening.

I arranged for my buddies Andy Lane and Jimmy Heycraft and their dates to meet Mary Ann and me at the corner of 48th and Market at 5:30 p.m. From there, a streetcar would take us most of the way to the Shrine Temple. But to make our streetcar connection on the way back, we'd have to leave the dance by 10:30.

When I came to pick up Mary Ann, I was caught completely off guard. I had never seen a girl so pretty! She wore a red party dress with high heels, and in her hair was a gardenia that I'd brought her. Speechless, I just stood and stared. How did I get lucky enough to go to the dance with this beauty?

We arrived early, and as soon as Mary Ann took off her coat, guys were lining up to sign her dance card. Thank goodness she cut them off early. After five dances, she would be mine for the rest of the night.

The evening was extra special. We danced, talked and sang the song of the night, "I'll Never Smile Again," along with Frank Sinatra.

We and our friends had such a good time that we missed our streetcar connection. The six of us had to walk 20 blocks in freezing weather. Worse yet, it was snowing—and Mary Ann was wearing heels for the first time.

She had only thin gloves on, which at least

FIVE YEARS LATER...
When James returned from World War II, he and Mary Ann were married. By then, over five years had passed since the Valentine's Day dance.

gave me a chance to be gallant. I took off my heavy right-hand glove, placed it over Mary Ann's right hand, then took her left hand in my right hand, and placed them in my right-hand coat pocket. Now, that was a move!

Despite the weather, it was still a beautiful evening, one of those nights where it seemed as if you could reach out and touch every star. We could hear ice cracking on the trees and see shooting stars cross the sky.

Love Blossomed

We reached Mary Ann's house well past her 11 p.m. curfew. She told her parents she'd returned, and that I was warming up inside before I rode my bike home.

Chilled to the bone, both of us leaned in toward the old steam radiator, holding our toes underneath it and our hands over the top, talking about the splendid evening and how much we had enjoyed the dance.

Soon, we ran out of words. We looked into each other's eyes, and leaned in closer. Our lips touched and lingered for several moments—nothing too passionate, but our very first kiss. I knew it meant there was something special between us.

Then she reached into her coat pocket and pulled out her dance card, which was shaped like a heart. She tore the dance card in half and gave me one piece. Then she said, "The heart we each have is broken, but if you put them together, they are one."

Well, that's when I started to shake all over. I didn't know if I was still chilled, or if it was from Mary Ann sharing her heart. Whatever it was, it left me both scared and elated.

I hardly remember my ride home, but I know the cold never bothered me. The bike flew as I sang "I'll Never Smile Again" in the cold night air.

Our lives soon changed dramatically. Within a year, all seven of Mary Ann's young suitors were off to fight in World War II. Only four of us would come home.

But during the next three years, Mary Ann wrote me every night—more than a thousand letters in all—while she waited for my return. We were married April 13, 1946, and enjoyed many rich and rewarding years together.

Mary Ann has been gone a few years now. Not long ago, I found some of her old scrapbooks. The pages held a lot of personal things: report cards, awards, letters from friends and souvenirs of high school days.

Toward the back of the book, one page stopped me cold and brought tears to my eyes. It was her half of the torn dance card. With a red pen, she had drawn in the other half of the heart—my half—and written inside it: "Dance Feb. 14, 1941. Went with Jimmie. Had a wonderful time." She had underlined the words "Jimmie" and "wonderful."

The sight of that card took me right back to our enchanted evening 70 years ago. That magical night, when I realized the improbable was possible, will live on in my heart forever.

Young Love

SHE WAS A SUCKER FOR HER VALENTINE

It was recess on my first day of fifth grade at a new school, Panama Union Elementary, in Bakersfield, California.

A pudgy girl approached and asked me who I liked, and I knew I had to answer so she'd leave me alone. The problem was, I couldn't recall any names. The teacher had called two boys up to her desk. One wore bib overalls and a striped T-shirt. He was only 12 but was already as tall as a man. I remembered him both for his height and his unusual name, Lavonne.

"Lavonne," I said. She was ready to pry further, but I was saved by the bell, and we all scurried back to class.

At lunchtime, the girl told Lavonne what I said, and he came over to the merry-go-round where I was sitting. By the end of lunch, I really did like Lavonne, especially his cute Southern accent.

I spent many lunches after that with Lavonne. Along with Milk Duds, Sugar Daddies and Fleer's bubble gum, he would often bring wild-cherry suckers for me—my favorite.

I lived with my brother, who was a beekeeper. We had plenty of honeycombs, so I started taking one of the sweet, sticky squares to school each day for Lavonne.

When Valentine's Day came, I expected a card from Lavonne. Nothing.

But when you're 12, disappointment doesn't last long. I just walked home after school, as usual, and pretty much forgot about it.

Later, my sister-in-law called and said I had a visitor. There was Lavonne. He shyly lowered his eyes and handed me a Valentine's Day card. Inside was a lollipop and the message, "Be My Valentine, Sucker."

It took 16 years, but that simple little sucker finally sucked me in, and Lavonne and I were married in 1963. We've stuck together ever since.

—*Norma Howell*, Ridgecrest, California

LOVE IS BLIND

I spent almost every summer day at the beach when I lived in Glencoe, Illinois, a Chicago suburb on Lake Michigan, in the 1940s.

One day in 1946, the summer after my freshman year at New Trier High School, I was bicycling to the beach when I saw six or seven sophomore girls cavorting on the lawn of a large brick Georgian-style house. One of the girls was Mary Campbell, a class beauty highly regarded by the sophomore boys.

The next thing I knew, I was lying on the gravel shoulder with all those girls around me asking if I was all right.

Entranced by the sight of Mary and her friends, I had failed to notice the car parked in front of the house, and I had ridden right into the back of it.

I was further embarrassed to find that the fork of my bike was badly bent, and I had to walk it away in front of all those girls.

—*H. Clark Dean*, Glencoe, Illinois

WATER BALLOON WAS HEAVEN-SENT

I was the "new girl in school" back in 1948, having moved from Chicago to a small Iowa town.

My new high school was putting on a carnival, and I got to run one of the booths. I wore an outfit I was proud of—a new pink blouse and gray slacks.

Some boys came by, and I noticed one whose picture I'd seen a few days earlier in a friend's yearbook. "I'd sure like to go out with that guy someday," I'd told her. "Not a chance!" she'd replied.

Those boys left the gym, and I didn't think much more about them…until I was suddenly soaked head to toe! They'd gone to the second floor above my booth and dropped a water balloon on me! When I looked up, there was "that guy," grinning broadly.

I was appalled, of course, but not for long. Despite my friend's prediction, I did end up going out with that boy. We've been married for decades and have two wonderful boys…just like their dad.

—*Arlene Brammer*, Cedar Rapids, Iowa

How Mom Saved My Senior Prom

IT DIDN'T LOOK LIKE SHE'D EVER GET TO WEAR HER BEAUTIFUL PROM DRESS—
UNTIL A RESOURCEFUL MOTHER TOOK OVER! *By Carol Beck, Indianapolis, Indiana*

I'd looked forward to June 8, 1945, for many weeks. Graduation from my high school in Indianapolis, Indiana, was scheduled for 6:30 p.m. that night, with the prom to follow at 9:30 in the school gym.

Though I'd never had a date with a boy at school, I still believed that one would ask me to the senior prom. After all, it happened in the movies all the time!

Unfortunately, the country had been at war all four years I was in high school, and many of my male classmates had already joined the military.

Until our prom, my best friend and I made do at our weekly sock hops in the gym, dancing together or just watching. So I was looking forward to a real dance with pretty decorations and everyone dressed up special.

Mother bought me a sophisticated dress with a black top, a sweetheart neckline and a light blue chiffon skirt. Oh, how I looked forward to wearing that dress!

Every day I went to school prepared to answer "Yes" to anyone who asked me to prom. But no one did. On the last day of the ticket sale, Mother gave me money to buy two tickets. She said they'd be "insurance" if someone asked me and couldn't get tickets.

Time Was Short

On the evening of our graduation, I walked out on the football field in my cap and gown to receive my diploma, still hoping some boy would speak up. Prom was less than four hours away! But after the ceremony ended, it was obvious I wouldn't be going to the prom. I was heartbroken.

Some friends and relatives came back to our house for refreshments. I didn't want these well-wishers to see my disappointment, but I'm sure they knew.

Mother thanked everyone for coming, then told me to put on my prom dress anyway so everyone could see it. I did as I was told, long black gloves and all. Then Mother told me to get in the car. I couldn't imagine what she was up to.

Mother drove me downtown to the Indiana Roof Ballroom and stopped the car in front. A long line of young women and servicemen waiting to enter the hall to dance to a prominent big band stretched on and on.

Mother told me to pick out a serviceman and ask him if he'd like to go to my prom. I only had to ask one young man, a handsome Canadian sailor. After I'd explained my predicament, he gallantly agreed to escort me.

Sailor Was Smooth

Back home, Mother gave him the corsage she'd bought for me and the keys to her car. Then the two of us drove to the gym and went inside. I couldn't believe I was really at my senior prom with a dashing young sailor who was a good dancer and a polite and refined gentleman.

My classmates were surprised to see us, but he and I acted as if we'd known each other forever. He made me feel so happy and special.

When the dance ended, my sailor could have taken me home and I'd have been more than satisfied. Instead, we joined some kids who were going to an after-hours place, where we danced until it closed. I felt like Cinderella at the ball!

The sailor drove me home, handed over the keys and said good-bye. I never saw him again. For all I know, he was an angel—he certainly was for me that night!

My graduating class recently celebrated our 50-year class reunion—at the Indiana Roof Ballroom of all places! That night, I couldn't help but think of that kind young man from Canada who made a young girl's dream come true...and a wonderful mother who couldn't stand by and see her little girl be disappointed.

Saved by the Bell

IN A CLASS OF HER OWN. "At the one-room school I attended," says Cordell Madel of Neenah, Wisconsin, "I was the only one in my grade for eight years." She's seated in the back of the 1946 photo above. "For graduation, I picked my own motto and corsage colors!"

SUNNY FACES. "Students loved picture day at Sunnyside School in 1946. Lucy Williams of Ephrata, Pennsylvania, (second row, fourth from left) remembers her school days as unhurried and pleasant, and still treasures the copy of *Anne of Green Gables* given to her by her teacher, Mr. Geib.

ALL IN THEIR PLACES. On October 3, 1940, pupils in fourth and fifth grades at Central School in Olivette, Missouri, took time out from lessons to pose for this photo, shared by Lillian Knoche of St. Louis.

STICK-TOGETHERNESS. "We five kids in this picture, taken in 1941, went from kindergarten through fifth grade together—only five of us in the class!" says Frances Ogden of Clinton, Washington. "My folks and I moved to the West Coast shortly after this photo was taken so my dad could work in the shipyards during World War II. I've always wondered what life dealt my classmates. Pictured from left are Jack Jones, Donald Frazier, Bernard Shaw, me (then Frances Smith) and Barbara Hunt. Behind us is Chesterfield School in Des Moines, Iowa."

Like daughter, like mother...

...and both of them really "alive"

A pair of Hemo girls!

D ON'T *you* sometimes wish you had the pep, the burbling-with-life your bright-eyed offspring radiates?

Then, take as good care of *you* as you do of her!

See that *you*, too, get enough vitamins every day. Three out of four folks may not, you know.

And get those vital vitamins in the glorious *food* drink—HEMO. We defy you to resist its "milk-chocolate" flavor!

Every luscious sip teems with vit and minerals you and your children have every day to feel and act "aliv

Tip: Have a *steaming* cupful of at bedtime to help you relax. *cold*, it's swell! Just 59¢ for a full jar at grocery or drug stores.

AND REMEMBER — Just 2 glas HEMO made with milk supply a f needs of all these vital vitam minerals!

JUST ONE GLASS of Hemo gives you:

The Vitamin A in 3 boiled eggs!
PLUS
The Vitamin B₁ in 4 slices of whole wheat bread!
PLUS
The Vitamin B₂ (G) in 4 servings of spinach!
PLUS
The Vitamin D in 3 servings of beef liver!
PLUS
The Niacin in 3 servings of carrots!
PLUS
The Iron in ½ pound of beef!
PLUS
The Calcium & Phosphorus in 2 servings of cauliflower
and 1 serving of cooked green beans combined!

HEMO exceeds adult requirements!			
Minimum daily needs set by U. S. nutritionists		2 servings of HEMO, made with milk, give	
4000 USP units	VITAMIN A	4900 USP units	
333 USP units	VITAMIN B₁	400 USP units	
2 milligrams	VITAMIN B₂	3 milligrams	
400 USP units (Nat set)	VITAMIN D	410 USP units	
10 milligrams	NIACIN	10.3 milligrams	
750 milligram	IRON	11.7 milligrams	
750 milligrams	CALCIUM	950 milligrams	
	PHOSPHORUS	750 milligrams	

Guaranteed by Good Housekeeping

Borden's
Hemo

Remember Saying?

STOOLIE:
tattletale

Welch's
or PURE *Enjoyment*

UNDER THE
WEATHER

THE CARAS GIRLS. Tootsie (left) and Elaine, are pictured in a childhood portrait, at ages 6 and 3, around 1941.

STRANDED ON THE FRONT PORCH

I remember that fateful day in the summer of 1943 when a man nailed a white sheet of paper to the telephone pole in the corner of our front yard. I was 6 and my sister, Tootsie, was 8. I asked her what the paper meant.

Tootsie said it meant we couldn't get off the porch all summer, or until the man came back and removed the sign. We had whooping cough, and the sign meant we were quarantined.

A sinking feeling came over me. Not only were we restricted for the summer—we were diseased!

Our days on the green-and-yellow-striped glider were sunny and warm…and long. We ate crackers, drank Kool-Aid and played Monopoly. Tootsie, being older, always won the game because she was not only the banker but was also in charge of distributing the property.

Tootsie would play board games with me, but she wouldn't play house. She liked to read, color and play cards.

But one day, probably out of desperation for something to do, Tootsie made me a set of paper dolls. They were beautiful, and I was delighted. We colored the clothes with all the colors in the box of crayons, and I played happily with my wonderful paper dolls and their stylish outfits.

I liked to play house with my real dolls, too, and one day figured out how to get Tootsie to play with me.

My mother had given each of us a stick of licorice, my favorite candy. Tootsie ate hers right away. I decided to save mine and offer it to Tootsie if she would play house with me. Tootsie took the offer. But she played with me for only as long as it took her to eat my stick of licorice, then said, "I quit." Now I was out a playmate and my licorice stick.

Summer finally ended and the man came and removed the sign.

We weren't happy to have spent all that summer on the front porch. But we were at least happy that we hadn't contaminated anybody else.

—**Elaine Caras Mugan,** *Flushing, Michigan*

IT WON'T HURT LATER

I was born in England in 1943, the eldest of seven children, and my mom had a surefire remedy for whatever ailed us. Be it a bump on the head, a grazed knee or a cut finger, she simply gave it a healthy rub and declared, "Never mind, it won't hurt when it gets better."

We took that at face value and didn't complain again, with the belief that it certainly wouldn't!

Now, if we had a burn, Mom would rub butter on it, and it had to be real butter, not margarine. Many folks back then used that remedy and other old-fashioned cures. You got honey and vinegar for a sore throat, and if you dared bite your fingernails, they were painted with hot mustard.

We also had to take a spoonful of cod liver oil with malt every day, but I honestly don't remember what that was for!

—**Joyce Chilson,** *Springfield, Oregon*

THE BABE WROTE BACK

The year 1941 was a bleak one for the U.S., on the brink of war, and for me, with rheumatic fever.

During a hospital stay, I began reading about the just-ended career of Babe Ruth, a hero to all us boys. I was in pain, so a nurse helped me write a letter to the Babe, explaining my problems. I didn't know then that he had his own pain at times, nor that cancer would claim his life in a few years.

To this 11-year-old's great pleasure, the Babe answered with a short letter, with the encouraging words to "hang in there."

I long ago verified the signature as that of the Great Bambino, and I will never forget that simple act of kindness from a revered man.

—**John Donofrio,** *Clarendon Hills, Illinois*

Mischief Makers

RUNAWAY'S BOLD PLAN LAID BARE

In 1940, when I was 8 years old, I decided to run away from home. With my suitcase packed and some peanut butter sandwiches in a brown paper bag, I started for the front door of our stucco bungalow in Wantagh, New York.

My mom asked where I was going.

"I'm leaving home," I said, with the suitcase and food in tow.

"If you want to run away, that's all right," she said. "But you came into this home without anything and you can leave the same way."

I threw my suitcase and sandwiches on the floor defiantly and started for the door again.

"Wait a minute," Mom said. "You didn't have any clothes on when you arrived, and I want them back."

This infuriated me. I tore my clothes off—shoes, shirt, socks, underwear and all—and shouted, "Can I go now?"

"Yes," my mom answered, "but once you close that door, don't expect to come back."

I was so angry I slammed the door and stepped out on the front porch. Suddenly I realized that I was outside, completely naked. Then I noticed that down the street, two neighborhood girls were walking toward our house. Looking for a place to hide, I spied the big spruce tree that took up half our front yard.

Hoping the girls hadn't seen me, I dived under the low-hanging branches face first. Ouch! After I was sure the girls had passed by, I ran to the front door and banged on it loudly.

"Who's there?" I heard.

"It's Billy! Let me in!"

The voice behind the door answered, "Billy doesn't live here anymore. He ran away from home."

Glancing behind me to see if anyone else was coming down the street, I said, "Aw, c'mon, Mom! I'm still your son. Let me in!"

The door inched open and Mom's smiling face appeared. "Did you change your mind about running away?" she asked.

"What's for supper?" I answered.

—**Bill Cozine,** Spring Green, Wisconsin

BUBBLEGUM PROFITEER

In 1945, when I was 7, many items were either rationed, scarce or nonexistent.

Several blocks from my home was a store named Huber's that sold ice cream, candy, milk, bread and even school supplies. One item we kids especially liked was Dubble Bubble Gum, but it was always in short supply. The owner usually received one box of 100 pieces each month, and I asked if someone could purchase the whole box when it arrived. He said yes, so my 9-year-old sister, Marsha, and I pooled our money to split the box of gum for $1. After what seemed like an eternity, the box was ours! I held back 20 pieces for me and left 30 to sell in a war profiteering venture. I set up shop near the store, and soon my customers began arriving.

My opening price was 2 cents for a piece, but that escalated to 4 cents. When I came to the last piece, a little blond curly-haired girl, no older than 5, came and asked if I had any more gum to sell. I said I did, and when she asked the price, I paused and considered that this was my last chance to profit.

I told her 7 cents, and she turned and went back to her father, who was standing a few yards away. Her father slowly turned and gave me a look of sad disgust that I remember to this day. I could hardly look in his direction as he counted out the 7 cents so his little girl could have her precious piece of gum.

Well, everyone got some gum, and I made a kid-size fortune, but my joy was tempered by the lesson I learned from that father. I learned that money isn't everything, and that some looks are never forgotten.

—**Terry Bender,** *Orlando, Florida*

BIG BROTHER PULLED A FAST ONE

One day in the early '40s, when I was 4 and my brother, Richard, was 5, we went for a ride on his tricycle. Richard was the "driver," and I stood on the back and pushed with one leg to help us go a little faster.

We rode to the end of the block and stopped at a funny-looking red metal box atop a shiny pole. Richard told me it was a gum machine and that by opening the little door I could get us both a piece of gum. He even held the bike still for me while I stood on the seat and opened the little glass door.

You can guess what happened next. The fire station was only a block away, and within seconds we had two fire trucks with flashing lights following us. We pedaled and pumped furiously in hopes of getting home first and maybe hiding before they arrived.

We both had early and long naps that afternoon!

—**Susan Keller**
Valdosta, Georgia

A LITTLE LARCENY LED TO UNEXPECTED LESSON

Just because I was a pastor's daughter didn't mean I stayed out of trouble.

At age 5, I hadn't yet grasped the meaning of one of the Ten Commandments, "Thou shalt not steal."

At a grocery store one day in 1943, I asked my mother for one of the candy bars on display, but she refused. I really wanted one, so when she turned away, I shoved a Baby Ruth into my coat pocket.

To my horror, my pocket had a hole in it, so as a result, I clutched that Baby Ruth tightly in my little fist as I followed Mother through the store and checkout stand, out the door and all the way home. The truth came out when I took my hand out of my pocket to take off my coat back at home.

"I have to go back and pay for this," Mother said, and she did so immediately. Her reaction surprised me; I thought she would scold me and return the candy, not go back and pay for it.

When Mother returned, Dad, Virgil and I sat at our dining room table while she cut the Baby Ruth into four pieces. I got a piece of candy the same size as everyone else's. I didn't get spanked. And Dad didn't bring out his Bible and pontificate on the evils of stealing. He enjoyed the chocolate as much as the rest of us. As you can see, my parents also taught us about mercy and grace.

—**Naomi Voorhees**
Whittier, California

REVEREND'S FAMILY. Virgil and Naomi wear angelic looks in this portrait with their parents, Mildred and A.J. Allen.

We Were Babes In
TOYLAND!

WHEN YOU GROW UP IN A TOY STORE, EVERY DAY IS CHRISTMAS. *By Marilyn Rack, Sinking Spring, Pennsylvania*

I suppose every child dreams of living in a toy store. For my brother, Jim, and me, that dream was a reality. From the mid-'40s, when we were growing up, until 1972, our parents, Billie and Frank Hummel, ran a bicycle and toy store from the basement of our home in West Lawn, Pennsylvania.

The business started by accident after Dad repaired a neighbor's bike. Word got around fast that Mr. Hummel could fix bicycles, and before long, Pop was in business!

During World War II, the only bicycles manufactured were Victory Bikes. They featured a regular-size tire in the rear, with a small wheel and a huge basket up front. The patriotic idea behind the design was for folks to do their shopping via pedal power, conserving gasoline.

We sold a few of the Victory models to adults, but since the other more popular styles were no longer being made, Pop started buying old bikes and reviving them with repairs and bright new coats of paint.

Folks came to our store from all over the county to buy those refurbished bikes. After the war ended, Pop was able to sell new bicycles again...although just like the new cars that were manufactured at that time, there was a long waiting list.

animal display! Soon there were dozens of animals hanging by an ear from the backyard clothesline. It made quite a picture—and when they finally dried, we had a stuffed animal sale.

The store had no regular hours, so business began with the first customer of the day (often waking my folks from a sound sleep) and ended when the last person left at night. There were even times when customers joined us for supper.

Today, a new family lives in the old place. They don't have layaways in the living room or stuffed animals hanging from the clothesline...and do you know what they keep in the garage? Their car. Imagine that.

Up to Their Elbows in Paint

One plaything I'll never forget was a toy carpet sweeper. Pop got a deal on the components needed to make 5,000 of them. Before the sweepers could be assembled, the parts had to be painted by dipping them into huge vats of lacquer. We could always tell which part was being painted on any given day by the color of our parents' arms...clear up to their elbows!

Once everything dried, the entire family joined forces and formed an assembly line to complete the sweepers. (If only I had one now, I'd have it bronzed and give it to my parents as a memento. On second thought, they probably don't need a reminder—blue arms are pretty hard to forget!)

Another unforgettable incident started with our washing machine, which was upstairs on the first floor. One busy Christmas season, the machine overflowed, and water leaked into the basement below—soaking the entire stuffed

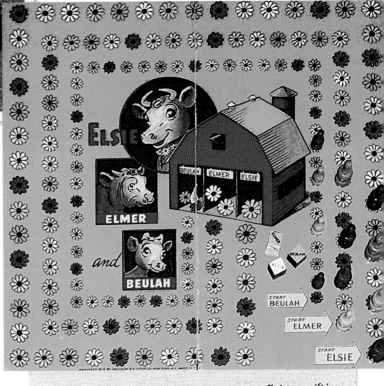

ENDLESS A-MOOS-MENT. "This Elsie game was a Christmas gift in 1941, when I was 5," explains Russ Richardson. "It was the first board game I ever had. It has been played with by three generations and is still used by the little ones."

Students' Shenanigans

A LESSON IN ALGEBRA

One day in 1946, my friend Blitz somehow persuaded me to back him up when he went to see our high school math teacher, Mr. Axtel, about the "F" he'd received in algebra.

"You know I try real hard," Blitz said to the teacher. "I never miss class. And my dad has a real bad temper. He could kick the stuffing out of me. And my mom has a weak heart, and I'm an only child, and she's got all her hopes set on me. This is really serious. Is there anything you can do for me? Please?"

Mr. Axtel sat immobile, peering without expression over his glasses at this humbled student. There never was an aura of good humor around Mr. Axtel, who was both a math teacher and head football coach in our football-crazy hometown of Beaver Falls, Pennsylvania.

Blitz was warming to the task. He blathered on about trying extra hard and working to be Mr. Axtel's best student.

Finally, Mr. Axtel held out his hand and said flatly, "Give me your report card."

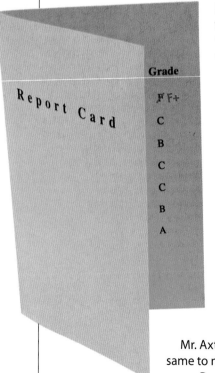

"Oh, yes sir, Mr. Axtel," Blitz said. "Thank you, thank you. I'll never forget this, and you won't regret it."

Mr. Axtel made some notation and handed the report card back to Blitz, who clutched it in his sweaty hand and backed out the door with many thanks, like someone leaving a royal presence. This performance was making me nauseated, but I had to give him credit for pulling it off.

We stepped into the hall and cautiously looked at the card. It now said "F-plus."

Mr. Axtel never looked the same to me after that.

—**Don Robb,** *Glendale, California*

LOOSE LIPS SINK QUIPS

In 1945, our brand-new, young and very pretty teacher, Miss DeMoss, was very close to the age of some of the fellows back from the war to get their Gresham (Oregon) Union High School diplomas.

The fellows would hang around the classroom door, which our new teacher seemed to enjoy but which made it hard for us girls to get in the room for her shorthand class.

One day while riding the city bus from downtown Portland with some of my friends, our conversation turned to our teacher. Some of the talk was a bit catty, including some remarks about her baggy stockings. (Nylons were hard to come by back then.)

The next day, Miss DeMoss read off our entire conversation to the class. She didn't miss a thing, delighting in every word. Embarrassed? Never in my life had I ever been so mortified!

It turned out her sister was on the same bus and recorded the whole conversation—in shorthand, of course. The rest of the class wondered what it was all about, but we five girls knew very well.

I've forgotten much of the shorthand I learned from Miss DeMoss, but I have never forgotten the lesson I learned riding the bus that day.

—**Violet Lambert Petersen,** *Oregon City, Oregon*

IMPERFECT TIMING

In 1940 I entered a country school called the Mudrun School. Since there were no other children in first grade, my teacher, Hal Guthrie, put me in second grade with three other kids.

Like most young boys, I got into some mischief while attending the one-room school. Mr. Guthrie often left his pocket watch on his desk while he walked around the room, teaching groups of students. One day while he was busy, I slipped up to his desk and set the watch ahead an hour. Class was dismissed early!

That afternoon, as Mr. Guthrie drove through town, everyone looked at him quizzically, wondering why he was out so early in the day.

The next day, I aimed for another early dismissal. I did not consider that Mr. Guthrie might have wised up to the prank and was keeping a close eye on his desk from across the room. I received a good tanning, and I certainly learned a good lesson.

—**Richard Ellinger,** *Lewiston, Illinois*

APRIL FOOLS ON PARADE. Every April Fools' Day at Milwaukie Junior High School in Milwaukie, Oregon, we had "Dress-Up Day." We'd follow the school band and parade through downtown Milwaukie and back. In 1945, I won a prize for my Little Bo-Peep costume, and my friend Dean Binn got one for his hula dancer outfit (the two boys are "looking pretty" in the top row).

GUM IS NOT BECOMING

A strict rule for my fourth-grade class in 1941 was no chewing gum in school.

One day, my teacher caught me chewing and asked if I had gum in my mouth. I said no, of course, but she asked me to come up to her desk and open my mouth. The evidence was plain as day.

My teacher told me to take the gum and stick it on the end of my nose. I know my face turned 10 shades of red. I had to return to my desk and wear the gum for the rest of the class period. Naturally, this brought laughter from some students.

Then the worst part happened. The principal entered the room, saw me with gum on my nose and asked me why I was wearing it, so I had to explain. If I could have disappeared, never to be seen again, I would have been happy.

—**Judy Beaman,** *Merced, California*

Snow Days

WHEN THE FLEXIBLE FLYER REIGNED SUPREME

A cycle of snowy winters into the '40s delighted kids in my Long Island, New York, hometown. Adults didn't look forward to the first snowfall, but it sent us kids scampering to garages, sheds and barns to pull out our trusty old Flexible Flyers.

On Saturday mornings, we'd line up a "train" of a dozen or more sleds and prevail on an adult to pull us around the block with his or her car. It was undoubtedly dangerous and probably illegal, but it sure was fun.

After the road was "ruined" by town sanding crews, the action moved to a nearby golf course that had plenty of hills and some challenging wooded areas. If natural hazards were lacking, we'd create barriers of packed snow to plow through or vault over.

Stacking as many bodies as possible on one sled and trying to reach the bottom of the hill without tipping over was a popular pastime. Multi-sled trains inevitably crashed at the end of the line.

We also raced to see who could reach a designated finish line first—or fought for supremacy of the hill by upsetting opponents' sleds (grabbing a rear runner and pulling sideways worked best).

When my family moved to the north shore of Long Island, the terrain provided longer and steeper hills. From the top of a favorite sledding spot called "Suicide Hill," we had a spectacular view of the New York City skyline, some 20 miles distant.

Plunging down the steep incline, we'd try to negotiate a sharp curve to avoid plowing into a thick stand of sturdy oaks. Sled trains usually didn't make it!

As we kids passed from grammar school into our teen years, the tenor of our sledding activities changed. For one thing, boys were more likely to

SNOW FOOLIN'

Back in 1940, my friends and I built a two-story-tall snowman!

We rounded up all the kids in our Kirwan Heights, Pennsylvania, neighborhood, put up a tall pole and began packing snow around it. Even the man running the county snowplow got into the act— when he saw what we were up to, he dumped a few loads of snow nearby.

After the snowman grew to around 8 feet tall, we got Dad's ladder and carried more snow up in bushel baskets and buckets. For the snowman's arms, we nailed some boards near the top of the pole, then packed snow around them.

It took two days to reach the top. We used tin cans for his eyes, a long stick with a can for his pipe, coal for his mouth and cardboard and a bushel basket for his hat.

When we finished, Dad took several photos. That's him on the left (the neighbor lady is doffing his hat). I'm at the very top, just under the snowman's pipe.

—**Ken Gastgeb**, *Norman, Oklahoma*

SNOW PILE O' FUN. "How we loved to play in the snow," says Karen Eichner of Torrington, Connecticut. "This photo was taken in March 1947 at a neighbor's house on Guerdot Road (now Meyer Road) in the Newfield section of Torrington. Pictured in front, from left, are neighbor Harry Blackburn, my brother Paul and I. The Eichners in the back, from left, are cousin John, brother William and cousins Billy and Bobbie. Those surely were the good old days."

choose girls as the targets of mischief rather than their buddies.

Boys would stand at the top of the hill with sleds at the ready, waiting to chase the first girl foolish enough to start downhill. Then the race was on to see who could make her sled spin out! If a boy wanted to impress a particular girl, he might become her protector, cutting off or intercepting attacking sleds.

Often at the foot of the hill there'd be a fire for warming up and roasting marshmallows. With our sleds standing upright in the snow to shield us from the wind, we'd sip from thermoses of hot cocoa.

Sometimes we were invited to a friend's home for snacks. Parents may not have been eager to have their homes invaded by hungry snow-covered teenagers, but I think they appreciated having their kids safely at home.

As a north wind blows and the snow begins piling up, I find myself fighting an urge to clean the rust off my old Flexible Flyer. Maybe I could show my grandchildren how to form a sled train and how to cook marshmallows over a fire in the snow...

—*George Smith,* Avon, New York

CARDBOARD WAS KING

I remember winters during the '40s when we'd take an empty cardboard box, pile as many kids in it as possible and slide down a big hill by our house until the whole thing fell apart.

Then we'd each have a piece of cardboard to slide on. We'd stay out for hours in our wool snowsuits and mittens, then go home and sit behind the wood cookstove to warm up.

The smell of wool drying was terrible—but the warmth of that wood stove was wonderful.

—*Darlene Standiford,* Onalaska, Wisconsin

MUSH! Katie Mace of New Franken, Wisconsin, shares this photo of her father, Russell Jacobs, sometime around 1941.

The Teacher Who CHANGED MY LIFE

MISS VICKERY MAY HAVE BEEN STERN, BUT SHE KNEW EXACTLY
WHAT A SHY STUDENT NEEDED MOST OF ALL.
By Helen Goodman, Wadesboro, North Carolina

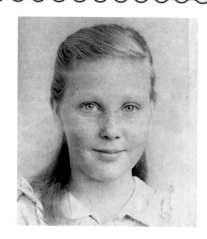

Her name was Miss Vickery, but to us seventh graders in Otsego, Michigan, she was known as "Old Miss Vickery." The nickname didn't denote age so much as her reputation for being stern, mean and witchlike.

Upperclassmen spooked us younger kids with stories about mean Old Miss Vickery, imitating her shrill voice, hunched shoulders and the way she used her deadly ruler.

It was 1944, and my junior high years were shadowed by the grim possibility of being assigned to Miss Vickery's homeroom. Of course, that's just what happened.

There I sat with 25 other dismayed students, listening to her lay down the rules of behavior. Her gray hair was pulled back in a tight bun and pierced through with a No. 2 pencil. A sideways glance from her cold black eyes could rivet us to our seats.

I'd always loved school and had made good grades in spite of an embarrassing handicap—many sounds were unpronounceable for me, so I'd learned to communicate using fractured words and my own sign language.

A Longtime Problem

Through sixth grade, I'd attended a small country school where the teacher knew everyone's family. Since one of my uncles had had the same difficulty, my speech problem wasn't considered unusual. It was said to "run in the family."

I always wrote my assignments and never had to recite in class. Friends who'd learned to understand me served as interpreters when I had to speak to others. I thought I'd adapted nicely, but everything changed in Miss Vickery's class.

She called on me often during discussions and even made me give oral book reports in front of the class. My face burned in humiliation at the snickers from the back of the room.

I begged my mother to explain to Miss Vickery that I couldn't do those things. Why didn't she just leave me alone?

One day, Miss Vickery asked me to stay after class. Her wrinkled face somehow softened. "Helen," she asked, "have you ever been to a speech therapist?"

I shook my head. "I gueth not. Wat ith it?"

"A speech therapist could help you pronounce words and sounds that are difficult for you," she said.

Was a Cure Possible?

No one had ever suggested that my speech defect might be curable. Could someone really help me?

Miss Vickery put a hand on my shoulder. "It'll take a lot of work on your part, but I know you can do it. Just don't give up."

That evening I waited until my brothers left the supper table to tell Mom and Dad about Miss Vickery's suggestion. (I had to write out "speech therapist" because I knew I couldn't pronounce it.)

My parents listened carefully but looked skeptical. Dad muttered something about "busybodies meddling in private affairs." Still, after some debate, they agreed to give it a try.

It took months of drills and exercises, but slowly my speech improved. There were frustrating days when no matter how hard I tried, the right sounds just wouldn't come. But there were glorious days when I conquered a recalcitrant sound.

I remember my thrill at learning to say "z." I went around singing wonderful words like "fizz," "buzz" and "sizzle" until my brother complained I sounded like a bee with a bellyache.

One day my therapist asked me to talk to some incoming students. I told them what Miss Vickery had told me: "I know you can do it. Don't give up."

I don't think I ever properly thanked Miss Vickery for changing my life. I just hope hearing me give the opening address at graduation was thanks enough.

Palms Full of Puppies

"I didn't have many toys as a child, but I had nine brothers, four sisters and lots of animals to play with on our farm near Ephrata, Pennsylvania," writes Mary W. Martin of nearby Akron. "With this group of puppies in 1949, we didn't even have to share, because there were enough for everyone—with a few extras! From left are Titus, Clarence, Jim, me, David and Martha."

CHAPTER 5

Popular
PASTIMES

PAGE 117

PAGE 126

PAGE 123

PAGE 118

When it came to hobbies in the 1940s, many guys—and lots of girls, too—turned to sports. We were "game" for starting a pickup game in the street or heading to the stadium to watch the pros.

"As a teen in Brooklyn during the '40s, my friends were of at least 10 different nationalities, and we all played together in harmony," says Arthur Kennedy, now of Boca Raton, Florida. "We played 'hockey' on roller skates, slap ball, handball, softball and stickball.

"Our footballs were so beat up they had to be stuffed with paper. And the old basketballs we used usually weighed a ton from being waterlogged. Anyone hit in the face by a pass risked ending up with a broken nose!

"When we tired of our neighborhood games, there was always Ebbets Field and the Brooklyn Dodgers. Bleacher seats cost 35 cents, but there were times during World War II when you could get in the ballpark free if you turned in 10 pounds of scrap metal. On those days, the trolley cars looked like rolling junkyards!"

Sports weren't the only activity filling our free time. We enjoyed making music, dancing, riding bikes—even collecting antiques. What were your pastimes?

Grandmother Got Her Antiques From
THE SOURCE

IN THE MID-'40S, BEFORE ANTIQUE SHOPS WERE COMMON, THEY HIT THE BACK ROADS LOOKING FOR OLD TREASURES.
By Jeanne Barbour, Topsail Beach, North Carolina

The story goes that my grandmother, Sally Dennis Paulette Ferguson, had an ulcerated stomach in her 40s, and the doctor told her to find a hobby. So she decided to collect antique pitchers. By the time I was old enough to remember, Grandma, whom I called Mama, not only had pitchers, but her collection had broadened to include antique furniture and all sorts of glassware.

The collection kept Papa, my grandfather, busy adding shelves to the sunroom, caning chair seats on the back porch and refinishing furniture in one of the buildings on their farm near Union Level in Mecklenburg County, Virginia.

One of my fondest memories of Mama and Papa is of them on the back porch—Papa caning a chair, and Mama shelling butter beans.

In the mid- to late '40s, I accompanied Mama many times on her antiquing days. It was always a day full of adventure and surprises, because we never knew what we'd find or what interesting people we'd meet.

The day started after the morning chores. On the way out the back door, Mama would stop at her

FUTURE BARGAIN HUNTERS. This photo of the author and her grandma was taken in 1938, before they started taking antique-buying trips in the Studebaker.

PHONOGRAPH: JAMES MORRIS; VASE: BETTY MORAVEC; LAMP: RUTH GROHLER; BENCH: MARK CHRISTOPHERSEN

pine and poplar bachelor's desk and take out a roll of bills from the middle drawer. She'd tuck the bills in her double-handled black leather pocketbook and drape it over her right forearm.

In Search of a "Find"

Then we'd settle into her robin's-egg blue Studebaker and head out into the countryside of southeast Virginia. To Mama, antiquing meant driving about 40 miles to some backcountry road and pulling up to a house.

If there were barking dogs in the yard, Mama would honk the horn to see if anyone would come to the front door. Sometimes, she'd send me up to knock on the door.

Mama only got out if someone came to the door. Then she'd ask, "Do you have any old dishes or furniture that you'd like to sell?"

The response was usually something like, "I've got an old table on the back porch that I might sell. I think there's an old churn back there, too, that I haven't used in years."

Mama would chat with the owner and ask to look at the pieces. She never left without asking, "Do you have any other old furniture or maybe some old dishes inside that you may not want anymore?"

Inside the house, if Mama saw something she liked, she might say, "Would you take $5 for that?" She seldom came away without buying something. If she bought a piece of furniture that was too big to fit in the Studebaker, Papa would drive her back the next day in his pickup truck and bring it home.

Mama and I repeated this procedure at every house for several miles or until the road came to a dead end. When we got hungry, we'd find a little country store and buy a Coke, a package of saltines and a can of Vienna sausages.

Ended the Day Content

About 4 o'clock, we'd head home. If Mama was especially pleased with our finds, she'd sort of whistle as she drove. Mama got supper ready when Papa got home from fishing. We ate on the side porch, with the windmill slowly turning on the other side of the large oak that shaded the porch. We always used at least one piece of the glassware we'd found that morning to add the day's magic to supper.

Mama filled her house with her collections of glassware and furniture. When she died, my mother loaded a packing barrel with one of the antique glassware or china collections for each of Mama's great-grandchildren to have when they married.

They were so excited. As they unpacked those barrels, each great-grandchild knew they were receiving very special and valuable antiques and also making a loving and lifelong connection with a great-grandmother they could only vaguely remember.

Mama would've been pleased.

A Batting Lesson
FROM THE BABE

IN THE SUMMER OF 1944, BASEBALL'S GREATEST HERO GAVE THESE
YOUNGSTERS SOME UNFORGETTABLE TIPS ON BASEBALL...AND LIFE.

By Bruce Sweet, Rochester, New York

From 1939 through the '70s, my family spent our summers at Greenwood Lake on the border of New York and New Jersey. One sunny afternoon in 1944, when I was 8 years old, my friends and I were playing baseball in the parking lot next to the Happy Landing grocery store.

As Billy, Brian and I were trying to hit the ball into the lake (and not through the Happy Landing window), a tall man in shorts, with thin legs and a large belly, came over to watch. After he'd seen us hit for a while, he began asking questions. He spoke quietly and easily in a gravelly voice. His wide-set eyes were large and very dark, almost like mahogany.

The man seemed to enjoy our company, because he had a broad smile and laughed a lot. When he asked if he could hold our Louisville Slugger, I noticed for the first time his immense hands.

"Don't squeeze the life out of it," he said, holding the bat up. "Think of the bat as part of you."

He held the bat away from him, then slowly drew it close to his left shoulder. His eyes grew coal-black as he stared at something that appeared to be very far away.

Watch the Ball

"Never take your eye off the ball," he said. "Never. You got that? Watch it leave the pitcher's hand. Never mind his eyes; watch his hand."

"Watch that ball wrap around the bat," he continued. "When you hit it, watch the stitches eat the wood...if you can."

He swung the bat. The whoop of his swing startled us and rose a tuft of dust in the lot. "Do one thing at a time," he advised. "Complete your swing, then run to first."

He licked his lower lip and swung again, then leaned on the bat handle for a moment, a faraway look in his eyes. "There's a split second there when you and the bat and the ball all come together," he said. "It's a timing thing, like you're all part of each other. Remember—no strain, easy does it, all in the timing."

He knelt on one knee before us and continued. "You guys are strong...lots of energy. But you try too hard. You push. You force it. Take your time. You gotta take it easy. Relax and have fun with it." He stood up, looked toward an imaginary pitcher and effortlessly swung the bat again. "It's only the three of you—you, the bat and the ball. Nobody else is there. One continuous swing."

The breeze from the bat cooled our faces.

"And then it's gone. Gone."

After "batting practice," he took us for milk shakes and Orange Crushes at the Mountain Lakes Inn, where we talked more baseball. He asked us about school and what we wanted to be when we grew up.

When it was time to go home for supper, we thanked him, and he said, "Remember now, pals, take it easy and have fun. Don't try too hard. Enjoy the swing."

I ran back to our cottage and told my mother about the afternoon. She asked if the man told me his name.

"Babe Ruth," I said.

"Do you know who he is?" she asked.

"He was a famous ball player with the New York Yankees," I replied. "But I'm a Brooklyn Dodgers fan, Mom."

"Get your father to tell you about Babe Ruth," she suggested. "There's more to life than Ebbets Field."

I spent more time with Babe Ruth that summer and the one following. Now, over a half-century after his death, I remember his love for the game and for kids.

I can still recall his grace, his dark eyes, his huge hands and his telling us, "Don't try too hard. Enjoy the swing."

We did, Babe. And we will.

At the Old Ballgame

ANNOUNCER MADE GAMES COLORFUL

There were two reasons why we were such die-hard Pittsburgh Pirates fans in the late '40s and early '50s. One was slugger Ralph Kiner, and the other was the colorful radio broadcaster Rosey Rowswell.

Rosey had us kids glued to the radio as he described the bases loaded as "FOB" (full of Bucs).

And a batter didn't just strike out with Rosey at the microphone. "It's the old dipsy doodle," he'd shout. "He swings and misses for strike three!"

Best of all was a Pirates home run, foretold with, "Open the window, Aunt Minnie—here it comes!" That was followed by the sound of breaking glass. We loved it!

—*Steve Pozar*, *Butler, Pennsylvania*

THE OLD BROOKLYN DODGERS KEPT US IN STITCHES

I was a big baseball fan as a high school girl in the 1940s. My best friend "Lucky" and I went to Ebbets Field every chance we got to watch our beloved Dodgers. We purchased 55 cent tickets for the bleachers, but used our "feminine wiles" to get better seats—often in the empty box seats!

We'd get to the park early to watch batting practice and talk to our heroes. Ballplayers were friendlier and more accessible in those days, and they were happy to sign autographs.

Lucky and I began collecting signatures on a pair of oversized shirts we'd carry to the park and wave at players. Back home, we'd embroider over the signatures to make them permanent.

Over time we added more names to our shirts and began wearing them to the games. We'd also lug along a portable radio to listen to broadcaster Red Barber do the play-by-play.

Lucky and I became such a familiar sight that one day we heard Red Barber announce our arrival at the ballpark! Everyone smiled at us…we were in heaven!

One day in 1986, I read in the *New York Times* that the Brooklyn Historical Society was looking for baseball memorabilia. I called the director about my shirt. She was delighted. It's still on display there today!

—*Leslie Sachs Sherman*, *Chestnut Hill, Massachusetts*

GIRLS ALLOWED. "As a young girl, I played sandlot baseball with the boys in my hometown of Winthrop, Massachusetts," writes Patricia Brown, still of Winthrop. "But when I became a teenager, I was heartbroken to learn that girls weren't allowed to play on school teams. Then, in 1948, I read an article about the All-American Girls Professional Baseball League. I wrote to the league inquiring about tryouts. Later, I got invited, at league expense, to a 10-day camp in South Bend, Indiana. At the end of camp, I was signed by the Kenosha (Wisconsin) Comets. I was later sent to the Chicago Colleens (that's me standing third from left in the photo above), and the next year I played for the Battle Creek Belles in Michigan."

PACKERS HALL OF FAMER WAS MY HERO

As a kid growing up in Milwaukee, Wisconsin, during the '40s, I saw many of Don Hutson's touchdowns when the Packers played at State Fair Park near Milwaukee and City Stadium in Green Bay.

On Oct. 7, 1945, Dad took me and a pal to the fairgrounds to watch the Packers play the Detroit Lions. Always hungry, my buddy and I went to the concession stand get hot dogs during the second quarter. When we returned to our seats, we wondered why the fans were cheering so wildly.

We learned that Hutson had scored twice while we were getting our hot dogs! (Incredibly, he scored 31 points that game—29 in the second quarter.) He was in his last season then, in the days when players played both offense and defense. At 32 years old, Hutson was considered "long in the tooth."

I tried my boyish best to emulate my hero. I ran all-out for passes and became adept at snagging them, even in "scrub" ball. I dreamed of catching the big pass to win the big game in the big time.

Now Don Hutson is gone. But my memories of him running, leaping and snagging passes will live on forever.

—*Bill Weekes*, *Spartanburg, South Carolina*

A Rip-Roaring Good Time

WICKET WATCH. "I'm the boy looking on, circa 1940, as my grandfather Charles Hatton prepares to strike a ball in a game of roque in Lancaster, Ohio," writes Robert Hatton of Columbus. "Roque, a form of croquet that dates back to the 19th century, was an Olympic sport in 1904 but eventually declined in popularity."

A GIFT OF WHEELS. Mollie Plush really had something to smile about in this photo taken just after Christmas in 1941. Mollie, of North Randall, Ohio, was living on the South Side of Chicago when she received this new Elgin bike. Her brother Don also looks pleased with his nearly new Ranger.

DASHING O'ER THE WAVES. Lonnie Arey sent a salty smile toward the camera while competing in an amateur boat race on Whiterock Lake in Texas. Sponsored by the Dallas Boat Club, this event took place in 1945. Lonnie's wife, Velma, shared this shot of her husband and his speedboat. They now live in Springville, California.

HAVING A FIELD DAY. These "hamateur" enthusiasts were out for the yearly field day, practicing emergency communications in case of disaster. The June 1948 photo was shared by Ed Willie and the Milwaukee Radio Amateurs' Club.

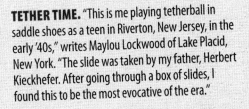

TETHER TIME. "This is me playing tetherball in saddle shoes as a teen in Riverton, New Jersey, in the early '40s," writes Maylou Lockwood of Lake Placid, New York. "The slide was taken by my father, Herbert Kieckhefer. After going through a box of slides, I found this to be the most evocative of the era."

Remember Saying?

BATHTUB:
motorcycle sidecar

ON THE DANCE FLOOR

LONG LINE AND LINDY HOP BROUGHT THEM TOGETHER

My friend Al and I came out of military service in 1946 and lived in the Bronx. One night, we went to the Paramount Theatre in Manhattan to see Tommy Dorsey's orchestra and one of Bob Hope and Bing Crosby's road pictures.

The line to get in was a block-and-a-half long, and I didn't want to stand in the bitter-cold December air. Al suggested we head to the nearby Hotel Diplomat, which held Saturday dances with good music and a lot of nice girls from the Bronx. The admission was just $2.

At dances, I'd always watch the floor to find a girl who could dance well, because I was a very good Lindy Hop dancer. I enjoyed watching the dancing of a pretty young lady who was about 5 feet tall. I'm not too tall myself, at about 5-foot-6.

A couple of numbers later, the band began playing my all-time favorite swing number, "Tuxedo Junction", so I immediately went over and asked the girl to dance. We did a terrific Lindy together, and then I introduced myself. Her name was Esther Silverman, and we spent the whole evening together on and off the dance floor.

We began dating, and in April 1947 I presented her with an engagement ring. We were wed in October, and enjoyed 56 years of marriage.

—*Ted Zukerman,* Towanda, Pennsylvania

CORRALLED BY A COWBOY

In 1948, I journeyed from Salix, Iowa, to Collbran, Colorado, in our old 1934 Chevy to visit relatives.

A cousin took my sister and me to a dance with a local cowboy. This cowboy, Henry Stanton, took a liking to me. Before I returned home to Iowa, he told me, "When the grass turns green, I'm going east."

The following April, I received a postcard with this simple message: "The grass is green."

The next day, he arrived. He never went any farther east. He got a job in a community near Salix and stayed until the cold weather set in.

We continued to correspond and a few months later, we married in Onawa, Iowa. After a short honeymoon, we settled in Ridgway, Colorado.

—*Allena Carroll Stanton,* Montrose, Colorado

BROTHER WAS A GREAT DANCER

When I was in school, my brother Bill said it was time for me to learn to dance. He wanted me to enjoy the upcoming dances to the fullest. We started with the two-step, and before long, I was learning all kinds of dances. We became a real team once the school dances came around.

One time when I felt really foxy in my steps, he stopped, looked at me and said, "If you want to continue dancing with me, stop flapping your wings." I was swinging my arms instead of my feet!

—*Virginia Jones,* Klamath Falls, Oregon

Fun on Wheels

A RINK 'N' ROLL AFFAIR

My husband, Edwin, and I were married on Jan. 10, 1941, a couple of weeks before this photo was taken at the wedding reception of Gordon and Doris Barrows.

My girlfriend, previously Doris Jones, got married on roller skates at the Shute Park Roller Rink in Hillsboro, Oregon. Everyone in the wedding party was a regular skater. Most of us drove from Portland to skate in Hillsboro several nights a week.

Behind the happy couple is Doris' twin sister, Dorothy, the maid of honor. To the right of Gordon is Al King, the best man. Next is the ring bearer, then bridesmaid Donna King, a groomsman named Frank, me (just 16), and another groomsman, Art Goodrich. I've forgotten the others.

The wedding was nearly delayed by auto fuel pump problems as Edwin drove Doris and me to Hillsboro. My husband was an auto mechanic, and after a few anxious stops we made it with a couple of minutes to spare.

After the wedding, we four newlyweds went to Seattle on our honeymoons and skated at several rinks. And yes, I still have my skates.

—**Florence Bell,** *Milwaukie, Oregon*

SKATING THROUGH LIFE

Roller skating was my favorite recreation back in the summer of 1942. I had my own skates and spent nearly every night at the rink.

During one of those fun evenings, I noticed two young ladies skating together. When the manager announced a "triple skate," which meant three people could skate together, I had no problem deciding who I wanted to skate with!

I approached the two girls and asked if I could join them. They agreed, and the three of us ended up skating together for the entire evening.

At first, I had my eye on one of those girls, but by the end of the evening, I'd switched my attention to the other! I could tell she was everything I wanted in a sweetheart.

We dated for two years and then were married. We have enjoyed "skating through life" for more than 50 years now…little did we know that a skate key would be our key to happiness!

—**Theodore Pfrimmer,** *Leland, Mississippi*

SHOE SKATES WERE A SIGHT

While Dad was serving his country in 1944 and '45, the rest of our family spent summer evenings at Ding's Pla-Mor roller rink in our hometown of Sleepy Eye, Minnesota.

We skated the hours away on a wooden floor under a large canvas tent. Mom bought her own "shoe skates" with the tips she saved from her job as a waitress at a local coffee shop. Those fancy skates cost $25!

Watching Mom's graceful moves in her new roller skates made such an impression on me that I've kept those skates all these years. I wish the old roller rink nestled under canvas was still around!

—**Marilyn Kay Hall,** *Glendora, California*

MUSICAL MEMORIES

TWIN TOOTERS. "That's me on the trumpet and my twin brother, Charles, on the trombone. We were 12 when this photo was snapped in 1943," says George Evans, of Reading, Pennsylvania. "We played in several bands in Reading and Kenhorst when we were growing up. It was great fun," George recalls.

PLUG-AND-PLAY DILEMMA

To my farm boy's way of thinking, I had big problems. It was 1940, and I'd been invited to play with the band that performed at Saturday night dances in the small New Mexico town of Elida. The dance, which drew folks from miles around, was the only local diversion aside from church services.

The problem was that I didn't have an electric guitar. The nearest source was almost 50 miles away in Clovis, and I had no car. For that matter, I didn't have any money to speak of, either.

The bandleader, "Pops" Jenkins, told me I could earn $8 a week, and that was a powerful incentive to get what I needed. So I hitchhiked to Clovis and found the Montgomery Ward store. The manager must have seen how determined I was to make the payments, because he ordered the guitar with no money down.

The instrument was scheduled to arrive in two weeks, and it came right on time. I hitchhiked both ways again and claimed my pride and joy.

At home, I gathered the family so I could debut my electric guitar. It was only then that I realized I was missing something vitally important. We didn't have electricity!

Nevertheless, I played with the band until Uncle Sam called me into the Army in 1943.

—**Alton Hare**
Amarillo, Texas

BUSING ACCOMPANIMENT

In 1948, I had helped Daddy clear out the old homestead in California and was taking a Greyhound bus back to college near Seattle.

As we drove through an area of magnificent redwoods, the bus driver asked me, "What was the very heavy suitcase you had me put on the bus?" When I told him it was my accordion, he pulled over, opened the storage hatch, brought my 120-button bass accordion inside and said, "Play for us!"

"Well, I only play gospel music," I said hesitantly, to which he replied, "That's great! Play for us."

As we continued north, I played and played, and soon many of the passengers joined in, singing the old hymns—one happy family enjoying the music of yesteryear. That's me (far left).

—**Bobbie Breedlove**, *Canby, Oregon*

SHUCKS, IT'S THE KORN KOBS! "'No, by gosh, we're not the symphony, we're just the Korn Kobs of Albert Lea. We've come to give you the best we know, so we hope you'll like it—let's go!'" writes Roger Naylor of Mesa, Arizona. "That was the theme song of our band, which started in 1946 with a junior high talent contest in Albert Lea, Minnesota. Standing, from left, are Rollie Green, John Sturtz, Darrell Meuser, Bill Kuchera and me, trombone. Seated is Eslie Bergstrom. At lower left is LeRoy 'Dutch' Van Proosdy, who joined the band later."

I Still Picture the Day When Color Came to Town

THE DAYS OF BLACK-AND-WHITE PHOTOS WERE OVER FOR THIS AMATEUR PHOTOGRAPHER WHEN SHE AND HER SISTER GOT THEIR FIRST ROLL OF COLOR FILM! *By Maxine Worth, Monticello, Minnesota*

Back in 1942, when the Eastman Kodak Company first introduced color print film, my sister, Connie, and I were ecstatic. We were both avid photographers, but the only film available up to that point was black and white.

We dashed to the drugstore where we bought all our film, only to find that the druggist hadn't yet received a shipment of the newfangled color stuff. But he said he was expecting an order soon.

Thus began our long wait. For weeks, we stopped by that drugstore almost every single day to ask if the film had come in. When it finally did arrive, were we thrilled! We bought a roll and raced home to load it into one of our rangefinder cameras.

A roll of film cost quite a bit back then, and it usually took us at least a week to shoot all the pictures. But this was a big occasion—we finished off our first roll of color film that same day!

And what a fun day it was! We couldn't very well wear the same outfits in all the pictures... after all, this was color film, and we wanted to make our pictures look as brilliant as possible. Connie and I must have changed clothes four or five times.

By the end of the day, we were both wearing slacks and taking the final few pictures at a local park. For the very last shot, we put the camera on a tripod and used the automatic timer so we could both be in the picture.

What a Thrill!

First thing the next day, we took the film back to the drugstore...and then endured another agonizing wait for it to be processed. Would our pictures "turn out"? Would they really be in color?

Well, they did...and they were! We couldn't believe our eyes—what a switch from drab black and white!

Nowadays, of course, color photos are common...few photographers use black-and-white film. But for me and Connie (and countless other amateur photographers), those first color photos we took were every bit as thrilling as the first "talking movie" or first radio broadcast or first television program.

The pictures shown here were reprinted from the originals Connie and I took on that fun day in the park. As you can see, the color is still great more than 60 years later!

'No Priest, No Foul!'

THAT CHANT RANG THROUGH THE OLD NEIGHBORHOOD GYM EVERY SATURDAY AS BUDDIES PLAYED ROUGH-AND-TUMBLE BASKETBALL.

By Herbert Lehmann, Euclid, Ohio

Rainey Institute in Cleveland will never be listed in basketball annals alongside such hallowed halls as Madison Square Garden. But to me and my buddies from East 71st Street, it was "hardwood heaven."

In the '30s and '40s, we could rent the third-floor gym for a quarter an hour, including the use of an ancient basketball, nearly oval in shape, with a protruding rubber bladder.

Our grade school, St. Francis, had a gym on its top floor, but getting the janitor to open it was a Herculean effort. So every Saturday during the winter, my buddies and I would scrape together the 25 cents and take the 20-minute hike to "Rainey's"...unless we could hop on the rear of a slow-moving trolley headed that way instead.

The gracious lady who kept track of the time at Rainey's often let us stretch our hour to 90 minutes, finally switching the lights off and on to signal when our time was up.

The only reason we'd ever dream of quitting on time was when another group of players waiting for their turn on the court looked mean enough to take it by force. Then we'd usually leave five minutes early!

Tough Place to Play

The backboards at the Rainey gym were flush with the walls, and we veteran players soon developed a lay-up shuffle that would have challenged any ballet teacher.

The baskets also had no nets, which sometimes made it hard to tell if the old ball had sailed through the goal or not. In those situations, the toughest player on the floor—usually a guy named Gus—had the last say. (All of Gus' shots were judged as good.)

We didn't know most of the official rules of the game, and those we did know were seldom obeyed. Our games contained a few aspects of basketball combined with the more punishing elements of football and tag-team wrestling.

Elbowing and hacking were treated with benign neglect, and few fouls were called unless the victim required the Last Sacraments. "No priest, no foul!" was our motto.

Bumps and bruises were fairly common and any player reclining stunned on the floor received our standard first aid treatment—a shout of: "Everyone move back and give him air!"

It would be fitting to relate that from this humble beginning several basketball stars emerged. Not so...none of us even played in high school, much less college.

As we grew older, girls pulled us away from this violent activity, and later the war came along and scattered us to all parts of the globe. After we were discharged, we rented the old gym once again for some games of "Married Men vs. Single Men." It wasn't the same. But the price was still reasonable, and the same lady manager was there, lenient as ever with the court times.

Even today as I drive past the old building, I sometimes imagine I can hear the faint shouts of the kids and the dull thud of that old basketball on the third floor. Once I even went up and rang the bell, but it was too early and no one answered. It was probably for the best—I feared I would have seen girls doing aerobics...or worse, nets on those old hoops!

Remember Saying?

SNAP YOUR CAP:
get angry

Part of the Team

ZOOK'S BOYS

In April 1946, our town of Hastings, Pennsylvania—population 2,000—decided to build a sports stadium to honor those who served in World War II.

As a 14-year-old lad, I looked upon this arena as being comparable to Yankee Stadium. And when the VFW announced that it was going to sponsor a team for boys 15 and younger, all the kids were ecstatic.

Frank "Zook" Walters agreed to manage our team (bottom photo at right), and Zook was something special. He had a vocabulary that made him another Casey Stengel. When referring to us, he said, "youse boys." When he brought the equipment for us to our practices, he would "fetch the tools."

It was a successful season, and we won most of our games. We practiced almost every day, even when there was an evening game. Zook slept through most of the practices, waking up only to roll a cigarette.

As summer wound down, a new teacher arrived in town. She was Miss Palmer—fresh from college—and boy, was she pretty. Zook returned our minds to baseball in a hurry. He'd slated a game to be played under the lights. Under the lights! We couldn't wait.

The night finally came. The first time I came to bat, Bill Fletcher announced my batting average of .545. I was in heaven. Three pitches later, I came back to earth. Strike three!

Later, a pop fly was lofted foul along the first-base line. First baseman Caesar Easly and I raced for it. Just before I reached it, I tripped on a bat that had been on the ground near the bleachers. I grabbed the ball but landed headfirst in Miss Palmer's lap.

I flipped the ball to Caesar and looked up. Miss Palmer had both arms wrapped tightly around me to keep me from falling, and she was laughing. She smelled so good! I didn't care if she never let go. From that moment on, she was my favorite teacher!
—**Harry Frycklund,** *Northern Cambria, Pennsylvania*

ALL-IMPORTANT GUIDE TO PICKING TEAMS

One night in 1944, we were playing an impromptu football game in Nashville, Tennessee, and our neighbor, a newspaper photographer, came out and took our picture. Each of us got a copy.

Seen at right in the top photo are (from left) Wayne Martin, Earl Piper, me (wearing a hat from one of four brothers in the Navy), James Witcher and Carl Martin. It reminds me of the games we played and the ways we chose sides.

For baseball, we picked two captains. One tossed the bat to the other, who caught it with one hand. The two walked their hands up the bat, and the person whose hand came out on top flung the bat first. Then the other captain flung the bat. Whoever tossed it farther selected first.

When we played basketball, the two captains shot free throws to determine who would pick first. For football, we had a punting contest.

We also played Kick the Can and Annie Over, which involved throwing a ball over the top of a house to someone on the other side.

We didn't have many organized sports, so we invented our own games. Picking teams was part of the fun!

—**Bob Martin,** *Livermore, California*

Striking Out

WHAT BOWLERS DIDN'T KNOW

My first job, in 1943, was working for J.B. Shear as a pinsetter at the eight-lane bowling alley at the Rozum Building in Mitchell, South Dakota. Bowlers paid either 35 or 45 cents a line, and I made a nickel per line for setting pins. As I became more experienced, I averaged about 100 lines a week, eventually setting pins for league bowlers on weekends.

Before a tournament, league bowlers would practice all week in the early evenings. They'd get frustrated in the tourney when they couldn't get strikes and spares as easily as they'd picked them up during the week.

What bowlers didn't know was that one of the workers,

Mr. Breck, took chipped or damaged pins into a back room and smoothed them on a machine. Some pins used for open bowling had been trimmed so many times that they fell through the racks when pinsetters tried to set them.

There was a real difference between these battered pins and those used for league bowling and tournaments. There was less need for Mr. Breck to smooth the edges of league pins, because they didn't suffer the abuse of those used for open bowling—for good reason.

The increased difficulty came from league and tournament pins being heavier than everyday pins. I wonder what the league bowlers would have thought if they'd known.

—*Denis Kurtenbach*
Vernal, Utah

BOWLING PINS: PHOTODISC/GETTY IMAGES

Knucks Down

This phrase was a common cry when kids hit the playground dirt at recess for a serious game of Playing for Keeps.

Long before the days of video games, cable TV, computers and other electronics, young ones had to get creative with finding ways to entertain themselves for hours on end. This usually involved some kind of outside play.

Marbles were a favorite pastime among children of the 1940s. If you were playing for "keepsies" that meant the winner got to keep all the marbles.

"This picture of the boys from Turner School in Grand Rapids, Michigan, was taken in '41 or '42," writes Lois Copeland of Cedar Springs, Michigan. "The boy taking the shot in the circle is my brother, Jack Denton."

FRUIT JU

CHAPTER 6

Around
TOWN

PAGE 132

PAGE 145

PAGE 140

Whether we lived in a big city, a village or a rural area, a trip downtown was one of our big thrills in the 1940s.

"My mother and I had a ritual every Friday night. We'd go out for dinner, then go to the movies," remembers Ann Bennett of Waldorf, Maryland. "The most exciting part of the evening, though, was afterward, when we stopped at the Bond Bread bakery on the other side of town in Mount Vernon, New York.

"They baked bread and rolls all through the night, and you could smell it for 10 blocks. We'd sneak in the back door, and even though they weren't supposed to, the bakers sold us bread and rolls right out of the oven.

"Mother would always say, 'These will be deliciously fresh for breakfast tomorrow,' but that never happened. On the way, we gobbled up at least a quarter of the loaf of bread, and once we got home, we spread butter on the hot rolls and ate every one."

In those days, we all treasured our communities, as the stories here show. Smile as you recall the cast of characters that made your own town great.

PAGE 139

Remember Syrup Squirts and
SODA JERKS?

THERE WAS A TIME WHEN THE OLD SODA FOUNTAIN WAS THE COOLEST PLACE IN TOWN. *By Julien Tracy, Carmel Valley, California*

A few weeks before the attack on Pearl Harbor, I began working in a drugstore making deliveries, cleaning and clerking. The owner, Mr. Brown, must have made quite an impression on me, since I eventually became a pharmacist myself.

I can still hear Mr. Brown's old oak swivel chair creak as he'd lean back and reminisce about the evolution of the soda fountain:

"The drugstore fountain arrived at about the same time as Prohibition. We already had mineral waters, particularly soda water, in our pharmacy stock, and we also carried flavoring oils, extracts and syrups.

"The development of refrigeration, ice cream and Prohibition all conspired to put the druggist in the fountain business. And as the syrups and flavoring agents moved from the pharmacy to the fountain, their ancient titles were often lost or forgotten.

"Syrupus Cacao, for example, became Chocolate Syrup, while Syrupus Cerasi became Cherry Syrup. Syrupus Rubi Idae was labeled Raspberry Syrup, and Syrupus Aurantii turned into Orange Syrup. Only Syrup of Sarsaparilla managed to cling to its pharmaceutical title for a few years before it was finally called root beer.

"By 1929," Mr. Brown concluded, "over half the drugstores in the country had their own soda fountain."

Heat Tough to Beat

Mr. Brown's little history lesson may have helped me appreciate the drugstore fountain a little more during the long, hot afternoons when the lines of tar in the pavement became soft and the surrounding hills shimmered in a heat haze.

That's when the local drugstore became a gathering place for our town's schoolkids. Back then, just entering the drugstore held a special presence of magic.

When the large oak doors with their beveled glass panes were swung open, the rays of the afternoon sun were refracted, sending a scattering of colored points across the white hexagonal floor tiles.

As you stepped inside, the fountain was the first thing you noticed—regally elevated on a marble step, it filled up the whole right side of the store. The counter's surface was a huge cool slab of white marble, lightly streaked with gray.

In front of the counter were the stools covered with padded leather cushions secured by a chrome ring, which swiveled on white enameled pedestals. Whenever I treated my girlfriend to an after-school Coke, the stools would creak as we turned nervously from side to side.

Soda Jerk Added the Squirts

After we'd ordered our Cokes, the fountain man would remove one of the round, black rubberized covers from the freezer cabinet and crack bits of ice into the glasses with a five-pronged pick. Then he'd pump in three squirts of Coke syrup and carefully add the carbonated water down the side of the tipped glass so as not to create too much foam.

If we'd ordered a lemon Coke or a chocolate Coke, he'd add a half squirt of the flavoring syrup. The final touch was a delicate swirl with a long-handled spoon.

Along the back bar of the fountain was a long mirror. While lingering over our Cokes, my girlfriend and I self-consciously studied each other's reflections between perusals of our comic books—*Wonder Woman, Flash Gordon* or *Mandrake the Magician*. Meanwhile, the nearly constant drone of the compressor was a pleasant accompaniment through the warm afternoon—sweet music from the "Golden Era"…the good old days of the drugstore soda fountain.

SODA FOUNTAIN ROMANCE

After serving three years in the Army's 90th Division in Europe during World War II, I returned to my hometown of Gardenville, New York.

I decided to find some old friends at our local drugstore and soda fountain. I'd worked at the fountain when I was in high school, so when I stepped back inside the door, the owner, Lefty, sat me down to talk about old times.

Soon a beautiful young lady came to our booth to serve us. For me, it was love at first sight!

Lefty introduced me to Louise, and from then on I'd show up at the fountain on the nights she worked. I'd help her wash the dishes just to have a chance to escort her home.

On our first date, we went to the Ice Follies. After many dances, trips to the roller derby and bouquets of flowers, Louise and I were married, and we've done many loads of dishes together since then!

—*Mel Schmidt, Colden, New York*

Community Celebrations

NEVER FORGOT THE ELEPHANT

I was 6 years old when the Ringling Bros. Circus came to Irvington, New Jersey, in 1940. It came right past our house on Grove Street and set up in Ollemar Field near my grade school.

The teacher let us sit outside and watch the action. It had rained for three days, and there was lots of mud. When a truck and trailer got stuck, a bulldozer was sent in.

When the bulldozer got stuck, they brought in an elephant. They hitched the elephant up to the truck and trailer, and he walked away with it. I was, and still am, impressed.

When the circus left and the big top was taken down, all that remained was colored sawdust. We kids used that to make our own circus.

—**Bob Dallmus,** *Brick, New Jersey*

AS BLOSSOMTIME GOES MARCHING BY

One of my earliest memories of springtime is standing on the curb in downtown Benton Harbor, Michigan, watching the Blossomtime Festival parade go by.

Every May, the twin cities of Benton Harbor and St. Joseph put on a huge Blossomtime Festival (except during World War II, when large gatherings were restricted and everyone had to save gasoline).

There were three parades during the festival. Friday afternoon was the Children's Parade, and any kid with a decorated "vehicle" or leashable pet could participate. The "Fun" or "Mummers" Parade was held that evening. With clowns, customized old cars, bands and comic entertainment, it proved to be a highlight. The big Blossom Parade on Saturday covered about five miles. After the festivities, a Queen's Ball was held at the Crystal Palace on Silver Beach in St. Joseph.

Most industrial firms in the area had floats, usually decorated with blossom-colored tissue paper. But almost anything could be considered a float. Local auto dealers vied to supply cars, usually convertibles, for the parade dignitaries. Most floats were populated with pretty girls, but everyone watched for that special large float carrying the queen and her court—I photographed these ladies (shown above) in 1948.

—**Paul Arent,** *Van Nuys, California*

DECORATION DAY SURPRISE

Cities and towns all across America had special celebrations planned for Decoration Day of 1946.

The parade in my hometown of Garrettsville, Ohio, ended at the cemetery, where speeches and other patriotic salutes were made for the heroes fallen in battle.

I was 6 years old, and though everyone in town was focused on this important event, my mind was on a loose tooth. I'd been wiggling it for two days, but it just wouldn't budge.

During a lengthy speech, I was concentrating on my problem…and was completely unprepared for the 21-gun salute that followed. At the deafening crack of those rifles, I jumped so hard that I pulled my tooth right out!

Few family stories have been re-told as often as this one has.

—**Dorothy Saurer,** *Kailua, Hawaii*

CRUISER AT THE CARNIVAL

Michigan's Upper Peninsula is noted for its snowy, cold winters. The art of ice sculpting is a long-standing tradition, but during the winter of '41, perhaps the region's most famous ice sculpture of all was constructed in Marquette.

That year's winter carnival featured a huge replica of a Navy cruiser christened the *USS Marquette*. Patriotism was the driving force behind the project as our community, along with the rest of the nation, was just entering World War II.

I was only 9 when my parents took my brother and me to view this magnificent battleship. It must have taken untold hours of packing and carving to create such a large sculpture, and it was strong enough so you could walk all over it.

Today, winter carnivals are still held in the Upper Peninsula. Although ice sculptures continue to be made, I doubt any will ever match the Navy cruiser we saw in 1941.

—**Donald Nelson,** *Lake Linden, Michigan*

ANGLED INTO FISHING DERBY

In the late '40s, our town held an annual fishing derby for kids. The year our daughter Carol, 6, wanted to participate, we couldn't afford a fishing pole.

I hated to see Carol so sad, so I cut a tree branch for a pole and used some string from meat packages for a line. I tied on a lug nut for a sinker and found a safety pin for a hook.

Next, I threaded a fat worm onto the safety pin so no one could see it wasn't a real fish hook.

Carol went to the pond and not only got in the derby—she caught a fish! The fish was too small and had to be thrown back , but Carol won a prize of $5 for being the most original fisherman!

At first, my husband didn't like me sending Carol out with that homemade pole, but after some of the guys patted him on the back for "his idea," the day ended well.

—**Constance Siekierski,** *Tucson, Arizona*

SHIP OF SNOW. Patriotism was running high in 1941 when ice sculptors in Marquette, Michigan, built this giant replica of a U.S. Navy cruiser.

Turning Trash to Treasure

THIS LOCAL GARBAGE LADY SERVED AS A TRUE "PICK-ME-UP" FOR KIDS. *By Joan Behm, Berlin, Wisconsin*

Everyone knew her as "Ash-Can Annie," and when she strapped on her stiff leather apron each morning, she certainly looked the part.

Annie and her husband (who walked with a severe limp) picked up rubbish in our town during the 1940s, before city garbage disposal took over in Weyauwega, Wisconsin.

Their route through town became a magnet for us kids, who followed this stocky, rough-looking Pied Piper. Annie's sweaty face was often smeared with grime, but we could always count on a smile, a little teasing and genuine interest in our spirited activities.

More important, Annie understood a child's curiosity with "junk" and often provided spare parts to build make-believe cars or equip a neighborhood circus, even though she knew those same pieces would be right back in the trash the next week.

Our inventive designs were never impossible once we presented the plans to Annie. Many parents scolded about the "trinkets" Annie allowed us to drag home, but others recognized the boost to our creativity. Her cooperation gave life to idle hours and kept us out of mischief.

Trash Met Its Match

When Annie saw a useful object among the castaways, she'd cleverly relocate it with another family. Sure, we could have offered my discarded tricycle to the young couple in the next block, but it was less embarrassing for them to accept a gift left by Annie.

Annie's tiny house was situated in a dense grove of trees at the edge of town. Out back was a vegetable garden and berry patch. In the summer, she carried berries or fresh vegetables to leave with families who didn't have much.

She Was a Role Model

Annie's ways taught us kids about life. She had no time for gossip, and we noticed how she politely greeted folks, even though most only nodded in return. She paid cash for her purchases or went without.

One tragic night, Annie and her husband were strolling along the sidewalk on Main Street when a driver lost control and jumped the curb. Annie's husband was struck and died instantly.

Each day as we kids waited for her truck to reappear on the block, we agonized over what to say to our friend. When the dreadful moment finally came, we just stood there, the words our parents had coached us to say clogging our aching throats.

What Could They Say?

Tears slid down the crevices of Annie's leathery face, and we learned what it meant, and how it felt, to share another person's grief.

Finally, Paul, the youngest of our troop, ran to Annie and hugged her. We followed his lead. No words were needed. Our friendship grew deeper, and we learned that love is not governed by physical attraction but by what the heart feels.

As the years passed, we said good-bye and left for college or moved away. When Annie later died, her house was torn down and the land became part of a new park. With picnic tables, swimming pool, playground, tennis courts, ballpark and even a toboggan slide for winter, it's now a haven for kids...just like Annie would have wanted.

Many of us come back for reunions in the park, but as we watch the children swing from the monkey bars, it doesn't seem right to call this fun land "Community Park."

We remember Annie's patience, friendship and warm smile and marvel at her keen understanding of how to keep kids out of trouble. In our hearts, this will always be Annie's Place.

When Columbus and I Went to Rotary Club

ACCOMPANYING DAD TO HIS MEETING WAS A VOYAGE OF DISCOVERY FOR THIS YOUNG SCHOLAR. *By Mary Chandler, Rancho Santa Fe, California*

IN THE CLUB. Rotarians discovered *Columbus* when Mary Chandler (left) accompanied her dad (above) to his meeting for her triumphant recitation.

Sparkling clean, with my pigtails tied in bright yellow ribbons to match my dress, I stood before my fourth-grade class and a panel of adult judges.

"Behind him lay the gray Azores…" I began.

Columbus Day was two days off, and I'd been practicing for weeks for this talent contest. The poem I'd chosen to recite was *Columbus* by Cincinnatus Hiner Miller. Today a winner would be selected, and that lucky person would get to be the guest of the local Rotarians for an evening.

Dad never missed a Rotary Club meeting. On "Fathers and Sons" night, my two brothers accompanied him. Off they'd go, laughing and joking. How I envied them.

"A light! A light!" I continued with the poem, shading my eyes with my hand, squinting into the distance, looking for the shore that Columbus had seen so long ago.

When I finished, Mrs. Tangren said, "Please wait in the hall. We'll let you know who won after the other contestants have performed."

Waited in Anticipation

My hands tingled as I opened the door and gazed down the vast, vacant hallway. Soon, others from grades four, five and six would join me…but no one could have been more excited than I was.

The minutes crept by as, one by one, the aspiring winners joined me in the hall. We waited and waited.

Finally the door swung open, and I heard the name of the runner-up. As I held my breath, I heard a voice announce, "Congratulations, Mary—you have been chosen to recite *Columbus* for the Rotarians."

"Oh, thank you. Thank you!" I said. Never had I been so happy.

A Magical Night

The evening soon arrived, and I held my father's hand proudly as we walked into that enormous meeting hall, where he introduced me to his fellow Rotarians.

During the business part of the meeting, I listened to how the club was arranging for surgery for a classmate of mine, and how a friend of my brother's was being fitted for a leg brace because of polio. My eyes brimmed.

Afterward, I feasted on buttery corn on the cob, mashed potatoes, meat loaf, mountains of orange sherbet and dark chocolate cake.

Then I climbed on a chair to recite the poem. But that wasn't good enough, someone thought. "Clear the table, Rotarians, so we can see Charley's daughter."

Dad grinned and lifted me onto the table. A sea of smiling faces greeted me. I stood proudly, imagining these men to be sailors on the *Nina*, *Pinta* and *Santa Maria*, sailing with Columbus to the New World. I implored them to, "Sail on! Sail on! Sail on and on!"

When I finished, I scampered off the table and stood beside Dad. There was silence…then thunderous applause! Rotarians surrounded me, shaking my hands, patting me on the head, smiling down at me.

A few minutes later, Dad and I left for home, hand in hand. Even though that was 50 years ago, I'm quite sure that my feet never touched the ground!

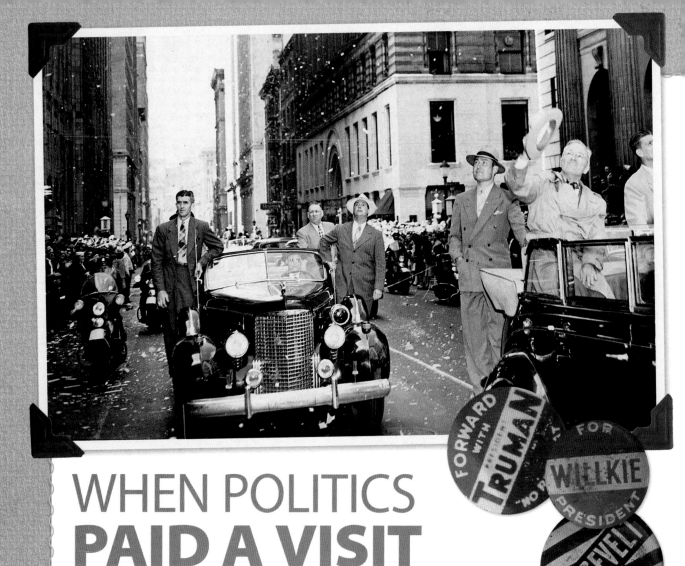

WHEN POLITICS PAID A VISIT

I COOKED BREAKFAST FOR HARRY TRUMAN

On a Friday in June of 1946, a week before summer vacation, several of us in my Boy Scout troop were called to the school office.

Our scoutmaster was there, along with a Secret Service man. I shook his hand and introduced myself. The friendly man said, "My name's Bob. No last name...No Mr....No Title."

Bob explained that the president of Mexico and his son were visiting. The Boy Scouts of Mexico had just been organized, and the president's son, Miguel, was a member.

The PR people thought it'd be nice if some local Scouts took Miguel on a camping trip...and one of our troop committee members, who worked at the White House, volunteered our troop.

We were dismissed from school by executive order! Bob drove us by bus to our houses for our uniforms and equipment. "Just Jim," another Secret Service man, arrived with Miguel in an Army truck.

The food was supplied by the White House stores, and we camped at what's now called Camp David, the wooded presidential retreat in Maryland.

We included Miguel in everything we did and found him a quick and eager learner. In fact, when we were told that we could fish on the property, Miguel proved to be an experienced angler and was soon teaching us. We had fresh-caught rainbow trout for breakfast.

On Sunday, we planned a tea and cake reception for President Truman and Miguel's father following religious services. But Miguel had promised his father rainbow trout for breakfast and had saved a beautiful 15-incher for him.

When the presidents arrived, Miguel said he wanted me to cook breakfast for his father. That was fine by me—I did most of the cooking on camping trips anyway.

Coffee was already served and I was building up the fire when, much to my surprise, President Truman came up. We were old friends at once, and

I was to call him Harry. He took a cup of our home-brewed sassafras tea, but only drank half a cup before switching to coffee.

I served Harry's coffee in a china mug from my personal gear. (The tin camping cups got too hot to hold, and paper cups spoiled the taste.)

Harry watched me cook for Miguel's father and decided he wanted a second breakfast. "Can you fix me breakfast?" he asked.

"Sure," I said. "We have everything we need— except the fish. You catch him and I'll cook him!"

Well, Harry caught his fish and I cooked it, along with eggs fresh from a nearby Amish farm, thick-sliced bacon and fried potatoes.

We also baked cakes, something most Boy Scout troops didn't do in the field. We baked to impress visitors…and because we liked cake. This day it was gingerbread with lemon frosting.

With a second breakfast under his belt, Harry wandered around camp, coffee mug in hand, marveling at our collapsible oven, homemade from tin cans.

We kept up a steady flow of cake and coffee until everyone had their fill. Then, after the dishes were washed and camp was broken, we lingered along the stream as long as possible.

Nowadays, when I walk along a stream near my home, I think of my "old friend Harry." I remember Miguel and wonder if he, too, recalls the good times we shared camping as Boy Scouts.

—**Jim Gosnell,** Clayton, Wisconsin

A HOT TIME IN HOOSIERLAND

During the summer of 1940, Wendell Willkie was named the Republican candidate for President. Soon after, his hometown of Elwood, Indiana, made big plans for "Willkie Day."

Mom, Dad, Grandpa Fid and Aunt Mary were all "red-hot Republicans" who dearly wanted to go see the presidential hopeful. Since we lived about an hour away and didn't own a car, that seemed an impossible dream.

About a month later, the dream came true. My boyfriend, who had a car, was visiting. Grandpa Fid knew if he hinted around long enough, my boyfriend would offer to drive us, and that's exactly what happened.

August 17 was a very hot day, and we piled into my boyfriend's '35 Ford Roadster convertible dressed in our best "bib and tucker" and "Sunday-go-to-meetin'" shoes. As we neared Elwood, the car's engine overheated and died. The men had me scoot behind the wheel while they pushed. "Get a

horse!" someone yelled…but we had no problem keeping up with the bumper-to-bumper traffic.

The motor finally cooled and everyone climbed back into the car. Thousands of cars were parked around Elwood, and the town was alive with excitement. Vendors were selling saltwater taffy, caramel corn, watermelon and cotton candy. As bands played and sirens wailed, we hurried to find a place to watch the parade.

The parade itself seemed pretty routine to me… until the hero of the day came by and the crowd went wild! Grandpa yelled out, "Hi, Wendell!" When Willkie looked right at him and waved, I thought Grandpa would faint on the spot.

He didn't faint, but Aunt Mary did. She was taken to a temporary first-aid station set up in the local mortuary. When she woke up in those surroundings, she was sure she'd died! (As you might imagine, this story was a conversation piece for years afterward.)

Despite our Hoosier enthusiasm, Wendell Willkie lost the fall election to President Roosevelt. After failing to get the nomination again in 1944, he retired from politics, but as each presidential election rolls around, I can't help but remember the "hot time" we had in Elwood, Indiana, on Wendell Willkie Day.

—**Doris Jordan,** Selma, Indiana

IT WAS A SNAP. "During the summer of 1945, I was 16 and worked as a copygirl for a newspaper syndicate," says Lynn Hartsell of Paradise, California. "One day while I was 'on loan' to the *San Francisco News*, President Truman's motorcade passed on the way to an address at the brand-new United Nations. The bureau chief had let me go out to the street a little early to 'get a good view of history.' The motorcade arrived 20 minutes ahead of schedule, and clutching my dad's old camera, I realized I was the only representative of Acme Newspictures on the scene! Dodging a policeman, I stepped into the street and 'shot' the president. Back at the office, the darkroom man emerged after 15 suspenseful minutes. Grinning broadly, he said, 'Hey, the kid got one!' My picture was sent out to our member newspapers all over California!"

Home From Service

MAKING IT OFFICIAL. Just to keep it all legal, the draft board wanted to make sure Ray had his battleship discharge papers. He did.

BUYING CIVVIES. Trying on civilian clothing at the local menswear store must have seemed a little bit odd for Ray. Imagine that. . .hats with brims!

THREE YEARS LATE FOR GRADUATION

My high school education was interrupted for three years during World War II while I served in the Navy in both the Atlantic and Pacific.

When I came home from the service, I was determined to finish my studies even though, at 21, I'd be the oldest student by far at Morristown (New Jersey) High School.

The local paper, the *Morristown Sunday Sentinel*, had photographer Joe Zeltsman tag along with me to chronicle my return to civilian life. Some of his photos appear here.

I finished high school in 1947, went on to Rider College and ended up with a degree in journalism. I later earned a master's degree, and after 17 years working for the *Morris County Daily Record*, I switched professions, becoming a teacher.

—**Raymond Goin,** *Boonton, New Jersey*

NO REVEILLE. His first morning home, Ray could get up when he felt like it, not when someone told him to. But 10:30? What a slugabed! After he was finally up and at 'em, he caught up with some school pals at the local sweet shop.

PRINCIPAL'S OFFICE. Being sent there was not punishment for Ray this time. He had to see Principal Wiley to get back in school. Once immersed back into his studies, Ray found history class to be a breeze. After all, he had a small part in making it while serving in the Navy in WWII.

Main Street Memories

GROCERY STORE WAS A COMMUNITY HUB

Customers got a broad look at scores of products when they walked up to the Bell Gardens Food Center in the Los Angeles suburb of Bell Gardens.

The entire front of the store opened up with a folding door. My father, Edward Carter, is the man in the front at left. Mr. Blau, the owner, is in front in the suit.

The store concept gave customers the feel of an open-air market. On the left, not shown in the picture, are the produce and meat departments. One of my memories is taking used grease from the meat department for use in the war effort. It was used in manufacturing ammunition for the Allies in World War II.

—**Lorraine Carter Beech,** Prescott, Arizona

A LESSON IN TRUST

I had so much fun when my mother sent me to the drugstore in the 1940s. When she did, she would give me a dollar to buy comic books.

Mr. Hooper, the friendly druggist, always smiled at me and then hummed while he put together Mother's order. Meanwhile, I'd busy myself looking over the new supply of comic books. If he finished first, Mr. Hooper would wait patiently while I made my selections.

Comic books were 10 cents each then, and I remember him saying, "How many today, Kathleen?"

Putting the stack on the counter for him to count, I'd answer, "Ten, Mr. Hooper."

He would smile and put them in a bag without bothering to count. I felt so proud that he trusted me!

Every time I went into Mr. Hooper's drugstore after that, I got a wonderful feeling…and I wouldn't have thought about cheating him for the world. He taught me a valuable lesson about trust—one that I carried on into adulthood.

—**Kathleen Hicks,** *Mississauga, Ontario*

LUNCH WITH DAD A SPECIAL MEMORY

Father was chief clerk in charge of registered mail for the Railway Mail Service during the '40s.

Once a month, he'd call Mother to bring me to meet him at the Oakland pier, then he and I would take the ferry across the Bay to deliver the registered mail to the San Francisco Post Office.

Afterward, we stopped at the Russian Tea Room for a lunch of cabbage soup and black bread. A violinist serenaded us with haunting Russian melodies, and a fortune-teller predicted my future in the tea leaves. These were great adventures in my preteen years.

On alternate months, Father took my younger brother to Piggly Wiggly for an "all-you-can-eat" lunch. As far as I was concerned, that didn't hold a candle to the Russian Tea Room.

—**Janet Zimmerman,** *Phoenix, Arizona*

NOW SMILE!

As a child of the 1940s, I thought having my picture taken at the local five-and-dime was a real adventure.

Mama and I would take the bus for 15 cents or the Rock Island train, an extravagance costing a quarter. We'd arrive in Joliet just in time for lunch. My Aunt Elsie operated a snack shop on Main Street, and her hamburgers were the best in town. With only one row of counter seats, people lined up three deep, waiting to pounce on the first available stool.

After lunch, we walked to the five-and-dime. I waited impatiently while Mama made several small purchases—new lipstick, a pound of candy orange slices for Dad and a shiny hair ribbon to match the dress I wore. The excitement mounted as we made our way down narrow aisles toward the back of the store. There, in a corner, stood a screen with a brightly painted backdrop and a swivel stool perched in front.

The salesclerk from the candy counter doubled as the "photographer." She'd turn the stool seat round and round until it reached the proper level, then lift me up onto it.

She'd pose me this way and that, occasionally pulling down a different backdrop for variety. After the photo session, if I'd been good, Mama would reward me with popcorn bought from a street vendor.

Today our family album still contains the results of these happy excursions—tiny snapshots preserved behind sheets of clear plastic.

—**Judy Landrey,** *New Lenox, Illinois*

ALL IN A DAY'S WORK

CASH ON A WIRE

I worked at the J.C. Penney store in Coldwater, Michigan, in the late 1940s. Along with my sales job for men's work clothing, I was also the sidewalk sweeper and window washer. Work clothing consisted mostly of overalls—either bib or waist—and blue chambray shirts.

After making a sale, I'd put the sales slip and money in the overhead trolley and pull on the rope to send it up to the cashier on the mezzanine level. If I didn't pull hard enough, the trolley would go partway up and then coast back down. Pulling too hard would send the trolley up to the cashier with a bang. She would make change and send it down, maybe with a note about not pulling too hard.

In 1949, I graduated from Tri-State College in Angola, Indiana, where Mr. J.C. Penney was the commencement speaker.

—**Eugene Lapham**, *Dimondale, Michigan*

HAVOC AT THE HARDWARE STORE

In the spring of 1946, I worked as a window designer at a hardware store. A young man was remodeling the store's interior. I felt the last thing I needed was advice from this recently returned Army veteran.

Though he was in no position to critique my work, he did so anyway. Finally, my response was to fling my shoe at him, which hit him squarely in the back. To my astonishment, he took a 16-penny nail and hammered my shoe to the floor, then walked off.

I tried to get the shoe loose, but to no avail. Later, my "knight" with shining hammer returned to pry it loose. As he handed it to me, he gallantly said, "I'm sorry I ruined your shoe. I'll pick you up tonight to buy you a new pair."

He arrived to pick me up in a new Pontiac convertible. Despite our rocky start, he proved to be quite a gentleman…and with that new pair of shoes, we began a lifelong relationship.

—**Mrs. Richard Stonesifer**
Hanover, Pennsylvania

OFFICE INNOVATIONS

I worked for an oil company in 1945, and office work has certainly come a long way since then!

The old Marchant calculator on my desk was heavy and cumbersome, but it did the job. When I look at today's tiny calculators, I'm amazed. The old rotary phone wasn't as quick and easy as touch-tones, either.

I learned to type quickly and accurately, since each evening I had to complete a report with seven carbon copies. Typing mistakes were a disaster—it was so much work to erase and retype everything!

If many copies of a report were needed, I'd have to use the mimeograph—a dreadfully messy, temperamental machine. I stretched a typed master made of porous material over an inked barrel that turned. With each revolution, it produced one copy of the master.

The mimeo machine jammed often and would sometimes wreck the master, which had to be typed all over again.

The Xerox machine was a wonderful invention!

—**Taye Waldron**, *Carson City, Nevada*

HAMMER: PHOTODISC

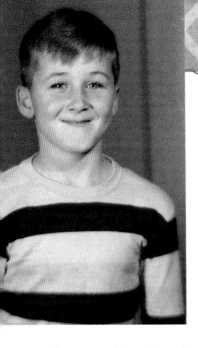

WE "FLEW" THE NEWS

Back when I was a paperboy in 1949 in Fort Worth, Texas, customers expected their papers on the porch—not on the lawn.

The key to successful airborne delivery, I learned during that boyhood career, was the proper fold. Folding newspapers was an art form passed down from the older boys.

On most days, a standard square fold worked best. Houses were far enough apart that I could fold the papers as I walked. I can still feel the canvas bag keeping cadence as it bumped against my hip…25 steps to the fold.

Thrown perfectly, a folded paper landed on the porch with a satisfying plop, then slid right up to the screen door. (Actually hitting the screen door brought little blue complaint slips from the route manager.) A standard fold wouldn't work on Thursday papers—they were too thick with advertising. Instead they were rolled into a baton and secured with a rubber band. Saturday's paper, on the other hand, was too thin for either the regular fold or the roll. It called for the old "dog ear," a triangular fold that could be thrown 100 feet on a windless morning. What Thursday and Saturday lacked in grace and finesse, they made up for in speed. On those days, if I dared, I could ride my bike.

None of us could fold papers and ride a bike at the same time—except for the legendary Joe Schuler. I can still see him coasting down Wabash Street, steering his bike with his knees. Joe could roll a Thursday paper, wrap it with a rubber band and get it away in the time it took to go the width of a 100-foot lot. He never hit a hedge or a porch light, either.

Aside from practical aerodynamics, I learned a lot about life from my paper route. I learned that the customer is always right and that if people like you, they will overlook your mistakes. (I also learned a lot about dogs.) Plus, I saw my first sunrise while waiting for my route manager at my bundle drop on Cedar Street. Ever since, I've been fond of morning's special sight.

—*Joe Wise, Santa Fe, New Mexico*

HEROIC HUSBAND

My husband, Les, was a rookie policeman in New York City in 1942.

One day he was approached by a hysterical woman who had accidentally locked herself out of her fourth-floor apartment and left her baby alone inside. Les advised her that he'd have to climb down from the roof to her fire escape and break a window to get in. She agreed.

Crowds gathered below as the young policeman swung into action. When he found one window covered by a storm window and the other not, he decided he'd rather just break the single window.

As he pulled out his gun to smash the window, he heard the noise of the crowd below. He thought they were cheering and couldn't help but think of the headlines in the next day's paper: "Local Cop Saves Baby."

He smashed the window and leaped inside…to find himself face-to-face with a terrified old man. He'd broken into the wrong apartment!

Shamefaced, he apologized, then left to break another window. Inside that apartment, he found the baby was fine. The mother was very grateful as he opened the door for her.

The crowd was still waiting outside when he left the building. They laughed, applauded and patted him on the back. He was so embarrassed he went straight to a glazier and ordered a new window!

—*Florence Paul, Santa Ana, California*

Remember Saying?

ABOVE MY PAY GRADE:
don't ask me

Soapbox Derby,
ALASKA-STYLE

"COFFIN CORNER" WAS REDEFINED AS A KID DROVE A PRISTINE DERBY RACER INTO ITS NEXT LIFE.

By Mike Foley, Loveland, Colorado

ONE NATURAL RACER, ONE NOT. The author's brother, Lowell, is pictured in his nifty Soapbox Derby racer above. The much less talented driver, author Mike Foley, is shown above, at 10 years old.

When I was growing up, we lived in Douglas, Alaska, a little island town across the Gastineau Channel from the capitol city of Juneau.

The Soap Box Derby was a much-anticipated event in Juneau, and when the contest was announced in 1947, my 14-year-old brother, Lowell, decided to enter. He persuaded Dad to sponsor his car.

As a 10-year-old copycat brother, I decided to build a race car myself, without a sponsor. Dad knew better. I spent a good 30 minutes designing my car, and it looked like it.

While Lowell's racer was progressing as a textbook example of a Soap Box Derby racer, mine looked like it was built by a 10-year-old with a short attention span—more like a soapbox than a racer.

A funeral home in Juneau offered their coffin-maker, Mr. Black, as a mentor for the kids building cars. We held our meetings in his workshop adjacent to the funeral home.

Mr. Black was tall, balding and dexterous. He used all his skills to build beautiful race cars as an example of what was expected but hardly possible from mostly 10- to 15-year-olds.

As it happened, the funeral home was at the top of the very hill that served as the official racecourse. So a special meeting was called at Mr. Black's shop, where he was going to let us drive his car to get the feel of a Derby racer and the course.

About 10 of us showed. Mr. Black left it to the group to select the first driver. Unfortunately for Mr. Black and the other boys, I was chosen.

I was not a typical 10-year-old. I had never been on a bike or roller skates.

Nervously accepting my fate, I climbed into the car and looked down the steep slope with fear.

I quickly glanced at the controls and was then pushed to the crest of the hill, where a communal shove and gravity started me downward.

Look Out Below!

The car rapidly picked up speed. I began turning the steering wheel back and forth, trying to find a track I liked.

But suddenly, where I hoped to see only a racecourse, I saw a curb and a telephone pole, which in an instant was embedded in the front of the car.

I was stunned for a second or two. Then I climbed out, nursing a cut chin.

The boys were not happy, picking through the remains of the car for anything salvageable.

Lowell was the only one who was concerned about the test pilot. He tried to comfort me. It could have happened to any other coward.

As we started home, we passed Mr. Black, who was standing in the midst of the debris that had once been his pride and joy.

He glared at me, and I sensed that he was conjuring up another project, a tailor-made creation, just my size, with three brass handles on each side.

The test-driving episode cured my Soap Box Derby fever. I was happy to let Lowell wear the family colors from then on.

County Fair Fun

A walk down the midway at the county fair in Boonville, New York, held colorful sights and curious sounds that remain memorable.

One Saturday Dad drove us kids to the fair in our old Essex, which wheezed and puttered the whole way. We headed for the grandstand to watch our favorite attraction—a stunt driver named Lucky Teeter. Dad told us he would meet us at the grandstand in 20 minutes.

Later, after Dad arrived and the show was about to begin, he told us to watch carefully. Suddenly our old Essex raced around the corner—speeding toward another car in an exciting head-on crash!

Lucky Teeter himself jumped out of the Essex and announced, "Thanks to Bill Savoy and his family for this stunt!"

The audience gave us a standing ovation! Afterward, Dad took us to meet Lucky and explained that he'd traded him the Essex for a better car. Such exciting childhood memories make me wish I could turn back the clock!

—**Bette Michik,** *Rome, New York*

CHAPTER 7

Keeping HOUSE

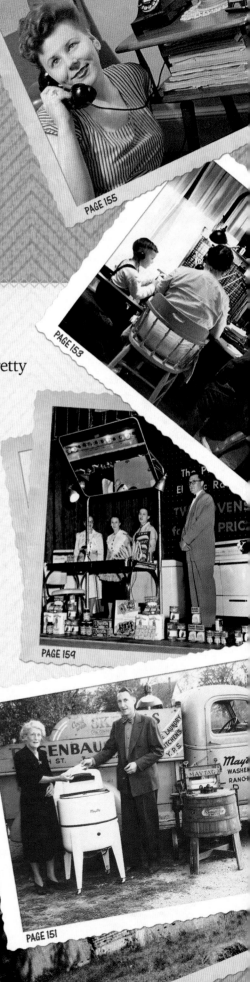

PAGE 155

PAGE 153

PAGE 159

PAGE 151

Finding a place to live was sometimes easier said than done during the postwar housing shortage. That put folks in some pretty amusing situations!

"We moved into our first apartment in 1946," writes Dolores Eggener of Marinette, Wisconsin. "We slowly transformed the apartment into a home as furniture started to become available in stores.

"In those early postwar years, you couldn't just walk in and buy a living room or bedroom suite—your name went on a list. When it was our turn, we got a call telling us what was available. We bought our living room furniture sight unseen. 'It's blue,' they told us. 'Fine by us!' we said.

"Refrigerators were especially hard to come by, but we were fortunate to have been moved up on the list because we had a baby. The problem was, when the refrigerator became available, the money wasn't. We decided to sell my husband Dick's large stamp collection to finance the purchase. We had our priorities!"

Whether we rented an apartment, lived with extended family or were lucky enough to have a house, a roof over our head was what mattered most. On the following pages, recall homes of the '40s and the amenities that we coveted.

HOME-TESTED. Jean Hobson (here with her family in the late '40s) never had to visit an appliance store. She got home delivery.

Her Home Was a
'SHOWROOM'

RIGHT AFTER WORLD WAR II, OWNING JUST ONE ELECTRIC APPLIANCE WAS A BIG DEAL.
BUT THIS HAPPY HOMEMAKER HAD A HOUSEFUL!
By Jean Hobson, West Vancouver, British Columbia

The year 1945 was catch-up time for many young families whose lives had been disrupted by the war. This happened to be fortuitous for my husband and I, as we owned a radio repair shop in Hamilton, Ontario, and we expanded our stock to include appliances just coming on the market.

In order to let potential customers see the appliances in operation, our home became a "tryout" center...and I was the demonstrator.

The gleaming white refrigerator came first. I shed no tears when my old icebox went to the dump. Who would miss wiping up the delivery man's muddy footprints after he sloshed a 50 cent block of ice across a newly waxed kitchen floor?

Soon I was blushing at my family's praise of my frozen desserts, cold milk and unsoggy salads. For their part, the neighbors were delighted to discover an ample supply of ice cubes when throwing a party.

When the washer and dryer arrived, my popularity increased. That night, our basement steps were filled like bleachers at a ball game as people sat knees to backs watching the machines work their magic.

Saw a Sudsy Spectacle

Our "fans" gasped in wonder as suds swirled and the garments tumbled toward cleanliness. Transferring the clothes to the dryer brought a chorus of "oohs" and "aahs."

But it was the television that clinched our popularity—it was the first set on the block.

Our living room quickly became a child-care center for neighborhood tots during the day and an adult theater at night for viewing boxing, wrestling or anything else that moved on that tiny 10-inch screen.

In those days before remote control, we often had to elbow our way through the audience to change channels or twiddle knobs to eliminate "snow." (Only the older kids were allowed to adjust the rabbit ears.)

Not only were we the first in the neighborhood

SIGN OF THE TIMES. Ads like the ones above boosted the popularity of automated household appliances, such as ovens, refrigerators, dishwashers, television sets, washing machines and dryers.

with a television, we were the first to be *on* television.

It all started when Dave Garroway was still doing the *Today* show from a New York studio with a street-level window. My husband and I were spending a few exciting days vacationing in New York, so we promised the family that we'd try to be in the front row of the sidewalk audience on a certain morning.

We did it...and when the camera moved across the crowd of eager faces, we waved frantically and mouthed, "Hi, kids, see you soon!"

Hometown Heroes

If that brief appearance on the TV screen back home was exciting, it paled beside the reception we got when we returned. We were stars in the eyes of our hometown fans!

Some years later, I had my last brush with fame as a home appliance demonstrator. The cooking columnist of our weekly newspaper somehow learned we were having a dishwasher installed. The woman called and asked for an interview about the dishwasher's benefits for the homemaker. I kept up a steady stream of "no's" until she wore me down.

"Couldn't you make that 'yes' and let me come over?" she pleaded. Sadly, I could...and she did—with her notebook and a professional photographer in tow!

No time to worry about the embarrassment to my husband and kids. No time to worry about my hair. There I was, standing beside the dishwasher with a stiff smile plastered on my face for the whole town to see.

But it turned out all right. Within a week, five new customers ordered dishwashers—an unexpected boost to our small business!

Nowadays, our grandkids master the mysteries of DVD players, smartphones and computers soon after they've learned to walk. Still, I doubt this generation will ever know the thrills we did when those first electric appliances arrived on the scene in the postwar years.

FIRST DISHWASHER MADE WAVES

Back in the '40s, I worked in a mining town store. We sold everything from clothes to groceries, hardware and electric appliances.

When we got in our first shipment of dishwashers, the store manager couldn't wait to see how they worked. He dragged one out to the middle of the store and hooked it up. He started the machine, then, as customers stood around watching, he opened the top to "see how it was doing."

The second he lifted that lid, water sprayed everywhere! Before he could close it, he was drenched from the waist up, and the rest of us got a good sprinkling, too. He didn't think it was funny, but everyone else did.

That early model was sure different from the one in my kitchen now!

—**Leona Lamon,** *Adamsville, Alabama*

Rolls Out to Load.. Rolls Back to Wash

Exclusive Westinghouse Roll-Out WASHWELL® holds more...does more...than any other Dishwasher

YOU CAN BE SURE..IF IT'S Westinghouse

My Only Wish Was A Washer

A WASHING MACHINE WAS THE ANSWER TO A YOUNG HOMEMAKER'S PRAYERS. *By Earleen Shorey, Kissimmee, Florida*

Back in 1949, I was a young homemaker with a husband, a 6-month-old child…and no washing machine. I was doing the family laundry on a washboard in the bathtub!

Bending over that tub and scrubbing away on a washboard made me feel like a pioneer. I couldn't help dreaming of just how wonderful life would be with my very own washing machine. Washers were readily available, of course. But like most other newlyweds, we were long on dreams and short on cash, so for us, a new washer seemed to be out of reach.

Then one Saturday afternoon I spotted a newspaper ad describing a sparkling white wringer washer on sale at a local department store. The price was a real bargain, but the clincher was that you could bring it home on credit. Just $5 down and $3 a month would make an aching back and scraped knuckles a thing of the past!

I talked it over with my husband, and though the payments would be high for us, he agreed that we could use a washer. If our credit was approved, he said, we'd manage to make that monthly payment somehow.

Awaiting the Call

At the store, the clerk gave us a sympathetic look when he saw our income on the credit application, but accepted our down payment anyway.

Back at home, while we waited for a call about our approval, I began saving our week's laundry, just in case. By the end of next week, I hoped, I'd be doing laundry in my own washing machine!

The following Wednesday morning, the credit manager called. After I promised him the $3 monthly payment would always come first, our credit was approved. The washer would be delivered that afternoon!

I was overcome with emotion as I replaced the phone in its cradle. "Thank you, God!" I sobbed, crying tears of joy over a simple washing machine. Something I had wanted and needed so badly was about to become reality.

Of course, the next day was wash day…and I've never been happier to do housework. Every washable item in the house was thrown into that wonderful white "maid."

As I hung each piece of clothing on the line, I was filled with pride…and gratitude. No more pioneering for me!

HER PATIENCE PAID OFF

Back in 1949, my grandmother, Mary Leith of Fond du Lac, Wisconsin, was happy she'd kept her old Maytag washer. That year, the local Maytag dealer, Rosenbaum Inc., had a contest to find the oldest Maytag washer in the area. Mary's, made in 1916, was the winner, so she received a brand-new machine as a prize.

In the photo above, Mary is receiving the washer along with her guarantee from L.E. Rosenbaum.

The new washer, of course, was electric. But there was a temporary hitch. When she won the new washer, the farm buildings and two houses on the farm were not yet completely wired. So, with her old washer gone, Grandma had to revert to the washboard for a few months while the new Maytag sat unused until the house was wired.

—*Walter Leith, Fond du Lac, Wisconsin*

We Fed Our Refrigerator
COLD CASH!

SIX BROTHERS AND SISTERS HAD A PLAN TO HELP OUT MOM AND DAD...
BUT IT MEANT FEEDING THIS CRITTER EVERY 24 HOURS.

By KerryAnn Sime, Bakersfield, California

Our distraught mom sat at the kitchen table, intently watching Dad try to revive our old refrigerator. Shaking his head, Dad pronounced the ailing machine dead.

What would we do now? The year was 1948, and our family didn't have a lot of money. The look on our parents' faces told us that things were pretty bleak.

My older brother, Bob, summoned his five siblings outside to chat. Mom and Dad needed help, and here was our big chance to contribute.

Sister Carol, age 17 and a true organizer, suggested a plan which would require all our efforts: A few days ago, she'd seen some shiny, new refrigerators at a store downtown. Each has a coin box attached. You could purchase the refrigerator with no money down, but to keep it operating, it was necessary to deposit two quarters a day into the box, or the refrigerator would turn itself off.

Then, at the end of the month, a man would come to collect the money and credit your account. At the end of 12 months, the coin box was removed and the refrigerator was yours.

Carol's proposal was this: The six children would commit to depositing two quarters in the box every six days for one year. We accepted her idea with enthusiasm. We felt an enormous sense of pride because we could help the family, and presented our plan to Mom and Dad. After a lot of persuasion, they accepted.

The refrigerator we chose, a brand-new International Harvester, was delivered the following week. As the delivery men rolled it down the ramp, the neighbors began to gather.

Mom's appreciation and pride made the whole plan worthwhile. No longer would she need to fret over the soured milk, rancid butter, moldy bacon or wilted vegetables that our undependable fridge had wrought.

At first I met my contribution obligation by collecting soda bottles for their 2 cent refund. But soon I turned 12 and got my first real job: a newspaper route. My brothers and sisters soon learned, too, that collecting two quarters every six days was no easy task. It had seemed easier during the enthusiasm of developing our "flawless plan." Still, difficult as it was, we stuck with our agreement.

By year's end, Mom and Dad never had to come forth with a single quarter. The appliance store removed the box and gave us kids a paid-in-full receipt for $180. The refrigerator was ours! Each of us knew we had been part of accomplishing something special.

OUR LITTLE SECRET

We didn't have much money when I was young in the 1940s. But my mom loved beautiful things, and although our belongings were old, there was always a special grace to the way she arranged them. She hid our aging sofas with vibrant floral slipcovers. Many people commented on how nice this looked.

One day I arrived home from school earlier than she'd expected, I saw Mom sitting on a sofa with a pink crayon in hand, coloring a big pink flower! When I walked in, she looked embarrassed, and when I asked her what she was doing, she replied, "Nothing."

I told her that I'd seen her coloring the sofa, and she asked me to promise not to tell anyone she was brightening up the fading slipcover. I kept my promise. When she received compliments on the slipcovers, we would glance at each other with a smile.

—Lorraine Hiester-Smart
Lehighton, Pennsylvania

PERSON TO PERSON. Listening in on the party line wasn't his idea of a good time, so this man is having a call placed to New York via a private telephone system set up in a Walton, Indiana, home. Virginia Phillips of Independence, Missouri, sent the 1949 shot, which shows her captivated son on the left.

On the Party Line

EAVESDROPPING PAID OFF

I "met" my husband on an old-fashioned party line—he was listening in!

It was 1949, and I'd just graduated from high school. One night my sister's friend Alvina called on the party line, but my sister was gone. Alvina and I began talking, and she offered to take me along to a local snack bar for music and entertainment.

Suddenly, a male voice cut in on our conversation.

"Hi, Alvina," the voice said. "Who's your friend?"

Alvina introduced me to her neighbor Joe, then asked him to please get off the line!

That night when Alvina and I went to the snack bar, who should walk in but Joe. We were introduced again, this time in person, and my heart was pounding!

We dated practically every night after that. Two years later, we were married. The old party line may not have offered much in the way of privacy, but after more than 40 happily married years, I'm glad someone once listened in on one of my conversations!

—**Betty Dusicsko,** *Fairview, Pennsylvania*

How We Wanted a
PLACE OF OUR OWN

NEWLYWEDS WERE COUNTING ON A CABIN BY THE RIVER,
BUT THEY GOT MORE THAN THEY BARGAINED FOR!
By Ruth Benson, Corvallis, Oregon

When we married shortly after V-J Day, Herb and I discovered that not even love could conquer the postwar housing shortage. After weeks of futile house hunting, we accepted an offer by Herb's folks to move into their unfinished attic.

Grateful as I was for a well-meaning mother-in-law, I still longed for the freedom to bang dishes and clatter up and down the stairs. I yearned to cook for my new husband and sew curtains and wax furniture. I wanted the chance to begin really living by ourselves, in a place of our own.

I searched the newspaper rental ads and hounded the real estate office, over and over swallowing my disappointment when I heard, "Sorry, there's not a thing to rent."

I fought to keep up my spirits during the rainy Oregon winter. And when spring brought daffodils and violets, it also brought amazing news from one of the real estate agents—he'd located a rental!

The agent was very careful to make it clear that the place was not a house, but a summer cottage on the nearby Molalla River. It had a fireplace and no indoor plumbing. Sight unseen, I signed the lease and paid $35 for a month's rent.

Minor Hardships?
The cottage could have been a chicken coop for all I knew. But if it had a roof and four walls, it would be heaven to me!

I could handle minor hardships like a pump on my back porch and an outhouse in the woods, I told myself. I came from pioneer stock, and surely some of my ancestors' grit had rubbed off on me.

Rather than dwell on the cabin's lack of conveniences, I focused on how wonderful it would be to breathe cottonwood-scented air, fish, swim, pump water, chop wood and fall asleep beside the fireplace, listening to the soft rush of the river.

Later, when we inspected the property, my heart dropped to my toes. Barely 18 inches from the front porch, a creamed coffee–colored torrent raced and voracious currents boiled and churned. The cottage was very nearly a houseboat!

Herb cast a weather eye at the sky and noted that the spring rains had stopped. In a day or two, he assured me, the water would go down. I forced a smile and hoped he was right.

Ignoring common sense, we set up the house the following afternoon. After a late supper, we made our bed on the floor before the river-rock fireplace, where a cheery blaze kept us warm.

A Place to Call Home
But I lay awake, springing up again and again to gaze at the rampaging river, imagining the cabin and all our possessions sliding into a tangle of debris and floating away.

By morning, the Molalla had receded, and as the days passed by, the weather warmed and we began to truly appreciate the joys of having our own home.

Every day we awoke to a cheerful chorus of birdsongs against the soft murmur of the Molalla. The sun sparkled on the clear, clean water. Treks to the outhouse became nature walks as we drank in the smells of the cottonwoods, maples and firs.

The board-and-batten cottage was the beginning of many dwellings that Herb and I came to call home. After all these years, we've never forgotten that cabin—the first real place of our own.

STYLES OF THE 1940S.
This slide was rescued from the garbage at an estate sale in Binghamton, New York, by Bob Hughes of Lisle. The stylish combination magazine rack and table was perfect for keeping a phone, lamp and clock within easy reach. Chances are the cleverly designed piece was handy in cramped quarters, possibly in this young woman's first apartment.

A HOME FOR $13 A MONTH

After our 1940 wedding ceremony, my husband, Leslie, worked with his brother Lester painting houses around Miami. We lived on one side of Lester's small duplex. Our monthly rent was $15, and after three months we saved $100 to put down on the purchase of a house and some furnishings.

That house was just a shell, with bare two-by-four studs for partitions inside and no indoor plumbing to start with. We were without electricity for the first two weeks, and we had running water only if I ran to get it from a small hand pump just outside the house.

The monthly payment for our $1,300 house was $13. With $50 of our savings going for a down payment, we had $50 left to furnish the house. In a used-furniture store, we bought an icebox for $2.50, a couch and three wicker chairs for $12, a dining table with three chairs for $4, and a mattress.

Our stove was a two-burner kerosene model that we placed on orange crates. For laundry, we had two washtubs and a washboard.

I took my bath in a little tool shed in back of the house. The lock was on the outside, so Leslie locked me inside for privacy. One day a little mouse kept running around the base of the tub during my bath. When Leslie came back to unlock the door, I was still in the tub, yelling for him to hurry up!

—**Imogene Sheffield,** *Orlando, Florida*

HIS OWN PLACE FOR PEANUTS

My husband, Fred, came from a family of 10 boys and two girls and learned early that if you wanted something, you had to work for it.

In 1940 to '41, he built his first house. The cost: 10 acres of land, $312.50; abstract, $22; taxes, $3.73.

For construction materials and services: lumber from an old barn, $45, and hauling it, $9; nails, $3.75; tractor, $30; drag, $10; plow, $2.50; pump for the well, $16.50; hammer, 69 cents; slide rule, 25 cents; 25 gallons of gas, $3.76; clevises, 43 cents; gravel, $7.50; cement, $8.45; lumber, $103.60; square, $1.25; level, $2.25; saw, $3; pipe, $2.70; ruler, 45 cents; building paper, $1.50; brick for chimney, $6; seven sacks of mortar, $6.50; trim, $3.75; shingles, $39.39; windows, $29.54; paint, 74 cents; brush, 50 cents; siding, $69.74; electrician, $10.60; other labor, $54.50.

—**Meryl Bromley,** *Dowagiac, Michigan*

WE STAYED
WARM & TOASTY

THE MONSTER DOWNSTAIRS

Back in 1940, a coal-fired furnace was a familiar sight in almost every basement of our little Pennsylvania town.

We heated five rooms of our bungalow with this furnace. The asbestos-covered monster gobbled up seven tons of a mixture of "pea" and "chestnut" coal every winter.

Our coal bin stood 30 feet from the furnace—imagine carrying coal from the bin to the furnace one shovel at a time! That's why I built a box on wheels that held 500 pounds of coal.

I would fill the box, then roll it to the side of the furnace, as you can see in the photo. During a severe winter, that 500 pounds might last a week.

Tending a coal-fired furnace was a never-ending job. I "banked" the fire every evening and raked down the ashes once a day. Ashes also had to be shoveled out of the pit and carried outside to be hauled away.

For hot water, we used a small "bucket-a-day" stove. It heated the water like a charm but had to be "worked" just like the big one downstairs.

—*John Spangler*, Hanover, Pennsylvania

SNUG AS A BUG

A fond winter memory from my childhood is the thick, multicolored patchwork quilt that covered my bed. I can vividly recall the different patterns composed of old suits and dresses once worn by my aunts, uncles and grandparents.

There was a piece of Uncle John's blue denim work shirt, a section of Aunt Lola's favorite black dress and a piece of the flowered scarf that Aunt Bues wore on windy days when taking a meal out to my uncle working in the field.

I can also remember waking up in the middle of those arctic nights and hearing nearby trees creaking with the wind as the pale blue light of a full moon entered my bedroom.

In the moon's light, I'd see particles of powder-fine snow that had sifted through our loose-fitting window frames and come to rest at the foot of my quilt. Those tiny white snowflakes glistened brightly in contrast to the darker patches of the quilt.

How consoling it felt on those frigid nights to be warm and snug beneath the protective shelter of the friendly family quilt!

—*Joan Knapp*, Three Rivers, Michigan

A LAWN-MOWING MEMORY

My father used a Monta mower to mow our two acres back in the '40s. Because it weighed only 8 pounds, I could hold it straight out at arm's length…yet it cut better than any other mower I've ever used! Ironically, I'd never been able to find one person who had seen or heard of one, and it still puzzles me that an invention so vastly superior was not more widespread or enduring—but then I found this ad. Now I can prove I'm not crazy when I tell people about that marvelous mower!

Raymond Ridgell, *Royse City, Texas*

Remember Saying?

GAS:
a good time, something funny

In the Kitchen

IN PRAISE OF APRONS

Aprons worn nowadays are mostly ornamental. In the '40s, we wore them to protect our dresses—even the everyday ones. Most women had ones with two huge pockets. These carried clothespins out to the line, fresh peas in from the garden or crying baby kittens to be warmed indoors.

A corner of the apron could be used as an instant pot holder or to wipe away a child's tears. No tool ever had more uses than an apron in the hands of a loving mother!

—**Gail Martin,** *El Dorado, Kansas*

66*...we'd arrive early with groceries and cookware and take over the kitchen.***99**

DADDY'S KITCHEN STAFF

My sister, Barbara Ann, and I were in our early teens in the late 1940s when we started working with our father, J. Alfred Smith. To earn extra money, Daddy had begun selling Steelco cookware where we lived in Morgan Acres, north of Spokane, Washington.

His kit included a variety of stainless steel pots and pans, a set of which I still use to this day. A host family would schedule a dinner party for a Friday or Saturday evening, and we'd arrive early with groceries and cookware and take over the kitchen.

The main course was always the same: pot roast cooked with carrots and potatoes and seasoned with savory salt in a roaster, and wedges of cabbage steamed in a three-piece saucepan with steamer insert and lid.

While the meat and vegetables cooked, Daddy mixed the batter for steamed date pudding, which would be made when the cabbage was done. After dessert, Barbara Ann and I cleaned up and packed the cookware while Daddy took orders. I don't recall if we were ever paid for our work, but we enjoyed the special time with our daddy.

—**Arty Lee Scott,** *Spokane, Washington*

GLASSES SHATTERED HIS EXPECTATIONS

One day in the '40s, Father came home from the city with a large package and a mischievous grin. In the kitchen, he opened the package and pulled out a glass tumbler. Then, scanning the room to make sure everyone was watching, he drew back his arm and flung the glass against the wall!

When it shattered to pieces, Dad's face dropped in bewilderment. We all gasped, thinking he'd lost his mind!

It turned out a salesman in the city had sold Dad a set of "unbreakable" drinking glasses. In the store, the salesman had hurled one glass after another against a wall, and each had stood the test (much to the admiration of onlookers).

Poor Dad's set was obviously defective. But after all these years, it's still fun to recall the look of shock on his face!

—**Irene Pollock,** *St. George, Utah*

Easy as Pie

Baking was a big part of Mary Fenton's career back in 1948, when she began conducting onstage cooking demonstrations for a company called Homemaker Schools.

Mary spent 14 years as a capable cooking and baking instructor, and on her cross-country travels she cooked up some luscious memories—but not always. "One night I was demonstrating a pie recipe when smoke came billowing from the oven behind me," she recalls. "I took out the pan and said, 'Ladies, this is how you burn a pie crust in one easy lesson!'" The audience roared with laughter.

Mary looks fondly upon her cooking adventures. She happily retired in North Hollywood, California.

Soft...
lovely...
longer lasting

Rilling

Koolerwave
The "vapor-veil" permanent

CHAPTER 8

Unforgettable
FASHIONS

PAGE 166

PAGE 170

PAGE 165

No matter our age back then, we all wanted to look our best in the 1940s. Some of us did some crazy things to ensure we were at the height of fashion.

"In 1943, my family moved from New Jersey to Connecticut so my parents could work in factories that produced war materials," says Marge Goral of Ridgefield, Connecticut. "Before school was to start, it was obvious that I needed a new pair of shoes, and I desperately wanted saddle shoes, which cost $8 a pair.

"My mother decided that, at age 14, I was old enough to go alone to shop for my shoes. So I took the bus into town and bought my shoes. They were perfect, and I could not wait to get them home.

"At the time, it was the style to wear dirty saddle shoes, so I spent the rest of the day rubbing my new shoes in the grass and driveway gravel until they looked just right. When my parents came home, my mother almost fainted when she saw what I had done. To this day, whenever I see a pair of saddle shoes, I can still hear my mother scolding me!"

From rationed fabric to postwar couture, the '40s certainly had a distinctive look! Here, we bring those styles back.

Wishes Once Came
IN THE MAIL

REMEMBER WHEN THE SEARS CATALOG WAS A "WISH BOOK OF DREAMS"?

By Ruby Sentman, Tonawanda, New York

While growing up, I always became something of a dreamer around late July or early August. That was when the Sears catalog of fall fashions appeared in Aunt Minnie's mailbox!

My family never ordered enough merchandise to get a "wish book" of our own, so we counted on Aunt Minnie to share. My sister and I, hot and tired from working out in the tobacco barn, would hurry though lunch, then run down the path to her place and wish our way through that thick book.

Sometimes Aunt Minnie even let us fill out the order blanks—just for fun, of course. One year, though, I vowed that instead of a dreamer, I'd be a real shopper!

I worked in a neighbor's patch for 25 cents a day, and got Dad to promise I could keep any money I earned by picking up the extra leaves of tobacco that were often left in the fields. By the time the catalog came, I had saved a whopping $25!

Agonized Over Choices

Never has greater care gone into choosing a Sunday outfit. I sought opinions on what hat

MAIL-ORDER MAGIC. Wishing and waiting were a big part of the fun back in the days when people ordered their clothing from Sears catalogs. When the order finally arrived, all the anticipation seemed worthwhile.

SEARS, ROEBUCK AND CO.

Spring and Summer
1941
CHICAGO

SATISFACTION GUARANTEED
OR YOUR MONEY REFUNDED

would look best with which suit, and what blouse would make the perfect accent.

Should I go with the high heels of my yearnings, or opt instead for the more sensible lower ones that wouldn't be as abused as I walked to and from church? Finally, the tough decisions were made and the order sent out. Then the waiting began. Each day as I came in from school, I'd nonchalantly ask, "Any mail for me?" At night, I'd dream about my order.

When the box finally arrived, I took it upstairs to open it in privacy. Turning back the tissue paper, I caught my breath …

Where was the hat? And the shoes? I scrambled downstairs to the kitchen but before I could say a word, I saw my mother with a mischievous smile on her face, holding another box. I shrieked, "How could you?" Then I grabbed my treasures and rushed back up to my room.

Pretty as a Picture

One by one, I reverently tried on my purchases. The stockings were so sheer that only the seam gave away their presence. Next came the elegant slip, the bright white blouse and the skirt of herringbone tweed with all the browns and reds of fall. Finally, with the jacket in place, I turned to the mirror to give the hat just the right tilt.

There I stood, feeling so gorgeous that I simply had to have a wider audience. After clunking

down the stairs on the wobbly heels, I made my way down the path to get Aunt Minnie's stamp of approval.

Along the way, my family members smiled and nodded. That was reassuring, but I wasn't truly convinced until I'd heard Aunt Minnie exclaim, "Well, look at you!"

With that final pronouncement, my dreams came true. Like Aunt Minnie, I was a veteran wish-book shopper!

So NEW!

they give you a headstart in style!

79¢

The Jolly Crest Hat

FIRST in this row of headlin comes the Crest hat! A jo crushable pull-on hat of soft Wool Zephyr yarn! Knitted like French beret cloth! It merits tip top place because of the t that gives it new height. Color ball pin. Stitched adjustable br 78 D 6688—Fits 21¾ to 22½ inc headsize.

Colors: Chamois (med. Beige, Royal Blue, Burnt (me Brown, Runyotone (dark wine re Hindu (med.) Green, or Black. M sure and state color. Not prepa Shipping Weight, 8 oz.

B "Ruffles"—a new madca

69¢

WHO says the new high hats haughty? "Ruffles" shows h gay and adorable they really a It's knit of sparkling Rayonandcri knotty Wool Boucle, and shows knowing tendency to dip toward front.
78 D 6692—Fits 21½ to 22½ inc headsize

$2.00 Post Paid

- Lovely 3-eyelet tongue tie
- Attractive snake design leather trim
- 1¾-inch covered wood heel
There's nothing like an oxford for that neat, tailored appearance—it goes so well with any frock. "Chassis-Bilt" quality.
15K2594—Black Kid
15K2595—Patent Leather $2.00
Sizes, 3½ to 8. Medium wide widths. Be sure to state size. Postpaid.

New Reduced Price

Rubber Sport Sole

- Fine grain, retanned, smoke color leather with attractive brown leather trim.
- Tough rubber sport design sole
- 1½-inch heel with long wearing rubber top lift "Chassis-Bilt" quality throughout.
15K2561—Sizes, 3½ to 8. Me- $1.88 dium wide widths. State size.......
When not included in a $2.00 order, send 12¢ for postage.

BLACK KID OR PATENT LEATHER

—Very pretty cut-outs and side buckle
—Fashioned on our Marcelle last
—1¾-inch covered wood heels
Proving popular this year for its attractive appearance and its fine quality. It keeps its style and wears longer because its "Chassis-Bilt."
15K2534—Black Kid
15K2535—Patent Leather... $1.59
Sizes, 2½ to 8. Medium wide widths. Be sure to state size. When not included in $2.00 order, send 10¢ for postage.

The Ghillie Tie
—Soft chrome tanned brown leather
—Latest design pierced perfora-tions
—Correct 1½-inch Military heel
—Long wearing rubber top lifts

CHRISTMAS IN JULY

Mother kept telling me that I was expecting it too soon. But every day for a week, I walked down our hot, dusty road to the post office to see if my order from the Spiegel catalog had arrived.

Dad had made the order on credit—it would be a tweed winter coat and it would be the first brand-new coat I'd ever owned!

On July 10, 1940, I took my walk to the post office once more. And I could barely believe it when the postman pulled out a package! I grabbed it, thanked him and quickly started for home. I was so eager to see that coat and try it on for the first time!

The excitement mounted as I carried the package back up that dusty road. I was about halfway home, nearing our little one-room schoolhouse, when the excitement became too much to bear.

I decided to duck into the school outhouse and try on my new coat!

Unless you've been inside a little outhouse in July with a winter coat on, you have no idea how hot that can be. But I didn't mind the heat a bit. The coat was a perfect fit, and it was mine!

—**June Spaw,** *Science Hill, Kentucky*

Refined Retailer

SHOPPING WITH CLASS

No matter what time of year I visited Arbaugh's department store in Lansing, Michigan, the employees always treated me special. My dad was the display director in charge of decorating the windows and all five floors of that elegant store.

Jewelry, gloves, handkerchiefs, hosiery, cosmetics and notions were displayed in glass cases, which the clerks opened to serve you. They didn't chew gum or act uninterested, either.

The store housed clothing, furniture, a beauty shop, a bargain basement, a photographer's studio, a grocery store, soda and lunch counters, and shoe and watch repair shops.

I wish department stores like the old Arbaugh's were still around.

—Annie-Laurie Robinson, *Williamston, Michigan*

Mom Was a Shoeshine Girl

GROWING UP IN A CITY SHOESHINE PARLOR LEFT HER WITH LOTS OF SHINING MEMORIES.

By Carolyn Pauls, Goddard, Kansas

If you lived in a town of any size during the good old days, you likely heard that call from a corner stand manned by a hardworking shoeshine boy. But if you lived in Springfield, Missouri, during the '40s and '50s, you may well have had your shoes shined by a young woman instead—my mother!

My parents ran the K&K Shoeshine Parlor back then, when a shoeshine was still considered a must before going to work, school or church.

Perfectly polished shoes were also required of the soldiers at nearby Fort Leonard Wood. On Saturdays, the GIs would line up to have Mom shine their shoes for 15 cents.

For most of the men, it was a strange experience to have a woman shine their shoes. But Mom had been at it for years and was good at what she did.

When Dad first opened the shop in 1942, Mom pleaded with him to let her help out. Dad was reluctant to let her handle a job that was considered "men's work," but when he finally relented, Mom really liked the job. And, more importantly, the customers loved her work.

The Three-Minute Shine

Mom could shine a pair of shoes neatly in three minutes flat. That figured out to about 20 pairs an hour, and she often worked that hard. Once, when she had to spend a lot more time on a farmer's muddy work boots, she was rewarded with a remarkable $1.80 tip.

Eventually, my parents hired a full crew of young lady shoeshiners! First-time customers were often surprised or even embarrassed when they entered our all-woman shop, but they always left satisfied.

As a youngster, I spent every spare moment in that shoeshine parlor. Every one of the customers was kind to me. Some of them even took time to play checkers with me.

I always loved to sit on the shoeshine bench next to one of the customers and listen as Mom buffed hard and made her rag "pop." The smell of the polish, the snap of her cloth and the friendly conversation remain etched in my memory.

Mom said the shoeshine parlor was almost as popular as the local barbershop for gossip and idle conversation. People just liked to talk while their shoes were being shined.

Occasionally, they had something exciting to gossip about. Many big-name country-western performers came to Springfield to appear on the Ozark Jubilee stage, and it wasn't uncommon for stars like Red Foley or Porter Waggoner to stop in for a shine!

For 33 years, my parents made a small but honest living shining shoes. When they retired in 1975, a shoeshine was still only 35 cents. Nowadays, except in airports and fancy hotels, it's hard to find a shoeshine parlor. But I'll always have a soft spot for the few folks who still shine shoes—and do it with pride. Whenever I hear the snap of a shoeshine rag, I recall our friendly K&K Shoeshine Parlor!

SHINES OF THE TIMES. Carolyn Pauls' mom and dad (in the rear of the shop) did brisk business, as the 1946 photo shows.

ISN'T SHE LOVELY?

THE PERFECT POUT

Does anyone remember Tangee lipstick? It has been gone for years, but I still think about that almost-colorless cosmetic in its plain black tube.

When I was a child, my mother said I was too young to wear regular lipstick, but she'd let me wear Tangee! It left the faintest ring around my lips and made me feel so grown-up.

Though there are thousands of lipstick shades available today, Tangee is still my favorite!

—**Janis McCann,** *Pond Eddy, New York*

HEY, WHERE'S OURS?

My brothers were jealous when they heard I was getting an "endcurl." They didn't know what it was, but they knew it cost $1, a lot of money for a nonessential in 1940.

When my mother and I came home from the beauty parlor, after a little shopping, my new hairdo was lost on my brothers. Their main interest was to rummage through our packages looking for that endcurl I'd gotten.

—**Mae Brehmer,** *Litchfield, Minnesota*

Mail-Order Mannequins
FASHIONED MIRTH

In 1943, you needed ration stamps to buy most anything—shoes, sugar, coffee, gasoline. But that didn't stop us girls from wanting new clothes.

Tube (or sack) dresses were a popular way around the dress shortage. You started with two yards of tubular jersey and sewed two seams at the top, leaving a space for your head.

Then you cut two armholes and hemmed the bottom. In less than an hour, you had a dress ready to accessorize with scarves and jewelry.

To make a truly stylish dress, you needed a dressmaker's mannequin, but only the affluent could afford one. So when my sister and I saw an ad for mail-order mannequins for just $5, we took the bait.

Itchin' to Stitch!
Neither of us knew much about sewing, but with our new mannequins on the way, we figured we could make our own stylish dresses easily enough.

Meanwhile, we visited the department store and waited our turn to look at the pattern books that were published by Simplicity and McCall's.

We copied the number below our selections, gave them to the clerk, and walked out with fabric and patterns in our hands and enthusiasm in our hearts. We could hardly wait for our mannequins!

Eventually, two packages about the size of greeting card boxes arrived. If these were our mannequins, we thought, they had to be for puppets!

We tore open the parcels. Each contained two rolls of thick brown mailing tape, a piece of tubular cheesecloth about a yard long and instructions for assembly—emphasizing that it was a two-person job.

Taped Into a Tube
As we carefully followed the instructions, our project took on the air of a professional comedy act. Step one was to strip down to your underwear, put the cheesecloth over your head and pull it down about midway across your backside.

Next, your helper soaked the mailing tape, cut it into short strips and plastered it over the cheesecloth,

overlaying each strip until all the tape had been used.

This sodden "body cast" slowly grew heavier and heavier. Even worse, the instructions warned it could not be removed until it had fully dried and was hard to the touch.

Were they kidding? It would take at least four hours for that tape to completely dry—and during that time you couldn't sit! You had to remain in a standing position. If nature called, tough luck.

As the tape dried, the body cast gradually grew lighter, but that's the only good thing I can say. The tricky part came when it eventually dried. Then your helper had to cut you out of the cast.

The manufacturer suggested going straight up the back from the bottom. If you were unfortunate enough to be ticklish, as I was, this method proved to be a real ordeal.

After escaping the cast, you retaped the seam and stuffed the mannequin with crumpled newspaper. Finally you had a duplicate of your own body on which to custom-style dresses.

My sister mounted her mannequin on an old floor lamp. I decided I had no desire to see my body cast displayed. I named my mannequin Matilda and relegated her to the closet.

I don't recall what happened to Matilda. She was probably thrown out with the ration books after the war. I do remember how we laughed as we made those mannequins, and how we howled at the results. During the war there wasn't often much to smile about, so I figure it was $5 well spent.

—**Rita Haban,** *Reynoldsburg, Ohio*

KIDS' CLOTHES

HAND-ME-DOWN BLUES

When I boarded the school bus that day in 1946, I was proud as a peacock over the "new" hand-me-down coat that my aunt had given me. It was purple with green sleeves and gold-trimmed cuffs, and there was a big red tulip sewn on the front.

"Johnny's got a girl's coat!" called out the other boys on the bus when I got on. My heart sank. I didn't know the difference.

It was little consolation when an older girl offered me a seat. But it helped when she showed me that she was wearing a boy's coat and black buckle overshoes.

—John Mack, *Nelson, Pennsylvania*

FEED-SACK FASHION. The two "flour children" showing off their pretty feed-sack dresses are Margaret and Mary Eleanor Walker. Their father, Stanley, now of Loma Linda, California, snapped this photograph in 1948. The girls are sitting on a '36 Pontiac.

HOPPY DAYS

It's amazing that I didn't get a permanent rash from my old Hopalong Cassidy sweater. It did itch sometimes, but not enough to discourage me from wearing it day after day during the late '40s.

In fact, I was sure the sweater had attracted my first girlfriend in the fourth grade. She stood at least a head taller than I did when she sent me a note explaining that now I was her boyfriend and I shouldn't talk to other girls.

Like most boys at that age, I could brag about my knowledge of girls, but place one in front of me and I became a stammering idiot. A week passed before I decided to approach my "girlfriend."

It was at that point I received another note saying it was Paul she really liked. Although saddened, I was also relieved it was Paul's turn to sweat.

The worst part was her postscript: "You have mustard on your Hoppy sweater." *Hopalong Cassidy is a lot more important than girls*, I told myself as I scraped off the mustard and went on with my life.

I wish I could tell you that the Hoppy sweater is still in my closet, mothproofed and safe. But it was the victim of a wringer washer accident—a mishap that always seemed a little suspicious, since Mom was never properly sorry.

—Jack Miller, *Smithton, Missouri*

MILLINER'S DELIGHT. Festive hats were fashionable when Helen Blair was a member of the Emelita Elementary School PTA in North Hollywood, California, in 1944. Helen, who now resides in San Jose, is standing second from the right in the top row, wearing a fashionable pillbox hat.

Accessories
MADE THE OUTFIT

HATS WERE EVERYWHERE

When I was growing up in the 1930s and '40s, men, women and children wore hats. Little girls wore velvet bonnets, and boys sported Eton caps. Men usually chose fedoras, and women opted for kerchiefs or sunbonnets.

Shopping on Woodward Avenue in downtown Detroit always included a trip to Hudson's or Kerr's hat departments to try on their latest styles.

Some of the ladies wore fancier hats adorned with fruit, flowers and feathers. My friends and I watched for the most ostentatious hats. What a sight they were!

—**Sherry Black,** *Charlevoix, Michigan*

A SHOW OF HANDS

I recall a time when ladies wore gloves. I selected mine at glove counters that used to be in drugstores. Behind the counters were drawers filled with gloves of all different colors, styles and sizes.

I'd sit on a stool and extend one of my hands toward the saleswoman. She'd measure it before pulling a glove over each finger and drawing it over my wrist.

Some of the more elegant white gloves went over my elbows. Those gloves were reserved for more formal occasions, of course.

Another fascinating place was the handkerchief counter, fully laden with dainty linen and lace. Growing up, my elders told me I should always carry a clean handkerchief—and I did!

—Mary Brand, *Richmond, Virginia*

ARE MY STREAKS STRAIGHT?

I was a front-desk receptionist for a company in Los Angeles. I never had time to go to the beach to get a tan, so when liquid leg makeup came out, I was the very first one at work to apply this wonderful invention. I even used an eyebrow pencil to draw dark "stocking seams" down the backs of my legs. (Famous last words: "Are my seams straight?")

This worked fine, or so I thought. At noon, I discovered that crossing and uncrossing my legs all morning had caused the makeup to melt and streak down my legs—and the hem and back of my white skirt were a complete disaster. At least my fellow employees had a good laugh!

—Doraine Dittman
San Bernardino, California

VINTAGE COUTURE.
The early part of the 1940s may have been dominated by war, but the second half saw the rise of American fashion. Ads like the ones shown above showcased everything from dresses, hats, coats, scarves and gloves to undergarments, shoes, jewelry, accessories and more.

MEN'S
FASHIONS

DAD'S "SUIT OF IRON"

It was a dream come true. One day I was working behind my father's little luncheonette counter in New York City, making egg creams. The next day I was on tour with the Raymond Scott Band. The year was 1946, I was 18 years old, and I had it made!

I remembered my father's birthday one day as I walked past a posh men's store in San Francisco. Stepping inside, I picked out a suit for him. It was a sharkskin number that looked like a suit of iron. He lived through the Great Depression, and I knew he'd never buy something like that for himself.

But money wasn't my concern. After all, I was a "big star," making $250 a week, which was a nice salary for 1946. So I asked the salesman to send the suit to my father.

"What size?" he wanted to know.

"Well, he's bigger than you," I replied. The salesman sent a size 50.

BEFORE BLAZE ORANGE. "Every fall my dad, William Mahan, took a week to go hunting around Erroll, New Hampshire," writes William Mahan Jr. of West Roxbury, Massachusetts. "This year, around 1948, he took me and Mom along. Back then, hunters dressed in the traditional red and black plaid so they'd be more visible to other hunters and not be mistaken for game. I'm guessing Mom, who took the photo, picked out my wardrobe. That's our Terraplane behind us. While Dad was out hunting, Mom and I hung around the cabin."

My first night home after a long tour, Dad wore the suit. It was a perfect fit! Later, Dad laughingly confessed he'd had the suit altered—it was six sizes too big. Two decades later, the fabric was worn and a few buttons were missing, but that suit lasted, just as a suit of armor should for a hero.

—*Alfred Weisman*, San Diego, California

Dressed in Their Sunday Best

Palm Sunday was approaching in March of 1945, and I'd purchased a new Easter bonnet and a pretty fuchsia coat accented with a black braid trim.

I persuaded my sailor husband, Henry, to take me to Atlantic City, New Jersey, for the annual Palm Sunday parade on the Boardwalk. We packed a small bag and took the train from Philadelphia.

The day was sunny but cool. Crowds of people dressed in their Easter finery hoped to be noticed by parade judges, who were in old-fashioned wheeled basket chairs. When we joined the throng, little did we know that we were going to be among the featured couples on that memorable day. As it turned out, the judges were looking for servicemen and their wives.

Suddenly someone pinned a double gardenia corsage on my coat. Then I was given a white hand-painted scarf to place around my neck. We'd been chosen as one of six winning couples!

Later, we were escorted down to the Claridge Hotel lobby for a reception. Photographers were there to take photographs, which were published the next day in *The Evening Bulletin*.

—**Olive Hall Howell,** *Dunedin Beach, Florida*

CHAPTER 9

Life
TOGETHER

PAGE 183

PAGE 193

PAGE 185

PAGE 189

In the 1940s, we valued family ties, and to this day we cherish our memories of our parents, siblings and extended families.

"I was blessed to be a part of a wonderful family in the late 1940s and 1950s," writes Paul Sexton from Lake Worth, Texas. "My grandparents and three adult aunts lived in a very nice house nearby, and we were often invited to lunch or supper there, which was always a treat.

"Over the years our friends heard about these special events, so when we became adolescents, occasionally we would bring a friend along. It was at one of these dinners that I learned about 'FHB.'

"Noticing that the meal was vanishing with alarming speed, my sweet Aunt Pearl came through the dining room's swinging doors saying, 'Oh, FHB.' It was uttered audibly, but it would never occur to any guest that my aunt was sending a secret message to her family. The code simply meant 'family hold back.' My family uses it to this day."

Everyone has family lore that conjures up feelings of nostalgia. The recollections on the following pages do just that.

4TH WAR LOAN

REUNION Sept. 1

I Was a
GI WAR BRIDE

THIS WRITER HAS VIVID MEMORIES OF THE DAYS WHEN BOATLOADS OF BRITISH BEAUTIES SAILED TO AMERICA'S SHORES.
By Gladys Calderwood, Strongsville, Ohio

At the height of World War II, I worked as a teleprinter operator at a Royal Air Force base 14 miles from my hometown of Reading, England.

It was there on a cold January day in 1944 that I met an American military policeman stationed nearby.

Our first outing was a blind date. For the next eight months, Francis and I saw each other every chance we got. By September, we were married.

As newlyweds we lived off base for a few short months before Francis was shipped back to the United States. He was en route to the Pacific theater nearly a year later when the Japanese surrendered and the war ended.

I stayed back in Britain, where I waited and wondered. When might I be allowed to go join my husband in America?

It was in January 1946 when I finally received word that I could soon leave for the U.S. While it was an exciting time for me, it was a sad time for my family when departure day came. I knew they were filled with apprehension, not knowing exactly what kind of life I would live far away on the other side of the ocean.

Memories of Shipping Out
Our shipload of war brides—only the second to head for the U.S.—sailed from Southampton, and it took 14 days to cross the Atlantic. I didn't get seasick, but many others did.

Upon our arrival in New York Harbor on Feb. 17, 1946, we were all greatly inspired at our first sight of the Statue of Liberty, and then again when passing near it on our way into port. What a breathtaking sight!

We were given quite an unexpected reception. During our trip up the Hudson River, we were

welcomed by a boat of entertainers who sang "Sentimental Journey" and many other songs. It was just overwhelming and unbelievable that so much effort was being expended to make us feel welcome. I knew then that I would love America.

When we reached New York, everyone on board and those meeting us were terribly excited. Our ship, the *Santa Paula*, wasn't a large one, but since it was only the second boatload of war brides, the welcomers apparently felt it carried precious cargo. People were so kind and considerate in ensuring that we reached our correct destinations.

The next evening, I was personally escorted to the train station by a uniformed officer who assured me the train conductor would "keep an eye on me" and give me any needed help.

The following day, the train stopped at Leavittsburg, Ohio, just outside the city of Warren. There I was met by my husband and by reporters who interviewed and photographed me. For a while, I felt like a real heroine.

Trading Tea for Coffee

That fall, my husband entered college. While he was in school, I worked for an insurance company. There I got to know the American people a whole lot better. And I made a huge transition—trading in my teacup for a morning cup of coffee.

Compared with England, America seemed vast. I was simply amazed that people thought nothing of taking a ride of 40 or 50 miles. And it took me quite some time to remember that oncoming traffic was now on the opposite side of the road.

Like many other war brides, I was especially impressed with America's supermarkets and clothing stores. After so many years of austerity, it was unreal to see such a large variety of food and clothing.

In time, I even developed a real affection for the sport of baseball. It reminded me of rounders, a game I had played as a child. To this day I am an avid Cleveland Indians fan.

Francis and I returned to England several times over the years. We traveled through the British Isles by car, and I found that I still dearly love the land of my birth. But America is my home now.

I can truly say that life here has been good to me. How lucky I was to be a GI war bride!

A Banner Year for Marriage

THESE WARTIME PEN PALS SAID "I DO" IN 1946.

By Norene Wilhelm Grubbs, Akron, Ohio

PEN PALS. After two years of letter writing during World War II, Norene and Ray finally got together in 1946, and married shortly after.

With the servicemen returning home from World War II, 1946 calendars were full of weddings. My ceremony with my husband, Ray, was one of them.

As a young woman during the 1940s, I was picky. I told my family that I didn't want anyone who cussed, smoked, drank or told filthy jokes. (I still recall my dad saying, "Well, I guess you'll just have to live alone.")

Then a friend told me she'd taken the liberty of sending my address to her soldier cousin overseas. "He's perfect for you," she said. "He has no bad habits, and he can even draw and paint."

I didn't believe she'd really sent him my address until his first letter came. It was written in red ink, and he had enclosed a photo of himself—a young soldier with golden hair and blue eyes.

In my dreams, I'd wished for a boy with blue eyes and wavy black hair. However, Ray and I discovered through our letters that we both agreed on the true values of faithfulness, kindness, truthfulness and trust in God.

Though we never met, he seemed just right for me. Still, Mom and Grandma warned, "Just because this soldier has written to you, it's no sign he'll come home to you!"

Red-Letter Days

The mailman really enjoyed delivering the letters Ray sent me. His envelopes were pieces of art, with vines and flowers drawn through my name, and all sorts of illustrations, with scenes like soldiers doing KP or sightseeing.

Ray wrote nearly every day for over two years, whether from the back of a truck rumbling through France or from the latrine at night when it was lights-out in the barracks.

He wrote on cold, snowy days in Belgium and Germany. He faithfully sent letters from foggy England and continued writing on the ship coming home.

At first, he'd sign his letters "As Ever." Then it was "More Than Ever"—and, finally, "All My Love."

Though we were separated by the ocean, the songs from those war years kept us close at heart. Our favorites were "I'll Walk Alone," "I'll Be Loving You Always," "I'll Be Seeing You" and "Love Letters Straight from Your Heart."

His last of more than 350 letters said, "I could never have gotten through the war without you." When Ray returned to his home in Akron, Ohio, in March of 1946, he sent me a dozen roses. "For two years of happiness," the card read.

I lived in nearby Cambridge, and we planned to meet for the first time and spend a week together—with our parents' supervision, of course! (I was hoping that I'd at least get to meet him at the bus station alone, but Ray's brother tagged along.)

Twelve Dates Later

Still, we had a wonderful time together. After that, we had only 12 dates until Sept. 25, 1946, when we were married in a double wedding alongside our friends Flo and Bob.

It was nearly impossible to find a place to live after the war. Our first apartment was small, old and not very clean.

I'd never packed a lunch before and sent my new bridegroom off with a cookie, a cold scrambled egg sandwich and coffee. It's amazing he kept me after that lunch!

A few weeks later, we lucked into a government trailer court project. They were all an ugly greenish brown, so Ray painted the trim on ours a nice cream color and made an adorable wooden nameplate that looked like a little house with flowers and trees.

Now we have a nicer home, plus four daughters and sons-in-law, nine grandchildren and three great-grandchildren who all honor God.

My husband has been my "Ray of sunshine," and our life together has been greater than I could've ever hoped for. We thank God for our blessings every day.

SHIVAREE!

PAYBACK FOR A PRANKSTER

Safford, Arizona, was a close-knit community in the 1940s, and shivarees for wedding couples were almost mandatory. My 21-year-old cousin, Dean Hall, planned to beat this tradition.

He'd decided to pick up his bride-to-be, Elizabeth Skinner, early in the morning, visit a justice of the peace and get out of town before anyone knew.

Unfortunately for Dean, Elizabeth didn't keep secrets well. She confided in me and another friend about the elopement. We crossed our hearts we wouldn't tell, but somehow news of Dean's scheme leaked out. He admitted defeat and agreed to a traditional wedding.

Soon after, two other cousins, Bud and Jed, called a shivaree meeting at our grandma's house, where we concocted a plan.

Following the "I do's," Bud inserted himself between the newlyweds and linked arms. "Cut the cake, pose for pictures and throw the bouquet," he murmured.

"Then what?" Dean growled, sounding braver than he looked. Bud just smiled. Then he gave everyone the prearranged signal.

"Shivaree!" Jed shouted.

Bud led the parade to Main Street. There, as all our vehicles screeched to a halt, a rug-lined wheelbarrow appeared. Bud deposited Elizabeth (dressed in a sheet and lace curtains) therein, shoved Dean (wearing a pair of cutoff Levi's and shoes) toward the handles and yelled, "Move!"

Dean, never a poor sport when totally lacking choices, pushed the bridal chariot down Main Street, followed by a pot-banging, bugle-blowing, catcalling crowd that halted traffic in all directions.

We marched through the Safford Theater, back along Main Street and finally through the high school football field, accompanied all the way by wild applause.

By this time, Dean seemed close to exhaustion. Sinking to the ground, he leaned back against the wheelbarrow. "This party," he whispered, "is over."

And so our work was done.

Today, the word shivaree takes me back to a glorious day in 1949 when Dean, Elizabeth, a wheelbarrow and most of Safford, Arizona, marched down the street, joyously celebrating a wedding the old-fashioned way.

—*Barbara Abegg,* Safford, Arizona

SHIVAREE ME TIMBERS! Dean "Jackrabbit" Hall wasn't fast enough to escape his buddies who were intent on throwing a shivaree. So, with Elizabeth in a one-wheeled "chariot", they cruised Safford, Arizona.

SOUNDS LIKE FUN! Folks tended to get "carried away" during shivarees, as depicted in the photos above. In the bottom photo, June Blankenship of Kennewick, Washington, cradles a doll as her new husband wheels her down the street on their wedding night back in 1947.

Holiday Album

FIRST CHRISTMAS. It was bit cramped in their first apartment, in Benton Harbor, Michigan, in 1946, but it was a great Christmas for Gwenn Schadler and her husband, Harold. They now live in nearby St. Joseph.

SWEETHEART. "That's me in the early 1940s in costume for the Candyland Valentine's Day dance recital at a church auditorium in Niles, Michigan," says Sherrie Miller of Las Vegas, Nevada. "My cousin Barbara Loos, age 4, and I were in the recital together and wore similar costumes designed and made by my mother, Mrs. Alex Loos. I was a candy heart, and Barbara wore chocolate-colored satin as a candy kiss. I still remember the dance steps I learned then. Check out those tap shoes. My parents were convinced I was the next Shirley Temple!"

SURPRISING SANTA VISIT. "My mother told me this Santa Claus came through our neighborhood in Burbank, California, around Christmas 1947. My brother, Mike Sevier, was about 7 and I was 3 when the photo was taken," says Sue Anderson of Post Falls, Idaho.

CLOSE GIRLS. Posed at their Niagara Falls home with their mom, Caroline, on Mother's Day 1946 are the Walasek girls (from left): Bernadette, Renee, Theresa, Martha, Estelle, Celia, Clara, Kay and Sofie. The girls also had two brothers. Martha, who still resides in Niagara Falls, shared the photo.

A TRIO OF WINNERS. "My sisters and I were proud to win first prize in the doll carriage category at the 1947 Fourth of July parade in the Adams Shore section of Quincy, Massachusetts," remembers JoAnne Ferraguto Hacking, now of Venice, Florida. "I'm on the right, Ilene is on the left and Jean's in the center."

GRANDMA'S LAP. There was no better place to be for Christmas sing-alongs. Bob Bittick of Tulsa, Oklahoma, sent this '44 photo of his son, Bobby Lee, and daughter, Judith Ann (on the right), posing with their cousins.

HALLOWEEN HORROR. "In the fall of 1948, the Marble Hill Theater announced it would hold a Halloween costume contest with prizes," writes Virginia McManus of New York, New York. "My best friend, Marion, and I decided we'd go all out to win. She and I wound up winning second and first place, respectively. What an exciting moment when, as the runner-up, Marion was presented with a hollowed-out cardboard pumpkin filled with what seemed like every kind of candy ever manufactured! My grand prize: a mere 25-cent movie ticket."

BONNET BOYS. "We'd been at my husband's folks' house for Easter dinner," explains Ruth Larson of Batavia, Illinois. "After taking photos of the ladies, the men asked for equal camera time." Ruth's husband, Bill (standing center), his dad, Thure (to Bill's right), and three of the others borrowed the gals' hats to wear. Since there weren't enough to go around, two of the fellows donned lamp shades—a custom usually associated with overly exuberant New Year's Eve parties.

GOBBLE, GOBBLE. "In 1941, I was engaged to Norma Johnson. Her dad, Norman, is carving turkey for grandson Edwin," says Bob Spring of Bellingham, Washington.

out on a "Date"

In Love and War

SAILOR QUICKLY SETTLED THE COMPETITION

Having graduated from Michigan's Manistique High School, I was about to begin a new job as a Bell Telephone operator in Chicago in 1945.

Since I finished my training on Thursday, April 12, the day President Franklin D. Roosevelt died, my supervisor told me to wait until Monday to start work. With a three-day weekend, I decided to go downtown with my sister to the Garrick Theater Lounge.

My sister and I took the last two seats at the bar on the street level. The bleached blonde sitting next to me said, "You're going to have stiff competition tonight." I told her I didn't think so.

A nice-looking sailor who had been downstairs listening to jazz music in the Downbeat Room was on his way out but decided to take a last look around. He walked right over to me and stopped. Whee! After introducing himself as Gerald Harsh, he joined us for the rest of the evening and later took me home.

We went to the Chicago Theatre the next day to see Judy Garland in *Meet Me in St. Louis*. He had to get back to San Diego, where he was stationed, but we wrote to each other every day.

He was discharged in December of 1945, and we were married the following July. We've enjoyed a lifetime together.

—*Ellen Harsh,* Spring Hill, Florida

FASTEST BOY ON THE BUS WON THE PRIZE

Upon returning from a three-year stint in the Pacific in 1945, I was reassigned to Page Field in Fort Myers, Florida.

I arrived Sunday afternoon after a five-day cross-country train trip. While waiting for a bus to take me out to the field, I noticed a perky little brunette on the other side of the waiting room. She got on the Page Field bus, too, but it was so crowded I couldn't get anywhere near her.

Two weeks later, I went to town for a movie. I got to the bus station just in time to catch the last bus back to the field, and standing in line several places ahead of me was the same brunette. When we got on the bus, I almost bowled over five other guys in my rush to get the seat next to her!

She wasn't eager to talk with me, but I finally coaxed her into telling me that she was a Civil Aeronautics Administration radio operator headed to the field to pull the graveyard shift. She let me walk her across the field to the radio shack.

I spent a lot of time in that radio shack over the next few months, and Evelyn and I have been together ever since.

Since our romance started in the tropics, we celebrated our 50th anniversary by renewing our wedding vows in balmy Hawaii.

—*Jack Heyn ,* West Des Moines, Iowa

CARIBBEAN MAIL CHANGED HIS LIFE

One misty morning in 1943, the *USS SC-1302,* a submarine chaser, tied up to a pier off the island of Trinidad. For weeks, we'd been hunting the German subs harassing Allied freighters in the Caribbean.

Battered by salt spray, the sides of our little wooden ship needed painting, and I got the job.

"Mail call!" came a shout from the deck above. "Brownie," the sailor on mail duty said as he leaned over the rail. "You've been holding out on us. Who's this sweet gal you know in Brooklyn?"

"Brooklyn? I don't know anyone from Brooklyn," I said, examining at the fancy blue envelope he handed me. The address was correct, though, and the letter was definitely written in a feminine hand. My heartbeat picked up.

I'd visited Brooklyn once, aboard the heavy cruiser *USS Louisville.* In fact, that's where I saw my first snowfall. But I hadn't met any girls there.

When I opened the letter, I found out. It turned out "Mom" Macarrio, the lady I boarded with while in Navy gunnery school in Minneapolis, had visited her sister in Brooklyn and met my future pen pal, Anne. Mom convinced her it would be patriotic to write to a serviceman.

Three years of letter-writing followed. Then, on April 18, 1946, my six years of Navy duty came to an end. After I was handed my discharge at the Naval Air Station in New Orleans, my first civilian purchase was a train ticket to New York.

When I stepped from the train in Pennsylvania Station, I searched the crowd for a face I'd seen only in a photograph. Ahead of me, a young woman approached. She resembled the picture I had, but I was cautious—a mistake could be embarrassing!

When she came closer, she looked me straight in the eyes and smiled, and all doubts were erased. I quickly embraced my longtime pen pal!

We were married on Dec. 26, 1946, and have lived happily ever after.

I still think often of that first blue envelope. I didn't know it then, but that was the most important turning point in my life.

—***William Brown,*** *Fort Worth, Texas*

LUCK FOLLOWED IN PRIVATE'S FOOTSTEPS

In March 1945, my 49th Infantry Battalion was sent to Holland for some rest during World War II, and I was one lucky private: My name was picked in a drawing for several passes to Paris, London or Switzerland. I picked London, not realizing what a good choice it would be.

One of the sights I saw there was Hyde Park's famous Speakers' Corner, where an evangelist was preaching. When the singing started, an attractive English girl offered to share her chorus book with me. As we were about to part, I felt a strong urge to ask her if I could meet her again, and we made plans for the next day.

Hylda Mae Kitchingham and I started dating, much to her father's dismay. An American soldier was not his idea of a suitable beau for his daughter. But after Victory in Europe Day on May 8, and after a few more months of corresponding, I asked for Hylda's hand in marriage, and she accepted.

I immediately requested a short leave to get married, and arrived in London in December. Hylda was quite surprised when I knocked on her door. Though there wasn't much time for preparations, we had a lovely wedding. Even Hylda's father hurriedly bought her a beautiful wedding dress. The weather also cooperated, turning so nasty that no vessels could cross the English Channel. That gave us three extra days to honeymoon before I had to return to my outfit.

On March 18, 1946, Hylda arrived in New York City on the *Queen Mary* and took a train to my hometown of New Castle, Pennsylvania, where we began a long life together.

—***Robert Brown,*** *New Castle, Pennsylvania*

HAPPY COUPLE. Robert Brown and his wife Hylda pose for the camera on their wedding day in the fall of 1945.

Remember Saying?

FUDDY-DUDDY:
an old-fashioned person

FOR US, GRANDMA'S PLACE WAS HOME

SUMMER VISITS TO HER GRANDPARENTS' FARM MADE SWEET MEMORIES FOR THIS READER.

By Vernice Garrett, Texas City, Texas

Back in the mid-'40s, when school let out for summer, my whole family began talking excitedly about "going home."

We lived in Texas, but "home" was what we called our grandparents' farm back in Arkansas. Each summer, we'd spend two glorious weeks there.

As our yearly vacation approached, we'd eagerly make preparations. The night before we left, we could hardly sleep. The next morning at dawn, we'd begin the long drive that took us through Louisiana to Arkansas.

When we finally turned onto the dirt road that led to the farm, we would see Grandma and Grandpa running out the door to meet us. As we pulled up, they'd be waving and smiling with tears of joy welling in their eyes.

Dad barely had the car stopped before we three kids piled out and ran squealing to them, happy to be gathered up in their loving arms.

Welcome Back!

Grandma would draw each of us near and marvel at how big we'd grown since our last visit. Over and over, she'd tell us how much she missed us. Even now, I can still feel her warm embrace.

After we'd said our hellos, we kids would dash into the old farmhouse for a look around. Polished linoleum floors glistened in the sunlight, and lace curtains billowed from open windows. Gospel music came from the old radio.

When we got to the kitchen, heavenly aromas greeted us. Grandma knew we'd be hungry, and no one could fry chicken like she could!

There was so much to enjoy in the days that followed—the smell of fresh-mown hay ... the cool, sweet taste of water drawn from the well ... the clucking melody of the chickens as we fed them ... the smell of red Arkansas clay when we played hide-and-seek in the cornfield. Life was good!

Playing With Grandma

Grandma might have been elderly, but she knew how to play and pretend as well as any child. She'd put aside her chores to visit me at the playhouse I'd made near the barn.

She'd ask how I was "a-doing" and politely inquire if I had any coffee. I'd fix her a cup of muddy water, and she'd ask, "Mind if I sit a spell? That is, if you have time ..."

Of course, I always had time for a visit with Grandma. Sometimes, she'd ask how the weather was "a-treatin'" me. Before returning to her chores, she'd wrap her arms around me and say, "Guess who loves you with all her heart?"

I'd grin and answer, "You do, Grandma!"

Sweet Sunday Singing

On Sunday, we all went to the little country church that Grandma and Grandpa attended. Grandpa sang in the choir, and I can still see him standing tall in what they called "amen corner," his head proudly lifted, holding his hymnbook high.

I could hear his beautiful tenor voice rising strong and clear above the others. He was a man filled with the love of Jesus, a man who worked hard and leaned on the Lord to get him through many a hardship.

All too soon, vacation came to an end. On the night before we left, a still quiet fell over us. The next morning after breakfast, we hugged goodbye on the porch. Then Grandma and Grandpa followed us out to the loaded car. Tears flowed as we climbed in. Even Mother sobbed. (It was rough on Father, too, but he held it back a little better.)

As we backed down the driveway, we took one more look into the faces of those we loved so dearly. *Lord, please keep them safe till we see them again* was the prayer in all of our hearts.

Years later, even after we became adults with children of our own, the farewells never got any easier. We all knew that one day Grandma and Grandpa would no longer be there for us to go home to.

And that day did come. But I feel certain the Lord prepared them an inviting place when it came time for them to go home.

BABIES BOOMED

TAKING THE LEAP

Feb. 29, 1948, was a momentous day for me, as I was about to cut my first official birthday cake after four years of waiting for another leap year to roll around. Pictured with me (above) at our home in Cicero, Illinois, are my twin sisters, Lenore and Lorene, who are seven years older. Earlier in the day, I also got my first haircut, losing the long curly locks that were the style of the day for little boys. In 2012, I turned 17, or 68 in solar years. For many years I tried to get into amusement parks, movie theaters and so on at the children's rate, without success.

—*Jerome Lech,* Cary, North Carolina

A LITTLE MIRACLE

My husband and I desperately wanted to have a child. Unfortunately, for medical reasons, our dreams were not meant to be.

In 1949 we decided to adopt, but the adoption agency told us no children were currently in need of homes. This left us both feeling down.

One day shortly afterward, as I worked at home on a project for church, the pastor's wife stopped by. She told me that her husband had just counseled a woman who'd lost her husband and couldn't raise her baby girl. That woman had turned to the church for help in finding a good home for her child, and the pastor recommended my husband and me.

I will never forget the joy of seeing our adopted daughter for the first time just before Christmas back in 1949.

Because of the kindness of our pastor and his wife, my husband and I were blessed with the most precious gift any couple could ever receive—a beautiful baby girl!

—*Mrs. Donald Calhoun,* Spring, Texas

BONDED BABY

My son, Michael Guerin, was born during World War II on July 10, 1943. At the time, there was a drive in Bath, Maine, for war bonds, so we thought it would be fun to take a picture of Michael with some of the bonds we bought (at right). We felt that if we distributed the photos to friends and relatives, it would help the cause. It worked nicely. Michael eventually served in the Air Force.

—Barbara Burns, *Bath, Maine*

DAUGHTER WAS A "ONE-ALARM" BABY

My husband was a Baptist minister. When I was expecting our third child, a woman from our church in Hudson, Wisconsin, volunteered to stay with our two older kids when it came time to go to the hospital.

As luck had it, the time was 2 a.m. We called the woman's number, but the phone was downstairs and the family, sleeping upstairs, couldn't hear it ringing.

The telephone operator in our town was very helpful and knew I was more than ready to get to the hospital.

So she came on the line and asked if we would like her to ring the fire bell located in the home of the woman we were trying to reach. Each of the town's volunteer firefighters had a bell in their home that could be rung from the telephone office.

She rang the bell, which woke up the family so they could hear the phone ringing downstairs. My friend was soon at our house and we rushed to the hospital.

By the time my husband returned the next day, the operator had let the entire town know of our child's arrival. This picture (far right) shows me and my 4-day-old daughter, Barbara.

—Charlotte Woodson
Monroe, Ohio

The Day Dad and I Did the
'DRESS BLUES WALK'

WHEN HER DADDY CAME HOME FROM THE WAR, THIS LITTLE GIRL DISCOVERED THAT DREAMS REALLY COME TRUE.

By Anita Witt, Carbondale, Colorado

I was 6 years old in 1945, and I knew all about the war. I knew that Gen. Eisenhower was handsome and brave, and that Churchill and Stalin were allies.

I learned these facts in school and at the Civic Theater in Wichita, Kansas, which ran a newsreel called *The Eyes and Ears of the World* each Saturday afternoon. As I watched the soldiers march and fight, the war became very real to me.

Most of all, I knew about the war because my dad was smack-dab in the middle of it—with the Marines in the South Pacific. I didn't know exactly where this was, but I knew he was in the 5th Division, and that sounded very important and official to me.

I couldn't remember when he had left home to go to war, so it seemed like he had always been there. I lived with my mom, my Aunt Goldie, my sister and my cousin, and we talked about him a lot.

Never Doubted Dad's Return

No one ever told me there was a chance Dad might not come home from the war, so it never occurred to me that he wouldn't. I just figured that someday he'd call and say he was coming home soon. And that's exactly what happened.

After we got the call, our family's excited wait began. I daydreamed endlessly about how proud I would be to take my dad by the hand and walk him through our neighborhood.

We all dressed up on the day of his arrival. I wore my Sunday school dress and best shoes, and I waited impatiently, trying to look nice. It seemed like he'd never get there.

Finally, after dark, a taxi pulled up. And out stepped Dad, carrying an old, beat-up suitcase and a green metal box. He looked so tall and wonderful! All of us cried and tried to hug him at the same time. He picked me up, and I remember I could almost reach up and touch the ceiling.

After a while, Mama fixed him a big plateful of food and sat him down at the table on the back porch. She shooed us away and said we should let him relax and eat his dinner in peace, so we headed outside for a bit. That night, I could hardly sleep.

I don't remember telling Dad about the walk I wanted to take with him. But I must have told someone, because only a few days later, he came downstairs looking absolutely resplendent in his Marine dress blues.

As I looked him over, my eyes were as big as saucers—he looked more handsome and more important than Gen. Eisenhower ever did on those newsreels.

He had on a snow-white cap bearing the Marine insignia of the gold eagle, globe and anchor, a beautiful deep blue jacket and sky blue pants, a white belt and those shiny black shoes.

Dad said, "Girl, are you ready for that walk?" I couldn't move fast enough to take his hand.

It was a Saturday and it seemed everyone in the neighborhood was home. Perhaps my mom called ahead to tell them we were coming—or maybe it happened by itself, just as I'd imagined it would—but at each house, someone came out to shake my dad's hand and welcome him home.

The kids all gathered around, too. They were quiet and shy for once, just staring and grinning at us. I smiled and hung onto my dad's hand and felt like I'd grown two feet. I knew right then that dreams really do come true.

Wanted Moment to Last

We headed back toward our house, and I could see Mama, Aunt Goldie, my sister and cousin all watching from the front porch. I wanted to keep on walking, but Dad said, "Well, that's probably enough now—that was just right."

And it was. It was one of the most right things that could ever happen.

A few years ago, I went back to that old neighborhood. Everyone I had known there had moved away, but the houses still looked the same. The sidewalk even had some of the same old cracks.

I looked closely at everything and, with misty eyes, remembered the day my dad took me on the "dress blues walk."

Family Picnics

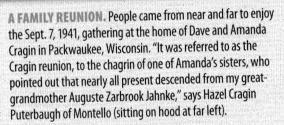

'CRAGIN REUNION' SEPT. 7 1941

A FAMILY REUNION. People came from near and far to enjoy the Sept. 7, 1941, gathering at the home of Dave and Amanda Cragin in Packwaukee, Wisconsin. "It was referred to as the Cragin reunion, to the chagrin of one of Amanda's sisters, who pointed out that nearly all present descended from my great-grandmother Auguste Zarbrook Jahnke," says Hazel Cragin Puterbaugh of Montello (sitting on hood at far left).

BARBECUE BASH. Though Floyd and Harriett Nicol Martin's loved ones had gathered in Chicago for their wedding on June 14, 1947, the beautiful summer weather prompted them to have a picnic, too! "My great-uncle Wilbur Beehler took the picture on the grounds of Watson Park Congregational Church," says James Martin of Fond du Lac, Wisconsin. "There was a large brick grill nearby that they often used for church picnics and youth group gatherings." Here, the happy couple (leaning in on the left side of the table) is dining with members of the bride's family. Her father, the Rev. Duane Nicol, was the church's pastor.

SAY GOODBYE TO CHORES. "Growing up on a small farm in Sheboygan County, Wisconsin, we didn't have much time for relaxation, so this Sunday afternoon picnic in 1942 was special," recalls Vernita Gessert of Sheboygan. "My sister, Evelyn Depping, was 13 and I was 8 when we visited the Kettle Moraine State Forest near our home."

SUNDAYS WERE A SCRAMBLE

WHILE MAMA PREENED, DADDY STEAMED...YET SOMEHOW, THEIR SUNDAYS ALWAYS ENDED UP HAPPY.
By Doris Allen, Harlingen, Texas

Sunday mornings at our house always simmered with predictability. The little wooden bird on the clock on the wall had barely finished his ninth cuckoo when Dad would bellow from the kitchen table, "It's 9 o'clock!" This was our signal to stop whatever leisurely fun we were having and get ready for church.

My brother, Don, and I would scamper to get dressed, leaving the funny papers scattered on the living room floor. But Mama always seemed to be oblivious to Daddy's announcement. She'd casually finish putting away the breakfast dishes before heading unhurriedly to her room.

By 9:15, Don and I would be sitting on the living room sofa, dressed in our Sunday best, with our hair slicked, our teeth brushed and our Bibles in hand.

Daddy would be pacing by the front door with his felt hat held firmly in hand, glancing at his watch. Finally, after he couldn't bear to wait any longer, he'd inhale deeply and call to Mama, "Aren't you ready yet, Lena?"

"Keep your shirt on, Fred!" she'd retort. Soon, I'd hear the familiar creak of the ornate dressing stool across the wooden floor and know that Mama was just sitting down to run the silver-edged comb through her beautiful finger waves. She'd then lightly dust her face with powder and dab on the slightest bit of pale pink lipstick.

Out to the Car

Meanwhile, Daddy would march Don and me out to the '37 Chevrolet waiting in the driveway. As he did so, he'd shout back over his shoulder, "I'm not going if we're gonna be late!" He would start the car and purposely gun the engine three or four times before bearing down on the horn. All this time, his face was growing redder and redder. A few minutes later, Mama would calmly walk out the door and down the steps.

As she calmly slid into the passenger seat of our Chevy, her floral perfume filled the car. No one dared speak a word until we got to church. Once there, Mama would hand my brother and me each a nickel. "Put the money in the collection plate," she'd say with a smile. Off we'd go to our Sunday school classes and then on to church, where Don and I were permitted to sit up in the balcony with the other young people.

When we stood for the hymns, I could lean over the railing and catch a glimpse of Mama and Daddy. They'd each hold half the hymnal, and Mama would sing like a bird. Daddy's eyes followed the words, but his lips never moved.

Service Produced Smiles

After the benediction, we kids raced down the stairs to shake the preacher's hand. "I enjoyed the sermon," I'd always tell him. (Mama had taught me that was a nice thing to say.)

At the car, I'd stand on the running board, waiting for Mama and Daddy. I could tell by the way they smiled as they walked out of the church that all thoughts of aggravation had evaporated.

On the way home, it became a tradition to stop and pick up hamburgers for lunch. At four for a dollar, they were a luxury—but that was our treat for the week.

Daddy never stopped trying to rush Mama on those frenzied Sunday mornings, and Mama continued to march to her own drumbeat. Even after all these years, I can still hear her call, "Keep your shirt on, Fred!"

Joke Hit the Funny Bone

I love the story behind this picture of my mother, Clara, and her two sisters, taken around 1940 by their brother George.

After shooting one rather somber pose, he wanted to loosen them up by telling a joke. I believe it worked! Here's George's story:

A rather simpleminded man approached the director of a small-town band as they prepared for a big parade. The man said that he wanted a position in the band, so the director asked him, "Do you play the trumpet?"

"No," the man replied.
"Do you play the trombone?"
"No."
"Do you play the drums or the flute?"
"No."
"Well, then what do you play?"
"I don't play nothing," the man drawled, "but I have a very large navel, and I thought maybe I could carry the flag."

—**Sarah Ann McNeilus,** *Knoxville, Tennessee*

CHAPTER 10

On The ROAD

PAGE 206

PAGE 203

From a leisurely Sunday afternoon drive to a trip clear across the country, our set of wheels kept us on the move.

"In the summer of 1947, our family traveled coast to coast on a two-month vacation adventure," says Charles Solomon of Roslyn Harbor, New York. "That was before turnpikes and interstate highways, so we had a chance to really see the faces and places that make up this great nation.

"We meandered through West Virginia, Ohio, Iowa, South Dakota, Wyoming and Montana. Some spots were chosen because they had restaurants or lodging recommended by Duncan Hines, the bible for tourists during the '40s. But other stops were dictated by the need for repairs to our family's weary prewar Chrysler.

"By the time we reached California, it was clear that our car would never survive the return trip, so Dad bought a new Kaiser-Frazer for $2,200. I'll never forget the closeness of our family throughout those two months. We savored the natural beauty of our wonderful country together."

Remember gasoline rationing, the year car production stopped, and the vehicles you drove in the 1940s? These writers do—read all about those times here!

PAGE 204

PAGE 199

The Year They
MADE CARS

WORLD WAR II BROUGHT SOME MIGHTY LEAN TIMES FOR LOVERS OF NEW AUTOMOBILES.

By Bill Schwartzberg, Flushing, New York

In fall of 1941, American carmakers introduced the 1942 models. I was only 4 years old at the time, but I was already an automobile buff.

I loved playing with toy cars, and our '38 Olds rarely left the house without me in it. The car often went on random rides to nowhere since that was the only way Father could get me to stop pestering him!

Visitors to our house got the same treatment. I'd often talk them into taking me for rides around the block in their cars.

I still vaguely recall Dec. 7, 1941, and the gloom that settled inside our house. I certainly didn't understand what "war" meant and how it would make life pretty grim for a little boy who loved cars.

For adults, the impact of the coming war was apparent in most advertising for the 1942 models. Those ads emphasized fuel economy, durability and conservation of scarce resources. Each manufacturer's contributions to the defense effort were highlighted.

A common theme among manufacturers was "choosing a better car for the long haul," a hint that soon, new cars wouldn't be available. In fact, new car production was halted at the end of January of 1942, just four months after the '42 models were introduced.

Built to Last—and Save Gas

"More durable" cars were desired by wartime motorists, but heavily built cars raised some concern—gas rationing was upon us! This change in the consumer's lifestyle wasn't lost on Oldsmobile; its ad said that its cars "Help you save America's gasoline."

Even whitewall tires were sacrificed for the war effort. But that didn't deter DeSoto from putting white plastic wheel trim rings on its popular model.

Although this International truck ad (opposite page, bottom left) appeared in *The Saturday Evening Post* on Oct. 25, 1941, six weeks before the war actually started, it illustrated only war products, not civilian goods—a practice followed by most car manufacturers during the war.

As shown by this wartime Packard ad, manufacturers stressed the durability of their products under difficult wartime conditions and the importance of regular maintenance.

The Lincoln ad was one of the few that didn't devote space to the company's war efforts. "This is a good year to buy a better car" and "no skimping on materials" are the only references to the world situation.

Return Was Slow

As the war years passed, shortages, rationing, scrap drives and no new cars on the streets began to seem normal to me. I couldn't even get toy cars in the stores anymore!

By 1945, the only new cars I remembered seeing were in a few dealerships near our home. Each one had one or two '42 models on display. They remained there for the duration of the war.

Toward the end of the war, car manufacturers returned to the matter of selling new vehicles to a car-starved public. The Buick ad, placed after V-E Day, emphasized the open road and a "bright and lively new Buick."

The caption underneath the convertible reads, "This is the 1942 Buick which sets the high standards to be surpassed by new models now being made ready."

I recall seeing that ad and being excited about the prospect of going to faraway places in a new car. But it took a while.

Finally, a year and a half after the war's end (and five full years after Pearl Harbor), I enjoyed the greatest experience of my short life—delivery of our family's brand-new 1946 Olds!

HARD-TO-GET HARDTOPS. When America's industries cranked up for the war effort, brand-new automobiles became unavailable. The ads shown here tout some of the 1942 models that were being sold late in 1941. The advertisements emphasized the cars' longevity, and they'd need it because there would be no more new ones for four years! Even when the war was winding down, the ads, like the one at left for Buick, showed the 1942 models. But they promised new and better models soon. It was the beginning of the automobile boom. When servicemen came home and moved their families to the suburbs, they needed transportation for work, school and pleasure.

MOTORING MEMORIES

WOODEN WONDER

Here I am in 1944 (above), next to my 1926-'27 Model T Ford touring sedan with a wooden body.

One day that year, my friend Dick Schroeder and I were heading to Glenwood, Minnesota, from our hometown of Starbuck when I realized I'd forgotten something. So I turned right down into the ditch and swung around to drive back the other way.

I glanced over at Dick. He was gone, and so was the passenger-side door. I swung the car around again and saw Dick lying on the door in the ditch, laughing. The hinge had ripped loose from the car. We had a good laugh, loaded the door into the back and continued on our trip.

—*Dean Dahlin, Denton, Texas*

MISGUIDED MECHANIC

My friend and I were leaving a funeral in Staten Island, New York, on a cold day in 1946, and her car would not start.

I informed her that when such a thing happened, my husband, Pete, used to work the choke. So with my learned instructions, my friend kept pulling out the choke.

With much manipulation, the motor turned over and then stopped. I told my friend that she had given it too much choke and flooded the motor. We sat for a while and tried the whole procedure again, to no avail.

Finally, we had to get out and start pushing the car out of the cemetery. A good samaritan spotted us and came to our rescue.

When my friend got home and recounted the experience to her husband, he told her that their new car had an automatic choke.

Per my instructions, all she was doing was turning the lights on and off!

—*Rose Gippa, Staten Island, New York*

OLD HABITS DIED HARD

My husband was a torpedo bomber pilot for the Marines during World War II, and he actually learned to fly an airplane before he could drive a car. Like many other Depression-era kids, he had grown up without the opportunity to get behind the wheel.

After the war ended, he finally acquired his own car. But his pilot habits died hard. Before "taking off," he'd tap everything on the dashboard, "checking the controls." Even the glove compartment got tapped, plus the cigarette lighter and every light and button.

Then, and only then, would he start the car.

—*Eliza Massa, Kansas City, Missouri*

HITTING CLOSE TO HOME

In 1940, when my family lived in Baltimore, our church in nearby Hamilton held a drawing for a new car—a navy 1940 Plymouth sedan—at its annual benefit carnival. Tickets were three for a quarter.

I was standing close to the raised platform where the priest was looking for someone to pick the winning ticket. "Here we have an honest little Girl Scout to pick the ticket," he announced.

I was 12 at the time, and I reached into a large wooden beer barrel to pull out a ticket as the priest said, "Dig deep." I pulled out a ticket, and the winner was my father!

We had never owned a car. My father, who was walking home when he heard his name announced over the loudspeaker, came running back to claim his big prize.

My father kept the car through the war years and beyond. It was his pride and joy. He kept it in our garage and spent a lot of time polishing it. I doubt a car was ever more appreciated.

—*Peggy Moore, Stewartstown, Pennsylvania*

BEANED IN THE HELMET

Motorcycling has always been my passion, so when I was offered the chance to ride for pay, I took the job. That's me kicking up dust in the photo above.

It was after World War II. The police department in Pittsburg, Kansas, had acquired a new 1949 Harley-Davidson motorcycle, and I was assigned to ride it.

"You are the traffic department," Chief Tom Stowers said to me. "Look for and apprehend any traffic violators."

That's just what I was doing one day when I stopped a very attractive young lady for speeding near the university. As she was signing the citation, a carload of teenage boys went by, and one of them threw out a beer can.

The can hit my helmet just as I was handing the lady her ticket. It took me two blocks, but I caught the car.

I told the boy who tossed the can he would be charged as a litterbug and could likely spend time in jail for having an open can of beer in the car.

I knew the empty can was not much in the way of evidence. So I told the boy that if he could walk all the way back and pick up the can, and show me by his walk that he wasn't under the influence, I would not charge him.

He walked like a very sober boy.

The incident remains fresh in my memory mainly because of how hard the young lady laughed when that can bounced off my shiny new helmet. I guess I would have laughed, too.

—**John Chester,** *Pittsburg, Kansas*

FLYING SCOOTERS. "During World War II, this Cushman scooter provided fuel-efficient transportation to Cushman Motor Works in Lincoln, Nebraska, where I worked in the defense department making bomb fuses in 1944," says Wilma Cramer of Healdsburg, California. "Cushman made scooters for the armed forces, including a specially designed heavy-duty model called the Airborne that could be dropped to troops by parachute."

7,000 Miles on PORK & BEANS

THE FOOD MIGHT NOT HAVE BEEN GOURMET, BUT THIS FAMILY'S TRIP WEST WAS DELICIOUSLY FUN.
By Evelyn Halligan Habenicht, Bettendorf, Iowa

ALMOST THERE. Mom and the kids pose on the Nevada line, en route to the California coast.

In July of 1947, my dad bought one of the first postwar cars delivered to Fort Dodge, Iowa—a burgundy 1946 Mercury sedan. It was our first new car!

During the war, we had only taken short trips to my aunt and uncle's farm. But with gas rationing lifted, my parents decided to drive our shiny new Mercury all the way to California to visit my brother, who was in the Navy and stationed in San Francisco.

Each day on the road started early so we could cover as many miles as possible before it got too hot. We stopped early every evening so we'd be sure to get a tourist cabin.

Sleepy Passengers

Before sunup, my sister, brother and I would be herded half-asleep to the car—where we would promptly fall asleep again. Thus we "saw" much of the beauty and grandeur of the western United States through half-closed, sleepy eyes each time an enthusiastic parent woke us up to share some spectacular sight.

We'd planned on eating breakfast and supper in restaurants and a picnic lunch on the road. But after a couple of days, we decided we preferred picnic suppers, too.

While Dad gassed up the car, Mom shopped in the little grocery stores along the way. Our meals consisted mostly of minced ham sandwiches, cold pork and beans, cottage cheese and ice-cold milk.

We subsisted on this fare for the 30 days we traveled. The route took us out to California, up the coast to Washington, then back to Iowa through Yellowstone National Park, the Bighorn Mountains and the Black Hills. We happily filled our back window with tourist decals from the 11 states we passed through.

Traveling with Mom was like having our own professional tour guide. Priming us with lots of information about the next attraction just over the horizon, she had us craning our necks to be the first to spot it. It didn't matter how many miles there were to cover each day. If there were interesting things to see every 10 miles, then we stopped every 10 miles.

Seeing the Sights

We read all the roadside historical markers, posed for pictures with each foot in a different state and walked through tunnels while our dad drove through and waited patiently at the other end. We had pictures taken on stuffed "bucking" broncos and took the scenic routes down scary hairpin turns.

I remember counting down the remaining miles to Wall Drug—and how we all loved reading those Burma-Shave signs! Dad's enthusiasm was catching, and we marveled with him at how old and how big the redwood trees were and how many zillions of years it took to carve out this canyon or make that mountain.

Along with our parents, we imagined the seemingly impossible task of building the Grand Coulee Dam—or what the first settlers must have thought when they came upon the Great Salt Lake or Yellowstone.

Many years later, Mom and Dad took my own children on a similar trip. I'll always be grateful my kids got to see the same spectacular sights I saw on that 1947 road trip and share their grandparents' love for the western United States.

Ridin' in a Rumble Seat

REVERSIBLE RUMBLE SEAT

This is me with the 1931 Chevy I drove to school in the 1940s. It had a reversible trunk lid and a rumble seat you could insert or take out.

The back window also rolled down so the people inside the car could talk with the ones in the "mother-in-law seat."

I bought the Chevy from our mail carrier for a hard-earned $85 from my part-time job and sold it a few years later for $125. A friend of mine now has one, in perfect condition, for which he has been offered more than $40,000. But he will not sell.

—**Allan Young,** *Springfield, Missouri*

AN UNEXPECTED SEATMATE

I'll never forget my ride in a rumble seat during the summer of 1940. I was hitchhiking through Montana when a couple vacationing from Chicago picked me up. They were on their way to visit Yellowstone National Park, so I went along for the ride.

We weren't in the park very long when a big black bear decided to take a closer look at their car, specifically at the rumble seat where I was sitting!

As the bear climbed into the seat beside me, I began to climb out. I pushed off the seat and quietly took a perch on top of the open lid of the rumble seat.

Old Mr. Bear tumbled into the seat and sat on my right foot. He looked up at me with what I thought was a friendly expression, and it seemed as if he wanted me to move.

When I tried to move, I found I must have misinterpreted his message, because the bear took my foot in his mouth and gave it just a little squeeze, then let go. I sat perfectly still!

Thankfully, he didn't hurt me a bit. Soon, he climbed out and ambled off.

I've thought about that bear often through the years, and have never considered our meeting a bad memory. The bear seemed so friendly that I almost wish I'd gotten to know him a little better!

—**Albert Cook,** *Erie, Pennsylvania*

MY FIRST CAR

THE DERELICT MODEL T SAT RUSTING IN A FIELD—UNTIL TWO ADVENTUROUS TEENS CAME TO THE RESCUE.
By Bill Fitzgerald, Weslaco, Texas

Back in 1940, when I was 14, I lived with my paternal grandparents in Hobart, Oklahoma. My best friend was W.D. "Dub" Wright. The thing I remember most about Dub was that he loved automobiles—any make, model, color or vintage, in any degree of disrepair.

I liked cars well enough, too, but since neither of us had a driver's license or a car, we didn't have much hope of enjoying a Saturday night cruise down Main Street.

Half of that teenage dilemma was solved the day we spotted a Model T Ford standing abandoned in a farmer's field. The farmer seemed surprised we were interested in it, and sold us the forlorn Ford for a mere $10—five hard-earned bucks apiece.

We figured we'd take care of getting driver's licenses later—first, we had some work on our hands. For the next month, Dub and I spent every spare moment rebuilding our first car.

What a Color!

The body of the sedan was badly corroded. To cure this problem, we headed for the hardware store to buy a gallon of paint. The owner sold us an unlabeled gallon he had in the back for just 75 cents.

That seemed like a real bargain until we opened it up and found an awful lime green color inside. Still, for 75 cents, we felt we could live with it.

The enamel was thick as winter honey. We dipped out huge globs of it and spread them on the driver's side, with Dub's little brother watching our every move. We had just finished the entire left side of the car when the little guy inadvertently kicked the can over and spilled the rest of the paint.

That's how we ended up owning a two-tone sedan—half lime green and half rust. That enamel was so thick it took three days for it to set to a tacky semblance of dryness.

A Lot to List

Besides its color, our old Model T had quite a few features that set it apart from other autos. One of the best of those was its reverse gear.

Reverse was not activated by means of a shift, but rather by a pedal located between the clutch and brake. Often, while Dub and I were rolling merrily down the streets of downtown Hobart, one or the other of us would purposely slam the reverse pedal on the floor. The Tin Lizzie would grind to a halt, shudder, shake and wheeze, then shoot backward like an errant cannonball!

We thought it was a great trick, because everyone in the car was thrown forward, then quickly snapped backward. Fortunately, I never heard the word "whiplash" until years later, when I roomed with a pre-law student at college.

Once, our car was stolen. We couldn't imagine anyone that hard up for a car that they'd steal our Model T, so we figured it had to be a prank.

After two weeks had passed, we considered reporting the theft to the police. But then who would believe a description of a missing Model T with "left side green, other side rust brown…no windshield…Auto War Stamp on inside roof… bathtub replacing missing backseat…both front doors unable to open…left headlight inoperable… horn working occasionally…and an out-of-date 1938 license plate, conveniently caked with obscuring mud"? Our car certainly wasn't inconspicuous!

Sure enough, Dub awoke one morning to find the car had been returned to the driveway. The headlight was repaired, and some screen wire had been installed in place of the missing windshield.

Also, all four tires had been painted a garish red. Since green and red were the colors of a rival high school, we easily deduced who the culprits were, but retribution was far from our minds, considering the repair work that had been done

Three years and 1,000 miles later, our first car was still running fine. But Dub and I, both bound for the service, had to bid her farewell. We donated that faithful old Lizzie to the scrap metal drive for the war effort. She was reluctantly accepted, bathtub backseat and all.

I never saw that Model T again, but during the war, I often daydreamed of a half rust-colored, half lime green army tank scaring the daylights out of a bewildered enemy!

CRAZY FOR OUR CROSLEY. Long before the invention of smart cars, the miniature Crosley attracted crowds wherever it went.

Our Tiny Car Was No Toy!

We often joked that we'd bought our first car at Macy's toy department. Weighing just 924 pounds, with a wheel base of 80 inches, the 1940 Crosley convertible coupe was certainly small enough to look like a toy.

My husband, Malcolm, and I really did buy that car at Macy's, which was a Crosley dealer. Stores that handled other Crosley products, such as their radios and famous Shelvador refrigerators, also sold the cars. For us newlyweds, still feeling the Depression's pinch, the little Crosley's petite price—$375—fit our budget well.

The Crosley was a novelty then, and on the ferry back to New Jersey, it attracted a curious crowd of fellow passengers. One burly truck driver squeezed into the driver's seat, and the poor little car sagged under his 240 pounds!

During the drive home on U.S. Highway 1, each big truck that passed nearly blew us off the road. But we made it safely, and the car soon became a popular curiosity in our small college town. All our friends wanted a ride in it—although one asked to be driven only on the back streets so she wouldn't be seen by anyone she knew!

We lived in an apartment in the center of town and parked the Crosley on the street out front. Passing college boys would often pick up the car and put it on the sidewalk! When that happened, the manager would call to ask us to move our car back onto the street.

One day after attending a lecture at the high school, we came out to find the little car blocking the door. Pranksters had carried it up the 20 steps, and we had to maneuver it back down in front of a captive audience that included my husband's boss.

The Crosley continued to attract attention wherever we went. In a parking lot in a nearby city, so many people crowded around the car that we had trouble getting to it and inside it.

Got 40 Miles Per Gallon!

Despite all the attention, the car was a joy to park, as it fit the smallest of places. Frustrated drivers who thought they'd found a parking spot had to change their minds when they discovered our little Crosley, initially unseen, hiding there.

Our first big trip in the Crosley was to Canada to visit relatives. With its two-cylinder, air-cooled 12-horsepower engine, the journey over the Pennsylvania mountains was a challenge, but we made it. The trip back was another story—the Crosley broke down in Buffalo and required a new engine. Luckily, we had relatives there with whom we could stay while the car was repaired.

We eventually made it home with no more problems. Later, we took a trip to New England, and the little Crosley behaved perfectly, getting 40 miles per gallon—just right for our thin pocketbooks.

By the time our tiny car had reached its second birthday, we were ready to graduate to a full-size model. We parted with the Crosley for the huge sum of $85 from a high school boy who was as delighted as we had been with the "toy" car.

From that time on, we blended inconspicuously into traffic. Our fun days of driving a novelty were over, but what unforgettable years we'd had with our "Car of Tomorrow."

—**Ruth Ferguson,** Port Charlotte, Florida

Fill 'er Up

KEROSENE DID THE TRICK

I grew up during the '40s in St. Albans on Long Island in New York. When gas rationing was in effect during World War II, we had only an "A" stamp on the window of our Model A Ford.

You'd think we would've done little driving, but that wasn't the case. During summer, Mom drove us to the ocean at Far Rockaway several times a week, and on weekends, Dad took us to state parks on Long Island.

We never ran out of gas because Dad would send us to get a can of kerosene, and then down to Bressler's Hardware for a couple of cans of cleaning fluid.

Working his magic, Dad mixed the gasoline with the kerosene and cleaning fluid, poured it into the tank and off we'd go. Clinton Maddock could do anything!

—*George Maddock, Agana Heights, Guam*

FRUGAL WAS HER MIDDLE NAME

My father bought this 1932 Chevy coupe (above) with a rumble seat for $35. A close look reveals a makeshift wooden running board and a damaged back fender. Some of the damage was due to my three younger brothers, all unlicensed, driving it around the farm and down to the big swimming hole that was on the back of our property.

But I was no angel, either—I loved to drive fast, and got the nickname Hot Rod Rita. More than once I was down at the township clerk's office paying a fine for my escapades.

One day, on the way to work with my sister and a friend, I drove into a gas station, where the attendant asked, "How much?" I answered, "One." He asked, "One dollar?" I quickly answered, "No! One gallon."

The three of us gathered up our nickels and pennies to pay for the gallon of gas, which at the time was about 27 cents. That was a lot of money to us, since my salary was $18 a week.

—*Rita Conte, Long Branch, New Jersey*

BOSS FUELED A SECRET

This was the last day I would pump gas from McCurdy's Atlantic service station on Chestnut Avenue and Ninth Street in Altoona, Pennsylvania. It was Nov. 6, 1940, and the building was to be demolished that day. Mr. Louse, the man whose car I'm filling in the photo below, was a longtime customer.

Working as an attendant, I learned a very interesting "secret" about the building. It was not only the office, but also the gasoline storage and pumping station.

In the top of the building was a large tank filled with water that was pumped into it and maintained at a constant level. Under the building was a gasoline storage tank.

The water was fed through a pipe into the gasoline tank. After about 15 minutes, the water and gasoline separated, with the water on the bottom. The water pressure pushed the gasoline into the pumps. There were six 4-foot-high red pumps on an island.

To refill the gasoline tank, the water was shut off and the tank drained of the water until the gasoline level was near the bottom. We measured the level with a stick painted with a special material that dissolved in water but not in gasoline.

The tank was then filled with gasoline, the water valve opened and in 15 minutes, we were ready to pump again.

In those days, a lot of filling stations had trouble with water in their gasoline. We did not, and in fact, we guaranteed there was no water in our gas. Still, my boss told me to never reveal how our pumping system worked.

This was the end of that system, since the building was replaced with a modern station and electric pumps.

—*John Kehoe Jr., Lockport, New York*

DOUBLE TROUBLE. When adventurous newlyweds (above) asked John Hanson and his wife, Ruth (right), about tagging along on a trip to Mount Rushmore in 1949, the wary Hansons had no choice but to say, "I do!"

Four's a Crowd

"Are you serious?" I quizzed newlyweds Charles and Avis when they asked to join my wife and me on a trip to South Dakota. "What about the honeymoon?"

Charles and Avis had been married that very day, and my wife, Ruth, and I were in the wedding party.

We told the couple we'd stop by their hotel early the next morning, and if they were ready, they could come along. Sure enough, we found them sitting on their bags in front of the hotel the next day.

Watch the Road!

We left Chicago for the Black Hills of South Dakota with Charles at the wheel. It didn't take long to figure out these newlyweds had eyes only for each other and not the road! I drove for the rest of the trip, and as we headed west, I wondered what kind of accommodations we'd find along the way.

There weren't any roadside motels in 1949, but there were reasonably priced tourist cabins. We scanned the road for a vacancy sign.

When we reached Pierre, South Dakota, we came upon an old house surrounded by cabins. Out front, a sign blinked "vacancy." No one was home, but the cabins were empty and their doors unlocked, so we took the first two, figuring we would pay later.

The others went into town to eat while I stayed at the cabin waiting for the owners to show up. By the time Ruth, Charles and Avis came back, the owners still hadn't arrived. But other travelers had—and I'd rented out every cabin and collected the money for the owner.

There still was no one home in the morning, so I left the money in the mailbox with a note.

A Sinking Feeling

We drove on toward the Black Hills, stopping at Deadwood too late, as all the vacancy signs had been turned off. Going on to the mining town of Lead, we saw a dim sign blinking "…ancy."

It was pitch dark by that time, and difficult to find our cabin. When I finally got the door open, we literally fell inside. After finding the light switch, we discovered the cabin floor had sunk!

Checking out in the morning, we learned the cabins had been built over an old gold mine and were sinking into the shaft! On that note, we headed on to some enjoyable visits at Mount Rushmore and Little Bighorn.

Charles and Avis were good company, but it was a chore getting the lovebirds up and out of their cabin every morning. My wife and I quickly learned that a vacation and a honeymoon have very different priorities!

—**John Hanson**, *Morton Grove, Illinois*

'40s-Style Car Phone

After Gene Marsh graduated from business college in 1946, her first job was with Southern Bell Telephone Co. in Knoxville, Tennessee.

"I was the executive secretary to Lt. Col. Lawrence H. Callaway," she says. "He'd just returned from World War II and was the district sales manager. This 1947 photo shows me with the first automobile telephone installation in Knoxville. What a huge difference in electronic communication compared to the high-tech mobile devices we use today!"

Gene later worked for the city of Knoxville as executive secretary for the director of engineering, and says she witnessed progress and innovation at its finest throughout her career.

My Own Memories